lonely planet

Buenos Aires

Diego Jemio, Federico Perelmuter, Rachel Tolosa Paz

MARCEL_STRELOW/SHUTTERSTOCK

Plaza de la República (p77)

CONTENTS

Plan Your Trip

FROM TOP: GUAXINIM/SHUTTERSTOCK, GABRIELA BERTOLINI/SHUTTERSTOCK

Feria de San Telmo (p100)

The Guide

Toolkit

Storybook

Empanadas

REED KAESTNER/GETTY IMAGES

Palermo (p160)

BUENOS AIRES

THE JOURNEY BEGINS HERE

There's nothing quite like Buenos Aires. From bookstores on every corner to glorious meals shared with *porteños* (Buenos Aires residents) that roll into the wee hours of the morning, to sprawling markets filled with arts and hand-crafted objects and live music everywhere you turn, it is a city full of life. Nostalgic and sometimes melancholic, it's akin to a tango; a deeply passionate tale of a longing for home.

I've spent the last decade regularly traveling to Buenos Aires, a journey I am sure to keep doing until the end of time. It doesn't matter how often I visit; the city slowly unravels a layer with each new trip. I first stayed in Chacarita in 2014 and it remains my favourite barrio – a growing area with hip bars, unique stores and innovative food, all shouldered by BA's great musicians buried in the cemetery.

Rachel Tolosa Paz

@racheltolosapaz

Writer and photographer Rachel Tolosa Paz is the author of The Food of Argentina.

My favorite experience is being swept up with the bohemian crowd at **El Boliche de Roberto** (p180) where tango musicians play long after midnight.

WHO GOES WHERE

Our writers and experts choose the places which, for them, define Buenos Aires.

JOHN DAMBIK/ALAMY

The city is full of *milongas* for dancing tango (pictured) and other venues to listen to live orchestras. **Los Laureles** (p119) is a place where you can truly breathe tango; here, this music is not just for export. Located in Barracas, right next to La Boca, it is a bar and restaurant offering authentic shows without the spectacle. Often, local neighbors come by to sing, making it feel like stepping into a time capsule.

Diego Jemio

@djemio

Diego is a book, letter and theater enthusiast and co-creator of the podcast Epistolar.

MARK GREEN/SHUTTERSTOCK

MALBA (pictured; p168) has an art collection to rival that of any top museum in the world. Frida Kahlo, León Ferrari and other greats of Latin American art are curated very tastefully and instructively in a building that, itself, could be called a work of art. My favorite piece is Tarsila do Amaral's *Abaporu*, a landmark of Brazil's modernist art movement.

Federico Perelmuter

@cementeriocc

Federico is a journalist and writer specializing in Argentine and Latin American culture and politics; music is his great passion.

URBAN DELIGHTS

Buenos Aires is complex and, at times, chaotic but if you stop to look, you'll find that the story of the city's last tumultuous centuries is revealed through its art, design and architecture. World-class murals and graffiti cover entire buildings, there's a museum for every taste, and the fascinating mix of architectural styles never fails to delight – from 17th century clay-brick homes to a skyline dotted with domes and colossal concrete works. Always look up!

Street Art Tours

For street art tours, contact walking tour company @graffitimundo. Check out lesser-explored street art spots like Coghlan, Villa Urquiza and Colegiales.

Homegrown Sign Writing

You'll spot the hand-painted flourishes of *fileteado*, BA's home-grown sign-writing style, on city buses. Wander Almagro, La Boca and San Telmo for more.

Brutalist Approach to Architecture

Pick up the *Brutalist Buenos Aires Map* to track down the city's concrete architectural beauties.

FROM LEFT: MARIANO GASPAR/SHUTTERSTOCK, ANIBAL TREJO/SHUTTERSTOCK, DIEGO GRANDI/SHUTTERSTOCK

Biblioteca Nacional Mariano Moreno (p141)

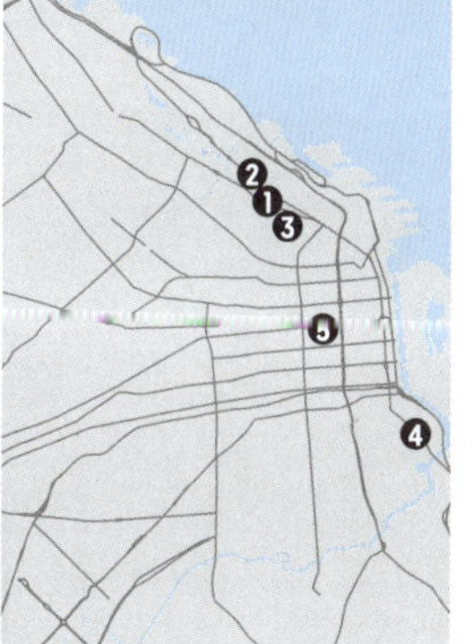

BEST URBAN DELIGHTS EXPERIENCES

Take a tour of Victoria Ocampo's former home the first rationalist residence, built in Buenos Aires by Alejandro Bustillo and now the ❶ **Casa de la Cultura del Fondo Nacional de las Artes** (p172).

Wander the cavernous halls of ❷ **MALBA** (p168), the largest museum dedicated to Latin American art in the world.

Step inside the brutalist beauty, the ❸ **Biblioteca Nacional Mariano Moreno** (p141), designed by famed local architect, Clorindo Testa.

Cycle ❹ **La Boca** (p120) to explore its street art and learn about the peculiarities of this football-crazed neighborhood linked to the port.

Tour ❺ **Palacio Barolo** (p76), a building entirely inspired by Dante's *Divine Comedy*. Discover details of its construction and climb the lighthouse for a dazzling view of BA.

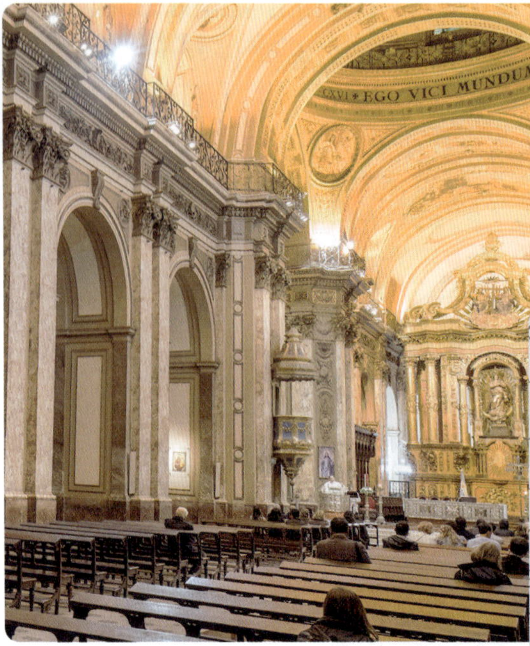

Catedral Metropolitana (p58)

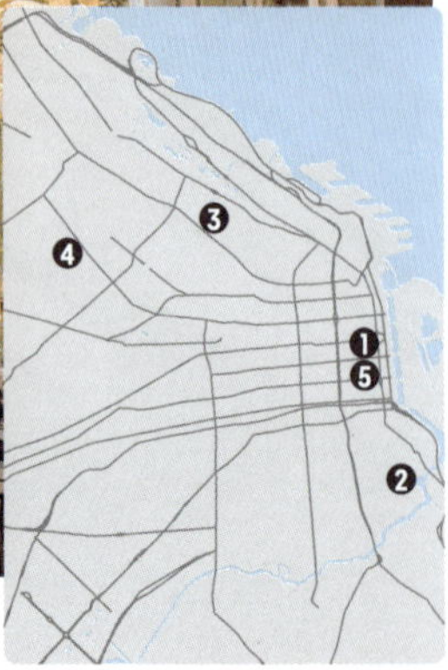

CULTURAL ICONS

Across sport, politics, religion and culture BA has its fair share of famous citizens. From Messi to Maradona, Evita to Pope Francis, Gardel to Piazzolla, and García, Cerati and Borges – *porteños* love nothing more than to kneel at the altar of an icon.

Martin Ron's Murals

Marvel at Argentina's football greats by visiting Martin Ron's soaring murals of Maradona (Av San Juan) and Messi (cnr Belgrano and Av 9 de Julio).

Charly García

Check out the messages on the facade of local rock icon Charly García's home (p146) in Recoleta.

BEST CULTURAL ICON EXPERIENCES

Visit the museum dedicated to Pope Francis at ❶ **Catedral Metropolitana** (p58).

Take a selfie with a Lionel Messi sculpture at ❷ **Cachafaz Caminito** (p117).

Learn all about Eva Perón at ❸ **Museo Evita** (p165) dedicated to her life and work.

Stand by the grave of legendary tango singer, Carlos Gardel, in ❹ **Cementerio de la Chacarita** (p178).

Say hello to ❺ **Mafalda** (p109) along the Paseo de la Historieta (Comic Strip Walk).

BACK IN TIME

First settled by Spanish colonizers in the 16th century, Buenos Aires is a city rich in historical layers. Its history encompasses indigenous, colonial and revolutionary criollo influences, alongside the diverse immigrant communities that contribute to this cultural melting pot. Volatile economics and notorious military dictatorships of the 20th century have also left their mark.

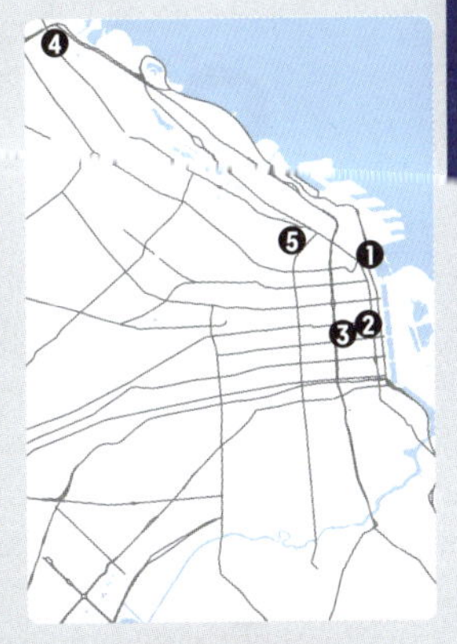

Criollo Identity

An important part of cultural heritage in Argentina, criollo identity blends influences from the local population, indigenous peoples, Spanish colonizers and other immigrant groups.

Spanish Influence

The Spanish attempted to settle Buenos Aires twice. The first attempt in 1530 was thwarted by local indigenous groups. Fifty years later, they tried again and succeeded.

Afro-Argentine Tours

To discover more about the little-known history of Black identity in Buenos Aires, take a community-led Afro-Argentine tour with local company Lunfarda Travel (p108).

BEST HISTORICAL EXPERIENCES

Discover the country's immigration history at the ❶ **Museo de la Inmigración** (p130).

Step back in time to the colonial era at ❷ **Manzana de las Luces** (pictured near left; p63), where the Jesuits settled in 1633.

Learn about Argentine colonial history at ❸ **Cabildo Nacional** (p58).

Shiver at the somber ❹ **El Museo Sitio de Memoria ESMA** (p155), a former clandestine torture site.

Wander the crypts of the ❺ **Cementerio de la Recoleta** (p140) filled with the remains of some of BA's most influential families.

FOLK CULTURE

Influenced by indigenous, African, and European traditions, Argentine folk culture is a unique blend of customs. From folk music and dance like *chamamé, malambo* and *zamba,* to hand-crafted silver and leather work – including the mesmerizing crafts of local horse whisperers *(doma india)* – it is all a vibrant expression of rural Argentina, the nomadic gaucho of the Pampa and criollo identity. Harder to see in the city, head to lesser-known cultural centers to catch a glimpse.

Gaucho Style

The gaucho uniform, still common in rural Argentina, consists of *bombacha* pants (tapered at the ankles), *alpagata* slippers and *boina* (a floppy knitted beret).

Peñas

Peñas are intimate gatherings of musicians to sing. Common in Northern Argentina, head to Pal Que Guste (p135) for a BA version.

Zamba

Different from the samba, the Argentine *zamba* is a folklore dance that involves waving a handkerchief.

FROM LEFT: PHILIP LEE HARVEY/LONELY PLANET, STATIKMOTION/ALAMY, MARTIN LINDSAY/ALAMY

Feria de Mataderos (p184)

BEST FOLK CULTURE EXPERIENCES

Listen and watch performances of *zamba* and folk music at ❶ **ATRODEN** (p108) in San Telmo.

Spend a Sunday at the ❷ **Feria de Mataderos** (p184), soaking up Argentine folk culture and shopping for leather bridles and hand-crafted knives.

Take a trip to ❸ **Campana** (p187), on the outskirts of Buenos Aires, and enjoy a day in the countryside with the gauchos and their horses at *estancia* Santa Susana.

Visit ❹ **Colección Histórica del Traje Argentino** (p108), an impressive collection of Argentine clothing from the 19th century to today with indigenous items and early gaucho wear.

Shop for unique artisanal pieces from across Argentina at ❺ **Facón** (p180) in Chacarita. It's Spanish for big knife!

EL GRECO 1973/SHUTTERSTOCK

Parque 3 de Febrero (p171)

NATURE CALLS

When the weather is nice, *porteños* flock to the nearest public parks. Many were designed in the late 19th and early 20th century by landscape architect Carlos Thays. The two largest green spaces are Palermo's Parque 3 de Febrero and Puerto Madero's Costanera Sur Ecological Reserve.

Green Spaces

If you're looking to combine running or access to green spaces with your visit, stay in Recoleta, Palermo or Puerto Madero.

Outdoor Activities

While BAEcobici bikes are scattered throughout the city, it is a system riddled with red tape for foreigners. Opt for local rental companies.

BEST OUTDOOR EXPERIENCES

Chill out in Palermo's peaceful ❶ **Jardín Botánico Carlos Thays** (p165).

Cycle ❷ **Parque 3 de Febrero** (p171), 400 hectares of sprawling parklands including a rose garden and lakes.

Explore the riverside nature sanctuary ❸ **Reserva Ecológica Costanera Sur** (p88) in Puerto Madero.

Board a ❹ **Sturla boat** (p112) to sail between La Boca and Puerto Madero.

Walk or cycle the riverside promenade to the ❺ **Parque de la Memoria** (p157).

BBQ BLISS

You'll know you're in Buenos Aires when you start to smell the heady mix of smoke and meat in the air. From humble, family-run *parrillas* (steakhouses) to Michelin-starred spectacles, every piece of beef you eat will be nothing short of glorious. But nothing quite beats the intimate ritual of an *asado* (barbecue) in an Argentine's home.

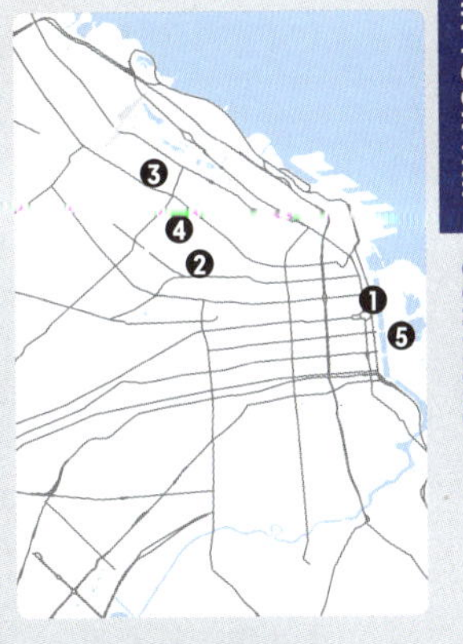

FROM LEFT: MARIA ELISA ROL/SHUTTERSTOCK, CARLOS L VIVES/SHUTTERSTOCK

Asado

Asado is male-dominated in Argentina, but the all-female team at @the_asado_ experience are mixing things up, teaching visitors all things *asado* from a woman's perspective.

Tasty Bites

The finest cuts are *ojo de bife* (rib-eye) and *bife de chorizo* (sirloin). For something leaner, order the *lomo* (tenderloin) Something small and tasty? Try the *entraña* (skirt steak).

Eat It With A Spoon

La Brigada (p105) has been in the heart of San Telmo since 1992. You won't find a steak knife here – the beef is so tender, you can eat it with a spoon.

BEST MEAT EXPERIENCES

Learn to prepare an *asado* with chef Diego Moyana in exclusive classes at ❶ **La Cabaña** (p90) in Puerto Madero.

Experience an intimate 14-course meat fest while chatting with the chefs at ❷ **Fogón Asado** (p165) in Palermo.

Eat *molleja* (sweetbreads) with Racing Club football fans in this rustic closed-door neighborhood *parrilla*, ❸ **El Secretito** (p164).

Send a WhatsApp message months ahead to make a booking at Michelin-starred *parrilla* ❹ **Don Julio** (p165).

Stroll ❺ **Costanera Sur** (p93) and enjoy a classic *choripán* (grilled sausage sandwich).

¡GOL!

A city bursting with spectator sport, BA won't disappoint fans. And we're not just talking football – tennis, hockey, polo, rugby, horse racing, volleyball and basketball all have their place in the city. For boxing fans, there's iconic stadium Luna Park where Evita and Perón first met and where Gardel's funeral and Maradona's wedding were both held. For car-racing fans, there's the Autódromo Oscar y Juan Gálvez, where the F1 Argentine Grand Prix was held until 1998.

Watch a Match

Keep expectations low if you want to see a football match. Clubs have more members than seats in their home stadiums, leaving little room for visitors.

Sporting Fans

The Paseo de la Gloria at Costanera Sur (near the *choripán* stalls) honors famous Argentine sportspeople like Fangio, Sabatini and Vilas.

Get Your Skates On

BA's biggest skatepark and rollerblading complex is found at the excellent Parque Deportivo (p158).

FROM LEFT: FABIDECIRIA/SHUTTERSTOCK, SIMON MAYER/SHUTTERSTOCK, THOMAS TROMPETER/SHUTTERSTOCK

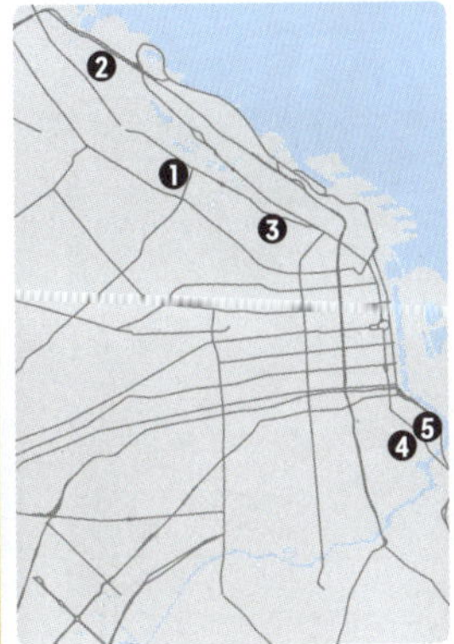

BEST SPORT EXPERIENCES

Marvel at the skill of the players and the power of the horses at the world's most prestigious polo championship at ❶ **Campo Argentino de Polo** (p170).

For die-hard football fans, visit one of the world's largest sports museums, ❷ **Museo River Plate** (p157) at River Plate's iconic homeground, Estadio Mâs Monumental.

Visit the museum in the ❸ **Automóvil Club Argentino** (p141) to see one of Juan Manuel Fangio's F1 Ferraris from 1949.

Experience the country's football madness up close; ❹ **take a guided tour to watch a match** (p212) including transfers, tickets and a snack.

Discover ❺ **San Diego del Barrio de La Boca** (p120), a piece of street art in La Boca dedicated to Diego Armando Maradona.

View over Buenos Aires

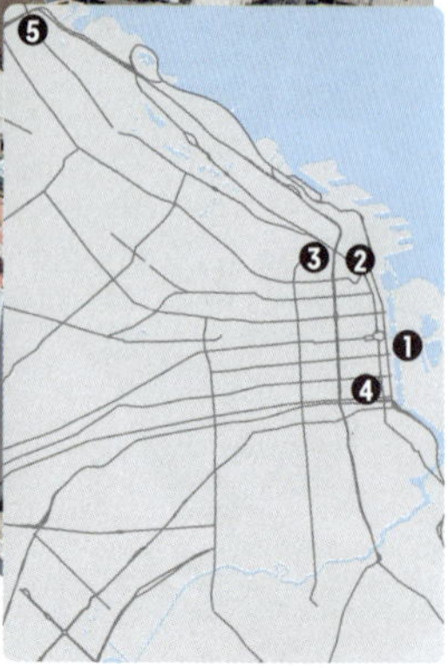

UP HIGH DOWN LOW

You'll probably spot the lack of hills in Buenos Aires, and these flat plains stretch wide across the province where there's hardly a hump to be found. To get up high, enjoy a drink with a view at one of BA's many rooftop bars or visit architectural monuments that give you towering perspectives over the city.

Sexto Panteón

This brutalist underground necropolis (p178) in Cementerio de la Chacarita, designed by Ítala Fulvia Villa, is one of BA's most awe-inspiring spaces.

Archaeological Discoveries

Colonial-era archaeological discoveries include the remains of BA's oldest home, Casa de Naranjo (p105), at Museo de Arte Moderno de Buenos Aires.

BEST EXPERIENCES WITH DIFFERENT PERSPECTIVES

Take in the panoramic city views from the rooftop ❶ **Crystal Bar** (p89).

Climb the ❷ **Torre Monumental** (p127) to take photos from one of the best vantage points in the city.

Enjoy more wonderful views at the ❸ **Alvear Roof Bar** (p147).

Go underground to discover historic tunnels at ❹ **El Zanjón de Granados** (p102).

Visit the grim detention basement at ❺ **El Museo Sitio de Memoria ESMA** (p155).

WITH KIDS

Argentina is a country where all generations spend plenty of time together, so kids are generally welcome and included everywhere. Best to stay in areas like Palermo or Recoleta which are central to most sites and have lots of parks and playgrounds to burn off energy. Top tip: book a spot with a pool in summer.

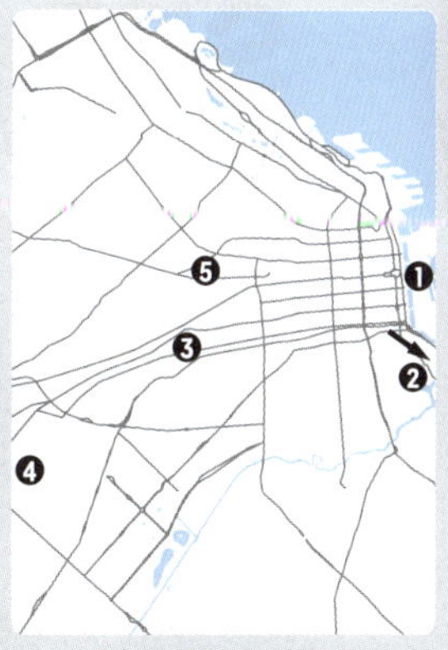

FROM LEFT: OLGA SMOLINA SL/SHUTTERSTOCK, JEFFREY ISAAC GREENBERG 4+/ALAMY

Kids' Dinner Time

BA is a late-night city with restaurants not opening until 9pm. Earlier dining options for kids include cafés, which are usually open from 8am to 8pm.

Snacking

For a quick snack for a hangry (or fussy) toddler, grab a ham and cheese *sandwich de miga* from a *panadería* (bakery).

Baby Essentials

BA is not the most stroller-friendly city with cobblestones, cracked and narrow pavements and plenty of stairs. Bring a baby carrier for little ones.

BEST FAMILY-FRIENDLY EXPERIENCES

Take the kids to ❶ **Museo de la Imaginación y el Juego** (p87), a fun museum dedicated to imagination and play.

Travel to La Plata's ❷ **República de los Niños** (p193), a retro kids theme park with a mini city, farm animals, a train and a plane.

Ride the antique ❸ **Tramway Histórico de Buenos Aires** (p180) in Caballito on weekends.

Head to ❹ **Feria de Mataderos** (p184) for a slice of country life; kids will love the site's music and dancing.

Marvel at the mechanical dinosaurs and spider exhibit at the ❺ **Museo Argentino de Ciencias Naturales** (p179).

SEDUCED BY TANGO

The Argentine tango bewitches many, be it the physicality of the connection, the intimate embrace or the sheer intensity of the dance. In Buenos Aires, tango songs were the anthems of the city's immigrants, telling tales of their yearning for home and the yesteryear. Nostalgic, intense and melancholic – tango is the perfect match for *porteño* culture. It's little wonder this slow show of seduction has stood the test of time.

Milonga

Milonga is the name given to the social gathering of people to dance tango. Venues often host tango classes before their *milongas* each week.

Chacarita Cemetery

Many legendary tango singers are buried in the Cementerio de la Chacarita (p178) including Carlos Gardel, Ángel Villoldo (the father of tango) and Roberto Goyeneche.

Tango Monument

Puerto Madero's Monumento al Tango (p89) is a metallic sculpture representing the *bandoneón* (small accordeon).

FROM LEFT: GARY YIM/SHUTTERSTOCK, 279PHOTO STUDIO/SHUTTERSTOCK, HEMIS/ALAMY

La Glorieta (p152)

BEST TANGO EXPERIENCES

Watch the dancers in the delightful ❶ **La Glorieta** (p152), an historic gazebo that hosts BA's only open-air *milonga*.

Attend the ❷ **Señor Tango** (p119) show in Barracas, close to La Boca. It is one of the most impressive in the city, with dozens of dancers and even two horses on stage!

Head to ❸ **Salón Marabú** (p68), an historic tango spot for live orchestras; **Parakultural** *(parakultural.com.ar)* hosts the *milonga* on Friday nights.

Nestle in with the bohemian crowd at ❹ **El Boliche de Roberto** (p180) where tango singers like Gardel and Pugliese once sang.

Book a spot at ❺ **Bar Sur** (p105) to watch an intimate tango show located in the oldest tango bar in San Telmo.

FOR FREE

Owing in large part to its periods of populist politics, Buenos Aires has plenty on offer when it comes to finding things to do for free. Most historic sites surrounding Plaza de Mayo are free to enter and if all else fails, wander the streets for free. It's the best way to get to know this complex city.

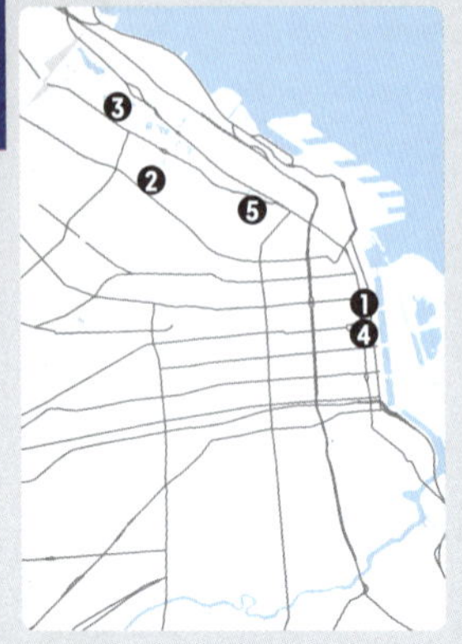

BEST FREE EXPERIENCES

Visit the ❶ **Palacio Libertad** (p60) and observe the city from its magnificent terrace.

Run wild in ❷ **Ecoparque** (p167), Buenos Aires' former zoo turned environmental education site.

Cheer on the horses at the Monday races at ❸ **Hipódromo Argentino de Palermo** (p170).

Check out the magnificent floor mural by renowned Mexican artist David Siqueiros at ❹ **Museo Casa Rosada** (p59).

Explore Argentina's largest collection of art at ❺ **Museo Nacional de Bellas Artes** (p147).

FROM LEFT: G. SOLER TOMASELLA/SHUTTERSTOCK, JEREMY GRAHAM/ALAMY

Donations Please

Keep in mind that when museums and sites in BA are free, they are also often under-resourced. If you can, leave a donation.

Amphitheater

The city's largest amphitheater in Parque Centenario (pictured; p179) has a huge schedule of free events. It's first come, first served. See @elanfi.ba on Instagram for schedules.

Wednesday Deals

Many museums have free (or half-price) entry on Wednesdays. Plan ahead if you have several days in the city.

UNDER THE RADAR

BA is the type of city that takes years to get to know. The top tourist sites are crammed with visitors, but it is easy to step away from the crowds and uncover other sides to the city. Head to lesser-explored neighborhoods like Caballito, Almagro and Chacarita to wander the streets and stumble upon hidden gems.

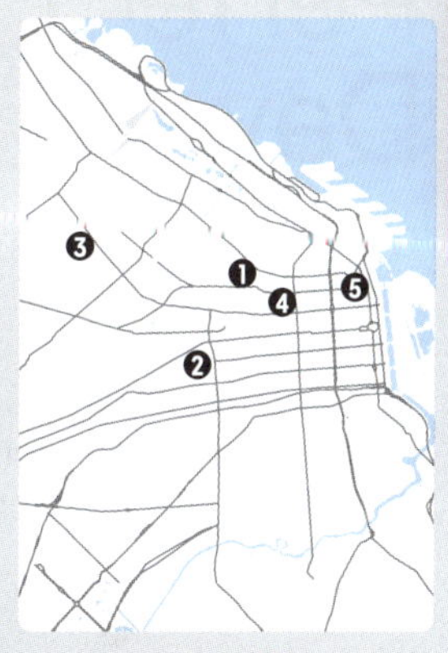

FROM LEFT: DIEGO JEMIO/LONELY PLANET, MARK GREEN/ALAMY

Local Tours

The best way to get under the skin of this city is to meet *porteños*. Always seek out tours or classes run by locals.

Speakeasies

Buenos Aires is home to a huge network of hidden speakeasies. Entrances are often out the back of restaurants or have cryptic passwords to gain entry.

Mundo Lingo

Mundo Lingo events *(mundolingo.org)* are a great way to meet locals wanting to practice English with native-speakers – and pick up some Spanish along the way!

BEST UNDER THE RADAR EXPERIENCES

Visit Xul Solar's labyrinth home and the most extensive collection of his works at ❶ **Museo de Xul Solar** (p144).

Step inside the impressive ❷ **Basílica María Auxiliadora y San Carlos** (p181) where Pope Francis was baptized, and Carlos Gardel sang in the choir.

Check out the underground necropolis containing 150,000 burial plots at ❸ **Cementerio de la Chacarita** (p178).

Discover the gigantic water tank disguised as a palace at the ❹ **Museo del Agua y de la Historia Sanitaria** (p81).

Pop into ❺ **El Legado** (p134), a piano bar that takes requests in Retiro.

Perfect Days

Discover Buenos Aires like a local with these punchy itineraries – each one a whirlwind tour through vibrant barrios, rich culture, and nonstop energy in the city that never sleeps.

Teatro Colón (p61)

NADIA_ACOSTA/SHUTTERSTOCK

DAY 1

Centro Histórico

From leafy **Plaza San Martín** (p126), walk south on pedestrian Florida to experience the bustle of the city. You'll eventually arrive at **Plaza de Mayo** (p58), the heart of Buenos Aires. This historic plaza is surrounded by **Casa Rosada**, the **Catedral Metropolitana** and the **Cabildo Nacional**, so spend the morning deep diving into the city's history. A block away, visit the Manzana de las Luces, a historic site where the Jesuits lived and where tunnels from colonial times can be seen.

Lunch Experience one of BA's historic cafes, **Café Tortoni** (p62) on Av de Mayo.

Centro Histórico

Tour the spectacular **Teatro Colón** (p61) – its stage has been graced by many of the world's great opera stars. Afterwards take a guided tour and climb the lighthouse at **Palacio Barolo** (p76), an architectural beauty inspired entirely by Dante's *Divine Comedy*.

Dinner Sip cocktails and eat sushi with breathtaking views at **Trade Sky Bar** (p69), located in the art deco Comega building.

Centro Histórico

Spend the evening downtown getting in touch with the city's tango roots. Try **Salon Marabú** (p68) for classes and *milongas* with a live orchestra or **El Beso** (p81), an intimate spot that will transport you back to the golden age of tango.

DAY 2

Recoleta & Barrio Norte

Explore Recoleta's famous cemetery; you can wander for hours among the crumbling tombs soaking up the city's history and visiting Evita's mausoleum. Down the road, visit brutalist national library, **Biblioteca Nacional Mariano Moreno** (p141), or visit the extensive Argentine collection at the **Museo Nacional de Bellas Artes** (p147) and the soaring metal flower sculpture, **Floralis Genérica** (p144). Be sure to pop into the entrance hall of the nearby **Facultad de Derecho** (p145): its scale is impressive.

Lunch Pop into **La Cocina** (p142), a hole-in-the-wall *empanada* joint that oozes character.

Puerto Madero

Relax in the **Reserva Ecológica Costanera Sur** (p88), the city's green lung with more than 350 hectares for walking and bird watching along the Río de la Plata. At sunset, take photos at the **Puente de la Mujer** (p87), one of the city's most famous bridges, designed to evoke a couple dancing tango.

Dinner Learn how to cook *asado* at **La Cabaña** (p90). Or for seafood by the river, try **Mare by Fran** (p86).

Retiro

Head out for a night at one of BA's classic speakeasies like **Florería Atlántico** (p131) or try **El Legado** (p134), a hip piano bar which takes requests and where famous musicians occasionally turn up.

DAY 3

Palermo

Wander the cavernous halls of **MALBA** (p168) to take in the Latin American collection. Afterwards visit **Casa de la Cultura del Fondo Nacional de las Artes** (p172), Victoria Ocampo's former home and the first rationalist residence in BA. Then take a stroll around the immaculate **Jardín Japonés** (p164) to marvel at the cherry blossoms (July) or azaleas (September).

Lunch Sushi on the terrace in the **Jardín Japonés** (p164).

La Boca

Walk along **El Caminito** (p115) and take in the iconic multicolored houses. Visit **Museo Benito Quinquela Martín** (p113), where the most famous painter of the neighborhood lived and view the scene from the museum's terrace. Visit **Colón Fábrica** (p113), the scenery and costumes warehouse of the Teatro Colón. And for football fans, **Museo de la Pasión Boquense** (p116) is located in the nearby Boca Juniors stadium.

Dinner Eat one of BA's best steaks with a spoon at **La Brigada** (p105) in San Telmo.

South of Palermo

Enjoy a bohemian night of tango music with the locals at Almagro's historic **El Boliche de Roberto** (p180) where the audience usually spills out on to the street. Afterwards head to **La Catédral** (p180), a tango institution housed in a grungy warehouse with lashings of character. Arrive in the wee hours of the morning when things get going.

WHEN TO GO

Buenos Aires is best in the travel-friendly seasons of spring and fall, but year-round there's always something to do.

Buenos Aires experiences a humid subtropical climate, with four distinct seasons. Summers, from December to February, are hot and humid, with occasional thunderstorms. The stunning *palo borracho* trees are also in full bloom. In fall (March to May), temperatures are milder, and the city is marked by beautiful foliage. Winters, from June to August, are cool and dry, with temperatures typically reaching 15°C (59°F) during the day. Frost is rare, but chilly winds can tunnel through. Spring (September to November) starts with the Santa Rosa storm and then the days start to warm. Jacarandas burst with flowers all over the city.

Accommodations

October to March is tourism high season in Buenos Aires. It coincides with the cruise ship season and with visitors passing through on their way to prime summers in Patagonia. Prices vary according to season so book ahead for peak periods. Many *porteños* take their holidays in January and February when some shops will be closed.

I LIVE HERE

BLOOMING JACARANDAS

Mariana Radisic Koliren is a born and bred *porteña* and the founder of *@lunfardatravel*

I love nothing more than when November arrives and the jacarandas start to bloom, painting the city with their lilac colour. The air tastes of optimism. One of my favorite early summer walks is from bohemian San Telmo to the soaring skyscrapers of Puerto Madero to arrive at the river. It's such a contrast but that's what I love about my city - every barrio has a strong identity.

Jacarandas in bloom

SUNSET SHOT

Standing on the bridge over Av Figueroa Alcorta, you can capture a top sunset shot. The university law faculty's neoclassical architecture contrasts with the striking Floralis Genérica (p144), all while the sunset bathes the scene in warm light and the traffic lights glow.

Weather Through the Year

JANUARY
Avg daytime max: **30°C**
Days of rainfall: **10**

FEBRUARY
Avg daytime max: **29°C**
Days of rainfall: **9**

MARCH
Avg daytime max: **26°C**
Days of rainfall: **10**

APRIL
Avg daytime max: **23°C**
Days of rainfall: **8**

MAY
Avg daytime max: **19°C**
Days of rainfall: **7**

JUNE
Avg daytime max: **16°C**
Days of rainfall: **7**

SANTA ROSA TORMENTA

The Santa Rosa Tormenta, occurring around early September, brings intense storms to Buenos Aires. Characterized by heavy rain, strong winds, and sometimes hail, it marks a shift in the seasons: afterwards, spring has arrived.

Classic Festivals

Buenos Aires Jazz Festival Internacional *(buenosairesjazz.org)* 16 venues including Teatro Colón (p61), the Anfiteatro del Parque Centenario (p179), small jazz clubs and cafes like Las Violetas (p185) are the stages for this staple of the city's cultural calendar. **November**

Festival Internacional de Buenos Aires (FIBA) *(fiba.ar)* Week-long arts and culture festival with theater, visual arts, dance and music events at venues including Usina del Arte (p114). **October**

La Noche de los Museos For one night, many of the city's museums, including MACBA (p105), stay open until after midnight; packed with fun events. **November**

Marcha del Orgullo *(marchadelorgullo.org.ar)* BA hosts South America's largest Pride march from Plaza de Mayo (p58) to Palacio del Congreso (p77). **First Saturday in November**

Yearly Celebrations

Carnaval A month packed with parades featuring *murgas* (traditional music and dance ensembles from each neighborhood) across the city. The main closing celebration takes place on Av de Mayo. **February**

BAFICI *(bafici.org)* Celebration of independent film, held in venues across BA, including Teatro San Martín (p78), with an extensive program of talks and events. **April**

Open House Buenos Aires *(openhousebsas.org)* Two-day festival of architecture and urban design opens the doors to many of the city's architectural beauties which are normally closed to the public. **October**

Quema de Muñecos Head to La Plata (p190) for this New Year's Eve celebration featuring a parade of huge papier-mâché effigies which are set aflame after midnight. **31 December**

I LIVE HERE

WINTERTIME MEMORIES

Juan Agustin Tolosa Paz was born in Buenos Aires and visits often. *@pangeagardens*

It might be an unpopular opinion, but I have many wonderful memories of the city in winter. The air is crisp, the crowds are light, and the days are dry. BA's architecture really pops in the chilly air and the Jardín Japonés is at its best, filled with cherry blossoms. Since our Independence Day is celebrated in July there are hearty dishes like *locro* to enjoy.

Jardín Japonés (p164)

EL NIÑO

This weather effect causes soaring temperatures and heavier than normal rainfall in Buenos Aires. Prompted by a cycle of warming sea temperatures in the Pacific Ocean, it usually lasts between nine and 12 months.

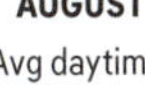

JULY	AUGUST	SEPTEMBER	OCTOBER	NOVEMBER	DECEMBER
Avg daytime max: **16°C**	Avg daytime max: **17°C**	Avg daytime max: **19°C**	Avg daytime max: **23°C**	Avg daytime max: **26°C**	Avg daytime max: **28°C**
Days of rainfall: **8**	Days of rainfall: **8**	Days of rainfall: **8**	Days of rainfall: **10**	Days of rainfall: **10**	Days of rainfall: **9**

Feria de San Telmo (p100)

GET PREPARED FOR BUENOS AIRES

Useful things to load in your bag, your ears and your brain.

Clothes

Dress code For most venues, smart casual will be sufficient.

Comfortable walking shoes or sneakers There are plenty of cobblestones and uneven pavements. You'll be glad of some cushioning.

Dancing shoes The best tango shoes have leather or suede soles without too much grip.

Mosquitos With the hot and humid climate in summer, mosquitos descend. Come prepared with repellent and light, long-sleeved clothing.

Umbrella Useful for the rainy days, of which there can be a few.

Manners

Porteños love to talk; conversation is somewhat of an obsession with discussions, arguments and heart-to-hearts easily rolling into the wee hours of the morning. If you want to get a word in edgeways, **butt in!** This is a totally accepted form of joining in.

However, some topics remain off limits, such as the Islas Malvinas (Falkland Islands). Treat these conversations **with respect**.

A cross-body bag or fanny pack Most *porteños* use these as their everyday bags to keep their belongings close.

Swimmers Beat the summer heat by booking accommodation with a pool.

READ

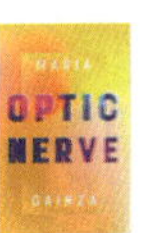

Optic Nerve (María Gainza; 2014) Seductively clever debut novel about a tour guide in BA obsessed with art and ways of seeing.

The Invention of Morel (Adolfo Bioy Casares; 1940) His breakthrough novel where a fugitive hides from tourists on an island.

Things We Lost in the Fire (Mariana Enríquez; 2016) Gothic short stories from Argentina's contemporary master of the genre.

Elena Knows (Claudia Piñiero; 2007) Elena travels across BA, attempting to solve the mystery of her daughter's murder.

Words

Buenas Short for *buenas tardes* (good afternoon) and/or *buenas noches* (good evening), you'll hear it everywhere post noon.

Boludo/a Once an insult, it is a very common, almost endearing term. Locals use it with their children, parents, just about everyone.

Bondi The bus in Buenos Aires, pronounced 'bon-dee,' as opposed to the famous beach.

Buena onda Someone (or something) that has good vibes.

Chabón/a or **Pibe/a** Slang for guy or girl.

Che A way to call attention to a mate or buddy

Estar al pedo Sitting around doing not much

Estar en pedo Very close but this one means drunk!

Guita or **Plata** Money

Hola Spanish for hello, pronounced 'o-la.'

Laburar A common way to say 'to work' in Buenos Aires, rather than the Spanish *trabajar*.

La cuenta, por favor. 'The bill, please.' Or simply make eye contact with the waiter and make the international sign for check by using your finger to write in the air.

Mina Slang for a girl or woman that you don't know.

Pelotudo Similar to *boludo*, but slightly stronger. Used to describe someone who is generally unpleasant to be around.

Piola Slang for cool or nice.

¿Qué tal? 'How are you?' in shops or cafes, a response is not expected.

¿Qué haces? ¿Qué onda? or **¿Como andas?** Informal way of asking 'how are you?' among friends.

WATCH

Wild Tales (Damián Szifron; 2014) Short tales that focus on explosive Argentine behavior.

The Clan (Pablo Trapero; 2015; pictured). Gripping true story of the Puccio family who kidnapped victims after the dictatorship.

Nine Queens (Fabián Belinsky; 2000) Cult classic that follows two con artists around the city.

La Luna Avellaneda (Juan José Campanella; 2004) Feel-good romp about a community trying to save their beloved BA social club.

La Ciénaga (Lucrecía Martel; 2001) Family drama from Argentina's most acclaimed female director.

LISTEN

After Chabón (Sumo; 1987) Italian-Scottish Luca Prodan's last album before his death.

Clics Modernos (Charly García; 1983) García's iconic second solo release with hits like Los dinosaurios.

From Argentina to the World (Atahualpa Yupanqui; 1996) Compilation album from one of Argentina's great folk musicians.

La síntesis O'Konor (Él Mató a un Policía Motorizado; 2017) Third album from this La Plata indie rock band. Él Mató for short.

FROM LEFT: FOCALFINDER/SHUTTERSTOCK, HULAHOP/SHUTTERSTOCK

Ezeiza International Airport

GETTING THERE

Most international flights land at Ezeiza International Airport, also known as Aeropuerto Internacional Ministro Pistarini, 31km southwest of the city. Most domestic flights arrive at Aeroparque Internacional Jorge Newbery in Costanera Norte. Overland travelers will arrive at Retiro.

Taxis

To catch a taxi from Ezeiza International Airport, exit the building and pass by the taxi touts where you'll see a clearly signposted taxi stand.

Airport Shuttle

The shuttle bus Tienda León is a great option if you are traveling alone; frequent shuttles are available between Ezeiza and the city center and between Ezeiza and the domestic airport, Aeroparque Jorge Newbery. There is a stand in the arrivals hall at Ezeiza.

SIM Cards

Either organize an eSIM or data pack and roaming before you arrive or pick up a cheap SIM card at a *kiosko* (corner shop). While there is some red tape to get through as a foreigner, it is a fairly simple process to set up and telecommunication companies like Movistar offer free WhatsApp and calls between Movistar users (a good option if you're in a group). You won't need to spend more than a few dollars on prepaid credit if you're in town for a couple of weeks.

SUBE cards

Neither airport is connected to the Subte, BA's underground subway system, but once you're in town it's a simple network to use and tickets are less than US$1. Hotels and hostels often provide a rechargeable SUBE card, or buy one at stations like Retiro and Scalabrini Ortiz (take your passport for ID).

FROM AIRPORTS TO THE CITY CENTER

From Ezeiza International Airport

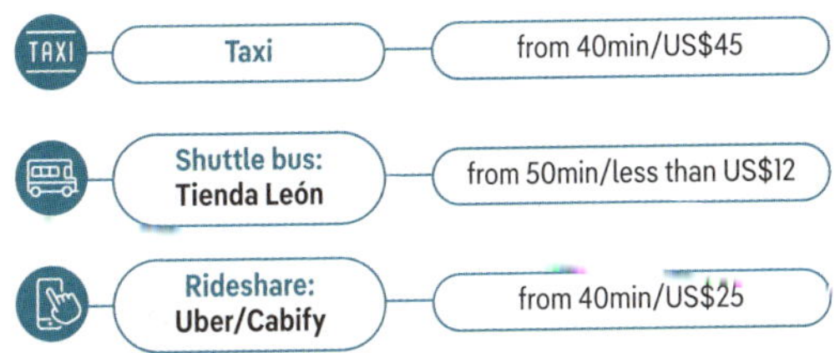

From Aeroparque Internacional Jorge Newbery

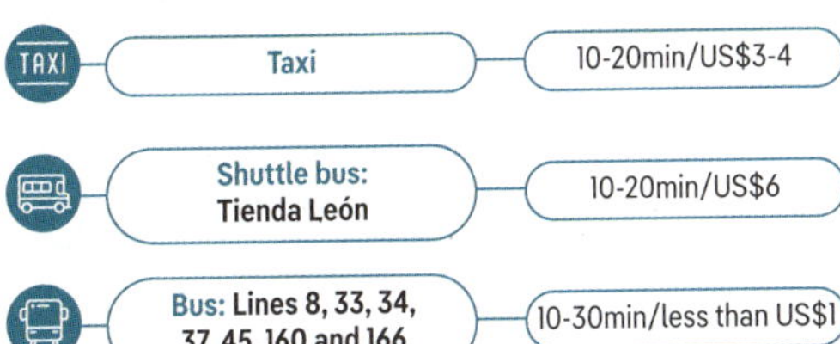

tiendaleon.com

uber.com

cabify.com

TIP

There's free wi-fi in both airport terminals. It's decently fast and can be accessed outside Terminal A in the pick-up and drop-off area close to McDonalds.

For subway, train and airport maps, visit **buenosairesmap360.com**

OTHER POINTS OF ENTRY

Boat

Modern and fast **Buquebus** ferries *(buquebus.com)* from Uruguay arrive at Puerto Madero, a 15-minute walk to Alem Subte station on Línea B (red line). The cheaper **Colonia Express** *(coloniaexpress.com)* ferries arrive in La Boca, from where you can take a taxi to your accommodation. Book online for cheap advance tickets.

Bus

Overnight sleeper buses are a comfortable and cheap way to travel. Most services arrive at the major transport hub, Retiro Bus Terminal. Here you can connect to BA's extensive bondi (local bus) system, two Subte stations (Línea C and Línea E), and train or regional buses that travel to La Plata and beyond.

Train

Estación Retiro is the city's main train station. There is a limited train service connecting Buenos Aires with nearby provinces. Book ahead; tickets often sell out in advance. For shorter trips (from Retiro to Tigre, for example), buy tickets in the station. For longer trips, you can purchase online at webventas.sofse.gob.ar.

FLORENCIA MAISONNAVE/SHUTTERSTOCK

Buenos Aires cycle path

GETTING AROUND

Buenos Aires is a flat city perfect for cycling and walking. Although the wider city itself is reasonably large and spread out, the areas that most visitors spend time in are in a relatively compact area, well serviced by cheap public transport.

Subte

BA's subway system, one of the oldest in the world (it's first line was built in 1913) is the quickest way to get around, though it can get hot and crowded during rush hour.

It consists of *líneas* (lines) A, B, C, D, E and H, each identified by a different colour. C runs north to south and connects the two major train stations, Retiro and Constitución. The other lines run parallel from downtown to the capital's western outskirts. If you're staying in Recoleta or Palermo, you'll likely be using the green line, Línea D.

You'll need a SUBE card. Trips are charged at a fixed price – you don't need your card to exit the station. Trains are frequent but only run until 11:30pm (10:30pm on Sundays).

TIP

While bus routes are numbered, each route often has variations that are signalled by a sign in the bus window saying 'POR' or 'X' destination, meaning via. Make sure you hop on the right bus.

Transport Tips

- The bus and train system may at first feel overwhelming but be brave, it's a great way to see the city.
- Take the bus during non-peak periods; sit close to the front and ask the driver to tell you when to hop off.
- Always use the yellow and black radio taxis; they're everywhere and safe.
- Hail a taxi or Uber home late at night; walking, especially alone, is not recommended in the wee hours.

Although in a state of faded glory in parts, each of BA's subway lines is themed and decorated with wonderful, tiled mosaics, murals and art installations.

Bus

City buses are referred to as *bondis* or *colectivos*. It is an extensive network with most bus routes running 24 hours a day. For navigating the routes, download Moovit which provides accurate schedules and live tracking. The system is cashless, so you'll need a SUBE card to board. When you enter the bus, let the driver know where you'll be alighting, then press your SUBE card to the machine and it will charge the necessary small amount.

TIP

A handy bus is the number 29, it runs from Núñez in the north, past Barrio Chino to Plaza Italia in Palermo, and all the way to San Telmo and La Boca in the south.

Walking

Being flat, Buenos Aires is a reasonably easy city to wander around, and this is by far the best way to discover hidden gems.

That said, there are some challenges. For the first few days, you'll be constantly looking down! Dog poo is a daily threat in BA and densely populated apartment block areas like Recoleta are the worst. You'll also want to watch for cracked and uneven pavements.

For those less mobile or traveling with strollers, Palermo generally has wider sidewalks. San Telmo is a minefield with narrow sidewalks, cobblestones and more crowded streets. As pedestrians, a crosswalk in Buenos Aires is not an invitation to cross – cars don't tend to give way to pedestrians. Wait for the crosswalk signal or stand close to a local, they'll show you how it's done.

PUBLIC TRANSPORT ESSENTIALS

SUBE Card

Most hotels and hostels provide SUBE cards for visitors but if not, head to the Subte station at Retiro or Scalabrini Ortiz where you can purchase a card for a small fee (bring your passport).

Validating Tickets

Tap your SUBE card when you enter the Subte station or board the bus. There are no zone systems for the Subte – you'll be charged a flat fare and don't need to tap off upon exiting. Bus fares vary depending on the zone you're traveling to – tell the driver your destination when boarding and you'll be charged accordingly.

Recharging

When your SUBE card runs out of credit it won't let you tap anymore and you'll have to recharge. This can be done at many stations in person (there are machines, but they often don't work with foreign cards) or at *kioskos* (corner stores) across the city. Many *kioskos* will only accept cash when recharging SUBE cards.

Discounts

If you're staying in BA for a longer period, register your SUBE card. After 20 trips in a month, the price per ride drops – a great incentive for anyone making multiple trips a day.

ART ON THE SUBTE

Check out José Hernández Station on Línea D for murals by Raúl Soldi (the artist who painted the dome of the Teatro Colón) and more recent Messi works.

Carlos Gardel Station on Línea B has impressive mosaics and *fileatado* murals. Also on Línea B, at Federico Lacroze Station, don't miss the 200m long mural that's an immersive Amazonian rainforest scene blending hyperrealism with surreal elements.

Facultad de Derecho-Julieta Lanteri Station (Línea H), opened in 2018, has a sleek, modern design and features contemporary works by artists such as Marcelo Toledo.

Cycling

While BAEcobici bikes are scattered throughout the city, it is a system riddled with red tape for foreigners. Opt for local rental companies. The city has an excellent network of cycle paths although take extra care at traffic lights, drivers tend to run red lights given the chance. Helmets are not commonly worn in BA but are recommended.

Taxi

Taxis are cheap and generally a safe way to get from A to B quickly, unless of course it's peak hour or there happens to be a transport strike (a relatively common occurrence). Rideshare companies operate in BA but they can be more expensive than taxis.

Train

The overground train network fills the gaps the Subte doesn't service. If you head to Núñez, you'll likely catch the train to Núñez or Rivadavia and for Barrio Chino, it is very convenient to hop off at Belgrano C. It's also a great option for heading north out of the city to Tigre or jump aboard the scenic Tren de la Costa that runs along the coastline.

Driving

It is not necessary to drive in Buenos Aires, public transport will often get you anywhere faster, cheaper and with much less stress. Parking is expensive and if you rent a vehicle, you'll likely pay for overnight undercover parking for security reasons. Fair warning: *porteño* drivers (and bus drivers) can be unpredictable, impatient and lackadaisical with road rules.

Ferry

A great way to connect between La Boca and Puerto Madero is to ride one of the cruises offered by **Sturla** *(sturlaviajes.com.ar)* called Postales de Buenos Aires (Postcards from Buenos Aires).

Apps & Maps

Moovit is a fantastic app for planning your trips. It provides real-time bus schedules and live tracking, ensuring you know exactly where to get off.

For maps of bus routes and details of route variations, visit Omnilineas. For subway and train maps, visit Buenos Aires Map 360.

Moovit

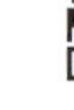

Omnilineas

Buenos Aires Map 360

FROM LEFT: AD-FOTO/SHUTTERSTOCK, JAMES ANDREWS1/SHUTTERSTOCK

Taxi

PREPARING FOR THE SUBTE

Peak Hours

From 8am to 10am and 5pm to 7pm, trains fill to the brim and personal space becomes optional. If you're uncomfortable in crowds, travel outside these hours. Always wear your bag on the front of your body, and avoid using your phone while riding.

Strikes

Transport strikes *(paros)* are a regular part of BA life and can throw the entire transit system into chaos. On these days, the Subte is usually your best bet since surface traffic comes to a standstill – but expect it to be overcrowded. Walking might actually be your fastest option.

Heating & Aircon

Heating and air-conditioning both in stations and on the trains vary depending on the line. In summer, a hand fan and a bottle of water can make a huge difference in comfort.

Hawkers & Buskers

Street vendors often walk down carriages, quietly placing items – pens, tissues, chewing gum – on your lap. Don't feel pressured to buy. The Subte is a stage as much as a transit system. Musicians, poets, magicians and performers regularly hop on to share their art.

TRAVEL COSTS

Subte
approx. US$0.60

Bus
approx. US$0.30

Bike rental
US$15/day

NEED TO KNOW

You'll notice that many people don't have their phones out while riding the subway. Snatching phones is a common petty crime and iPhones in particular are very expensive in BA.

ACCESSIBILITY

Buenos Aires is not an easy city to travel in for those with mobility challenges. Very few Subte stations have elevators, most are entered via flights of stairs or occasionally, escalators. Many BA buses have a manual ramp at the back door for wheelchairs or they 'kneel' and have wider spaces but not all bus stops have easy access or ramps. As an alternative, **OK Traslados** *(oktraslados.com.ar)* is a wheelchair accessible taxi service that provides rides and tours around Buenos Aires.

ALEX PHOTO STOCK/SHUTTERSTOCK

Barbecued beef

DINING OUT

The headline in Buenos Aires is the beef but there is a burgeoning food scene worthy of the world stage.

Buenos Aires is a melting pot of cultures and it's largely the immigrants – the Spanish, Italians, Russians, Germans, Armenians, Welsh and Japanese, to name but a few – who have so keenly left their mark on the dining tables of the city. The large numbers of Italians who emigrated to Argentina in the late 19th and early 20th centuries have had the biggest influence with staples such as pasta, *milanesa* (breadcrumbed veal), pizza and ice-cream being common everyday foods for many *porteños*. The Italian *panaderías* (bakeries) are also a daily stop for locals, who pop in for bread, *facturas* (pastries) bursting with *dulce de leche* (caramel) and *sandwiches de miga* (a light crustless sandwich) which hits the spot for afternoon tea.

You'll find the classics everywhere, but the Buenos Aires restaurant scene is innovative with plenty on offer for the visitor looking to eat their way through the city. From creative vegan joints to Asian fusion and tapas, there are plates oozing with flavor on every corner.

Beef

For the meat-eater, Buenos Aires is heaven. Everyone wants to wrangle a booking at one of the top *parrillas* (steakhouses), but the truth is, it simply doesn't matter where you go – you are unlikely to ever eat a bad piece of meat in Argentina.

It all comes down to the world-class beef, the simple preparation (just salt) and a slow-cooking process over coals. Many

Best Buenos Aires Dishes

BIFE DE CHORIZO
The choice cut of beef – equivalent to New York strip steak or sirloin.

CHORIPÁN
Grilled sausage wrapped in a crusty baguette and dripping with salsas.

MILANESA
Breadcrumbed veal schnitzels, the definition of comfort food.

FLAN MIXTO
Flan with lashings of cream and dulce de leche.

parrillas offer a traditional *parrillada* (mixed grill) and it's a great tasting smorgasbord with a little bit of everything. Expect appetizers like *choripán* (sausage), *chinchulines* (intestines), *molleja* (sweetbreads) and *morcilla* (blood sausage). For the main affair, there'll certainly be *tira de asado* (ribs) and other flavorful cuts like *vacío* (flank).

Vegans & Vegetarians

No longer the butt of the joke in Buenos Aires, vegans and vegetarians will be well fed during their stay. The city is crawling with innovative spots bringing veggies to the forefront. Some of our top picks include Donnet (p182), which specializes in mushrooms; Tita la Vedette (p183), for divine colored plant-based pastas in Chacarita; Sampa (p179) in Villa Crespo, for its small seasonal menu; Hola Chola Garage (p155) in Núñez, for plant-based meals in a fun garage spot; and stylish Gordo Vegano (p152) in Belgrano. For finer dining, try Anafe in Colegiales where more than half the menu is vegetarian. And they're not afraid to take risks, their delicious *chimichurri* coexists with rose water and sesame oil.

Gluten-Free (SIN-TACC)

BA used to be a celiac's worst nightmare but today you'll find plenty of options. Labelled on local menus as SIN-TACC, many cafes and restaurants have gluten-free meals. For ingredients, head to Mercado de Belgrano (p154) to shop gluten-free produce at Casa Polti. For those who don't want to miss out on the pastas, make a booking at Cucina Paradiso Senza Glutine, top Italian chef, Donato de Santis's 100% gluten-free outpost in Palermo.

Traditional Restaurants

Pulperías, *cantinas*, *boliches* and *bodegones*: all are versions of traditional restaurants, but the terms can be a little confusing. *Pulperías*, *cantinas* and *bodegones* all evolved from early general stores and immigrant delis that started to offer their clients a place to sit and sip after they'd purchased their produce. *Boliches* are for partying!

Puertas Cerradas

The *puertas cerradas* (closed-door) restaurant scene in BA was dying down prepandemic but there are still several

VALTER JUNIOR/SHUTTERSTOCK

FOOD & WINE FESTIVALS

Festival de las Parrillas In June each year, this roving festival plays host to many of BA's finest restaurants, which serve up innovative meat dishes.

Vinos y Boedgas Held in Buenos Aires' main conference and exhibition space, **La Rural** in Palermo. Festival to celebrate wine and wineries; annually in September.

Sabor a Buenos Aires Outdoor food festival offering held in March in Parque Thays in Recoleta.

Leer y Comer 'Read & Eat' is long-running food and literary festival held in October each year with food trucks, talks and live music.

La Noche de los Bares Notables In November each year, with events, special menus and fun for the whole family in *bares notables* (historic cafes and bars).

HELADO

Porteños are the true masters of the art of ice cream.

EMPANADAS

Delicious savory parcels filled with meat, cheese or veg.

FUGAZZETA

BA-born and bred pizza topping layered with a tonne of cheese and onions.

POSTRE VIGILANTE

Perfect post-meal combo of quince paste and cheese.

Empanadas, La Cabaña

DIEGO JEMIO/LONELY PLANET

TOP RESTAURANTS

Yiyo El Zeneize: Take a trip back in time to this family-run *cantina* (p183) in Parque Avellaneda.

La Sorellina: Nothing beats the mortadella at this top-rated pizzeria (p152).

La Cocina: Classic hole-in-the-wall *empanada* stop (p142). Try the Pikachu, a heavenly cheese and caramelized onion combo.

Anafe: Colegiales contemporary diner (p152); lots of tasty vegetarian options.

Basa: Local and Mediterranean-inspired dishes in a romantic underground setting in Retiro (p126).

Mare By Fran: Superb seasonal seafood by the river in Puerto Madero (p86).

La Cabaña: Quality meats and *asado* cooking classes taught by chef Diego Moyano (p90).

Tintorería Yafuso: Exquisite Japanese in an intimate setting (p179).

around. These spaces are generally in residential homes or buildings with no signage and limited seating. Some are held weekly, monthly or more sporadically. It is a unique experience – often hosted by some of the city's best chefs – and a great way to meet others as you generally eat at a shared table. Reservations are a must. Try @nectar.casa in Barrio Norte or long-running classic **Treintasillas**.

Learn how to cook an *asado* with the all-female crew at The Asado Experience (p168).

Michelin Stars

In 2023, the Michelin food guide made its way to Buenos Aires. There is a long list of recommended restaurants in town but very few stars have been awarded. Both Trescha (p178) in Villa Crespo and Don Julio (p165) in Palermo have one star each. The only restaurant with two stars, Aramburu (p144) in Recoleta, offers an 18-course tasting menu, a feast for the senses from chef Gonzalo Aramburu.

Food Shopping

Supermarkets in Buenos Aires aren't the dominating force that they are in Western countries. They're helpful for finding most things but locals still prefer to shop at the neighborhood *verdulería* for fruit and veg, the *carnicería* for meat and the *panadería* for daily bread. For visitors, it might be a hark back to the past, but it ensures a sense of community and provides ample opportunity for chats. Wait your turn (sometimes you need to take a number) and ask for (or point at) the things you would like to buy. To see a lovely old food market in action, head to Mercado

BA FOOD ONLINE

PICK UP THE FORK
@pickupthefork
Expat Allie Lazar has been eating her way through BA for over two decades and often posts about new and old dining spots.

MALEVA MAG
@malevamag
BA cultural magazine (in Spanish) that regularly reviews the city's new trends in food.

BUENOS PALADAIRES
*@buenospaladaires_*
Local Irina Widuczynski shares many of BA's top foodie spots on her wildly popular Instagram.

BUENOS AIRES PORTAL
buenosaires.substack.com
Weekly online newsletter packed with information about bars and restaurants.

del Progreso (p183) in Chacarita where locals line up to buy piles of *milanesas* for lunch or snack on fresh *empanadas* from the butcher's stands.

Café de Especialidad

BA is in the midst of a coffee revolution and, while some may rejoice at the ability to pick up a flat white (often made with a double shot here) on any given corner, the proliferation of these cafes means that the traditional coffee culture of the city is at risk of being lost.

A classic *porteño* order is a *cortado* and to order one, just catch a waiter's eye and make a 'C' with your thumb and forefinger. You'll be a local before you know it. To sip coffee at one of the city's many historic and lesser-known bars, check out @bardeviejes. The group have created a map so you can explore on your own and they organise monthly mass visits to old bars to raise their profiles.

When to Eat

Being a late-night city, most cafes don't open until 8am when coffee and bite-sized *medialunas* (croissants) are on offer for breakfast. Lunch is considered the main meal of the day when many locals tuck in to *milanesas* (veal schnitzels) or pastas. At 5pm, many stop to have a coffee and something sweet at a café or take *facturas* (pastries) and *mate* (tea-like communal drink) to a local park. Restaurants don't tend to open until 9pm when *porteños* are starting to think about dinner. If you can't stretch that far, cafes are often open from 8am to 6pm (or later) and serve food all day long.

Service & Tips

Service will probably be a little slower than what you're accustomed to. Sometimes taken for arrogance (or nonchalance), remember that eating in Argentina is for sitting, pausing and taking time out of your day. It is not an event purely for refueling and service reflects this cadence. *Porteños* also practice the ritual of *sobremesa* (the final course of the meal that is purely for chatting), so if the waiter leaves you alone for a while, they're only giving you space to talk.

The expected tip in cafes and restaurants is 10%. Pay your bill and then leave the tip in cash on the table.

RUBEN M RAMOS/SHUTTERSTOCK

Milanesas con papas fritas **(veal schnitzels with fries)**

OLIVERDELAHAYE/SHUTTERSTOCK

El Boleo (p93), Puerto Madero

BAR OPEN

Buenos Aires' bar scene focuses on the drama and theater of the space – and the quality of the cocktails.

There's nothing quite like a night out in Buenos Aires, it truly is the city that never sleeps. Restaurants, bars, late-night cafes and social clubs all come alive long after sunset – some would say, closer to sunrise.

For those seeking to taste the town, simply head out the door. With challenging import regulations, drinking in Buenos Aires is firmly planted in the local – you'll be hard-pressed to find international wines, spirits or beers. Pull up a pew at any establishment to sip and savor Argentina's national drink, *vino tinto* (red wine).

Outside of wine, craft beer and microbreweries are still flourishing but are slowly giving way to sumptuous cocktail bars that now proliferate the city. Buenos Aires is home to some of the world's best bars including one of the city's pioneering speakeasies, Florería Atlántico (p131), a basement bar entered via a florist in a residential area of Retiro. There are plenty of others to be discovered – just be sure to pack your sense of adventure.

Vino Tinto

By decree, Argentina's national alcoholic beverage is red wine. The most popular and well-known varietal is malbec, and there's no better accompaniment to savor with a feast of red meat. While Mendoza is traditionally the home of malbec, where the grapes are grown on the foothills of the Andes, today Argentina lays claim to several award-winning wine-making regions such as the high-altitude Valles Calchaquíes in Salta (northwestern Argentina) and the irrigated steppe of Neuquén and Río Negro where unique, light pinot noirs flourish in the Patagonian wind-afflicted landscape.

In Buenos Aires, there's not a bar or restaurant without an Argentine wine on the menu. For wine-oriented experiences, look out for

Lonely Planet's Top Bars

EL LIMÓN
Superb cocktails and easy listening in Villa Crespo. **p180**

TRES MONOS
World's best service from this pioneering Palermo hotspot. **p173**

LIBRARY LOUNGE
Intimate lounge at Faena Hotel with signature cocktails. **p92**

PRESIDENTE
Oozing charm and elegance, dress up for a night at this classic bar. **p131**

restaurants with *cavas* (cellars) or try Pain et Vin (p166), a wine-bar in Palermo run by a baker-sommelier couple (email info@pain-et-vin.com for group private tastings). Other great wine bars are Anchoíta Cava and Naranjo Bar in Chacarita (p184), Nilson (p109) in San Telmo and Amores Tintos (wines on tap by the glass; p166) in Palermo. For wine advice, pop into fun bottle shop, Sommelier en Bicicleta.

Fernandito

If *vino tinto* is the nation's official drink, the *fernandito* (Fernet & Coke) must be an awful close second. Though a traditional Italian liquor, made from a secret mix of herbs including myrrh, saffron and chamomile, Fernet Branca is so popular in Argentina that the brand built a distillery in Buenos Aires to serve the country (the only one outside of Italy). Unlike in Italy, where the drink is commonly served straight on ice, in Argentina it's a long pour cocktail, doused in cola and full of ice. Fernet Branca is bitter, like *mate*, and is an acquired taste – but the addition of sweet cola makes it an easy-drinking hit. You'll find the *fernandito* in bars throughout the city and in all *porteño* homes where friends gather before heading out.

Beer

The craft beer scene has been going strong in Buenos Aires for over a decade – bolstered by home-grown hops from the *chacras* (small independent farms) around El Bolsón near Bariloche. Patagonia, Blest, Buller and Antares are all classic breweries with a multitude of options on tap. Order a *porrón* and you'll get a long-neck bottle to share among friends in a round. *Chopp* is a mug of draft beer. For takeaways, head to the supermarket or a local *kiosko* (corner shop). It is legal in Buenos Aires to drink in the street.

Cocktails

After many years in a craft beer phase, Buenos Aires is upping the ante and is firmly in its reimagined cocktail era. Elegant, dimly-lit and immersive, they're all entirely atmospheric and with innovative cocktail lists, creating local spins on traditional drinks. Pop into LPV Las Patriotas Vilardo (p173) in Palermo for a menu inspired by female patriots from around the world. Be sure to try the Sargento Martina which honors an Argentine woman who captured British soldiers in her tavern during the invasions.

For home-grown classics, try a *clarito* – BA's answer to the martini (extra-dry gin and a splash of white vermouth, lemon peel and stirred, never shaken) or BA's own old-fashioned, which differs from others as local bartenders mix the sugar and bitters with water to create a paste.

Apéritifs

Bittersweet flavors are the signature palate of *porteños* so it's no surprise the city is home to a vibrant *aperitivo* culture. *Mate* (the ubiquitous hot caffeinated drink that Argentines imbibe daily), Fernet Branca, vermouth and Cynar (an artichoke aperitif) are all popular local bitter-heavy drinks.

NEED TO KNOW

Opening hours Vary widely but most bars are open from 7pm until after midnight, longer on weekends. Some close Mondays.

Booking Bookings are essential via social media for small or popular bars.

Service Many bars have table service. Be sure to leave 10% in cash as a tip.

Drinking culture Generally, *porteños* don't drink to excess; they pace themselves over a long night.

Clubs Most clubs have bouncers and dress is smart casual. For some clubs, book ahead via social media to receive a discount. Clubs are usually open from 2am until dawn.

Smoking While smoking is not permitted indoors in Buenos Aires, areas with access to open air allow smoking.

LPV LAS PATRIOTAS VILARDO
Head upstairs for this Palermo Chico locals' favorite with live music.
p173

TRADE SKY BAR
Breathtaking panoramic views and an amazing interior design in the art deco Edificio Comega.
p69

DOPPELGÄNGER
No wine, no beer, just cocktails from this San Telmo staple.
p109

LE CLUB BACÁN
Cocktail list inspired by rock and tango greats – try the Por Una Cabeza.
p131

Florería Atlántico

MARK GREEN/SHUTTERSTOCK

BEST SPEAKEASIES

Florería Atlántico (p131): Pioneering basement bar entered via a florist.

Uptown (p172): Immersive speakeasy where New York's subway comes alive.

Al Fondo (p159): Climb the stairs to discover this moody spot out the back of Piedra Pasillo.

Barcito Brutalista (p180): Tiny hidden bar beneath a late-night Villa Crespo pizza joint.

La UAT (p173): Fun 80s themed bar and dance floor at the back of Cacho Rotisería.

878 (p180): Laid-back hidden Villa Crespo bar.

J W Bradley (p170): Orient Express–themed time capsule in Palermo.

There are numerous *vermut* bars throughout the city – favorites like Los Galgos (p76), SIFÓN Sodería (p184) and La Fuerza (p184) are prime spots for a pre-dinner drink.

Speakeasies

Porteños are great storytellers (they have a lot of practice talking) so it's little wonder that the trend of speakeasies in BA has taken such a strong hold. The element of surprise, the drama and the dedication to theme are second to none. Most are found throughout Palermo Soho and Hollywood although they are starting to spread to Belgrano and Núñez as well. Some have cryptic passwords which you must decipher to enter while others are simply hidden behind existing restaurants or entered via nondescript doors.

Learn more about BA's historic *bares notables* on p153

Bar de Escuchas

There are several *bar de escuchas* (listening bars) in BA where people go to listen to DJs spin vinyl. Generally intimate spots for listening to music rather than dancing – try Gris Gris (p167) in Palermo or El Limón (p180) in Villa Crespo. Another fun spot with a musical twist is El Legado (p134), a piano bar in Retiro where requests are taken, and all (including famous musicians who sometimes pop by) join in to sing. Book ahead via their respective social media.

Clubbing

Buenos Aires is famous for its *boliches* (nightclubs). Every weekend – and even on some weeknights – the city's clubs come alive with crowds dancing to beats. Some of the most impressive spots are located in grandiose restored theaters, warehouses or factories – or perched on the banks of the Río de la Plata where partygoers can watch the sun rise over the water as the festivities wind down. Clubs are spread out over the city with main clusters in Palermo and on the Costanera Norte.

LGBTIQ+ Nightlife

There are plenty of LGBTIQ+ bars and clubs in the city (p172) – try Club 69 in Villa Crespo, Peuteo for drag shows, and the dance party Rheo held at Crobar.

For something more relaxed, visit low-key social and cultural club Feliza or head to El Despelote Tango to learn a few tango steps before taking part (or watching) the *milonga*.

MORE INFORMATION

MAPABSASGAY
@mapabsasgay
This map to LGBTIQ+ BA is regularly updated and covers bars, restaurants and other sites.

ARGIESMENT
argiesment.com
Check this website for discounts and free entry to some clubs.

TIME OUT BUENOS AIRES
timeout.com/buenos-aires
Best bar lists and events searchable by week and month.

BAIRES SECRETA
bairessecreta.com
Regularly updated with bars to visit and what's on in the city.

ALEXANDR VOROBEV/SHUTTERSTOCK

HOW TO... Drink Mate

For Argentines, drinking *mate* (pronounced mah-te) is an intrinsic part of everyday life, but to the uninitiated, it is a custom that requires some explanation. First, there's the confusion of the name itself: the word *mate* is used for both the drinking gourd and the butter tea infusion it holds. Then there are the complicated tasks of preparing *mate* and knowing how to drink it (through a metal straw with its own strainer, no less), not to mention the subtleties involved in sharing *mate* with friends (a minefield of *faux pas*). Read this guide to find out all you need to know.

When to Drink Mate

Many Argentines start their day with *mate*, but it's also common to drink it in the afternoon, perhaps accompanied by a *merienda* (afternoon tea snack) of *facturas* (pastries) or *chipa* (savory cheese balls).

Mate Equipment

First, you'll need a *mate*, a hollow drinking gourd traditionally made from a squash. It holds the *yerba*, the leaves of a plant that is native to northeast Argentina (look for packets of *yerba* in any Argentine supermarket). You'll also need a *bombilla*, a metal straw with a strainer at the end, and a thermos flask to fill with hot water.

How to Prepare Mate

Heat the water to between 75-80 degrees celsius but don't allow it to boil (electric kettles in Argentina have a special temperature setting for *mate)*. Pour some *yerba* into your *mate* and give it a shake to remove some of the dust. Put the *bombilla* into the *yerba*, so that the strainer is near the bottom of the *mate* and the opening is at the top.

And as for the taste? Well, it takes some getting used to. Some people add sugar and other flavors to the *yerba* to sweeten it.

How to Drink Mate

Holding the *mate* with one hand and the thermos in the other, carefully pour hot water into the gourd. Drink it immediately, by sipping the liquid through the *bombilla*. Keep the thermos near you and continue filling and drinking for as long as you like. The first *mates* poured are the strongest; after a while the *yerba* becomes washed (weakened).

HOW TO SHARE MATE

When drinking *mate* in a group, one person takes responsibility for serving everybody (the *cebador*). They will serve themselves first (it's polite to take the strongest hit), then pass the *mate* to each person in the group in turn. You should drink all the water in the *mate* (sip gently and avoid noisy slurping) before wordlessly returning it to the *cebador*. Saying *'gracias'* indicates that you do not wish to take part in the round anymore.

FROM LEFT: VALERIA VENEZIA/SHUTTERSTOCK, NORBERTO MARIO LAURIA/SHUTTERSTOCK

Luna Park

SHOWTIME

BA's a late-night city bursting at the seams with culture – there's live music of all stripes, theater, tango, dance and film.

Entertainment in Buenos Aires is a feast for the senses. In terms of live music, there are hundreds of venues dedicated to tango, jazz, *folklore* music and contemporary musicians and bands. Many cafes, bars, restaurants and neighborhood cultural centers also host packed schedules.

With one of the world's most acoustically perfect concert halls, the spectacular Teatro Colón (p61) is a must-visit for classical music, ballet and opera. Usina del Arte (p114) in La Boca is another fabulous venue, housed in a former power plant, with shows ranging from live orchestras to contemporary dance and tango.

Theater is a headline affair in the city with productions ranging from classic plays to multimedia performances and cabarets although, of course, most are in Spanish. You'll also find comedy clubs and film and writers' festivals in this truly cultural city. La Boca is not a nightlife option as it's unsafe to stay here after dark. Belgrano and Puerto Madero don't really have entertainment options other than eating and drinking.

Theater

Porteños love drama and with that, theater. There are hundreds of venues scattered across the city and annual attendance is in the hundreds of thousands. Traditionally, the theater district has centered around Av Corrientes between Av 9 de Julio and

Best for Live Music

SALÓN MARABÚ
Historic tango venue with popular *milongas* and live orchestras.
p68

PALACIO PAZ
Sumptuous palace at Plaza San Martin with live tango orchestras.
p129

CONGO CULTURAL CLUB
Music and fun outdoor garden in Palermo.
p170

THE NEW BRIGHTON
Character-filled *bar notable* with jazz, *boleros* and tango.
p74

Callao, but you'll find performances of all levels in every *barrio*.

Along Av Corrientes, BA's best-known theaters are Lola Membrives, El Nacional, San Martín (p78), Gran Rex, Metropolitan and Ópera – home to musicals, comedies, variety shows, children's favorites, tango and drama. For tickets, it is often easier to physically purchase seats at the *boletería* (box office; usually open 10am to 8pm) of the theater. Vouchers for discounted tickets are sold at Tickets Buenos Aires booth near Plaza de la Republica.

For off-Corrientes shows, independent theater or more experimental works (by both up-and-coming performers and more established actors), seek out theaters in San Telmo, Palermo and Abasto. Some theaters on the alternative circuit include Teatro Beckett, El Camarín de las Musas and Abasto Social Club. A good source for current non-mainstream performances is alternativateatral.com.

Live Music

It's not difficult to seek out live music in this city – many of BA's cafes and restaurants also have live music performances ranging from tango to jazz, rock and electronic music. Check their respective social media for details. For international artists and larger shows, classic venues are **Movistar Arena** *(movistararena.com.ar)* and **Niceto Club** *(@nicetoclub)* in Villa Crespo, **Luna Park** *(lunapark.com.ar)* in Centro Histórico and **Obras Sanitarias** *(estadioobras.com.ar)* in Núñez.

Buenos Aires has a thriving jazz scene with several iconic spots for late-night listening. In Palermo, drop by art deco beauty Virasoro (p170), Thelonious Club (p170) or Bebop (p170). In Recoleta, check out Jazz Voyeur Club (p147), Prez (p147) or Clásica y Moderna (p147). All are intimate and historic spots. Check their respective social media for schedules and tickets. Every November the International Jazz Festival sees shows happening with top local and global artists all over the city.

Outdoor Music Festivals

Anfiteatro del Parque Centenario (p179), BA's largest outdoor amphitheater, has regular live music and *folklore* music and dance performances which are mostly free. Built with the intention of being the location for Teatro Colón summer concerts, the quality is often very high, and the location can't be beat.

For summer music festivals, **Lollapalooza** *(lollapaloozaar.com)* has been held almost every March in the city since 2014, while **Primavera Sound** *(primaverasound.com)* is held in November. For electronic music fans, Buenos Aires plays host to **Creamfields** *(creamfields.ar)* in November and **Ultra Buenos Aires** *(ultrabuenosaires.com)* in February.

For regular dance parties, check out the cluster of outdoor clubs by the river in Costanera Norte (at the southern end of Aeroparque Internacional Jorge Newbery). Plan to turn up from 2am onwards.

Anfiteatro del Parque Centenario (p179)

TEATRO COLÓN
Historic opera house; the world's greats have graced its stage.
p61

CLÁSICA Y MODERNA
Intimate bookstore-cafe with a packed music schedule.
p147

PALACIO LIBERTAD
Incredible acoustics in this former post office building.
p60

VIRASORO
Iconic jazz venue housed in an art deco beauty in Palermo.
p170

Classical Music

With one of the world's most acoustically perfect opera houses, the spectacular Teatro Colón (p61) is a must-visit for classical music, ballet and opera. You can tour the building (arrive early for the first tour at 10am) and have lunch at the cafe where the pastries and dishes are inspired by great works of classical music. If you want to catch a show, check the schedule and book tickets online two to three months before your trip. The season runs from March to November with a break over summer.

Two relatively recent additions to the city in terms of excellent acoustics are Usina del Arte (p114), housed in a former power plant, and Palacio Libertad (p60) in the former central post office of Buenos Aires. Check websites for programs.

Tango

Nostalgic, intense and melancholic – tango is the perfect match for *porteño* culture. It's little wonder this slow show of seduction has stood the test of time. To see tango in the city, you'll be tempted to take in a mega spectacle – there are some fabulous shows like Señor Tango (p119), which has a couple of horses on stage! However, intimate shows are equally worthwhile. Try Bar Sur (p105) in San Telmo, Salón Marabú in Centro Histórico or visit a *milonga* (social tango evenings) where you can often combine a lesson with dancing, or choose to just watch. Check out hoy-milonga.com to search for *milongas*, classes and tango events in the city. For one week each August, BA bursts with more tango energy than usual when venues across the city host the **Tango BA Festival y Mundial**. Dancers from around the world descend on the city to compete in the tango World Cup at Usina del Arte.

Folk Culture

You'll find plenty of folk culture in BA with several venues showing *folklore* music and dancing. There are also several *peñas* (restaurants where folklore singers come together to sing, a tradition from Northern Argentina) like Pal Que Guste (p135) and Peña La Morena (p143) in Recoleta.

On Sundays, head to Feria de Mataderos (p184) to join in the gaucho festivities and enjoy performances of zamba on the

LEONID ANDRONOV/SHUTTERSTOCK

Teatro Colón (p61)

NEED TO KNOW

Plan Ahead
If you want to see a show at Teatro Colón, check out the schedule and book tickets online (at least 2-3 months ahead). Tickets sell out fast.

Mix it Up
Interested in cultural activities? Check out visitbue.com, which creates a monthly-round up of events and festivals coming up in BA.

Theater Tickets
Head to theater box offices or visit Tickets Buenos Aires, which sells vouchers for discounts of up to 50% on ticket prices.

ENTERTAINMENT BY NEIGHBORHOOD	
Centro Histórico	Home to the cultural strip that never sleeps (BA's theater district, Av Corrientes), Teatro Colón and a vibrant scene of tango, live music and cinema.
Retiro and Recoleta	Peppered with small live music joints from *peñas* (folklore music in a restaurant setting) to jazz and rock.
San Telmo	Wide range of tango shows from the stage to the streets and folklore performances at local cultural centers like Torquato Tasso and ATRODEN.
Palermo	Palermo's party scene includes iconic jazz, indie and comedy clubs, and *milongas,* while the racing track hosts large music festival events.
South of Palermo	More alternative scene with music venues such as Villa Crespo's Niceto Club, avant-garde theater, bohemian tango joints and drumming spectacles at Ciudad Cultural Konex.

open-air stage. Cultural centers are a treasure trove of cultural activities. In San Telmo, Centro Cultural Torquato Tasso (p108) on Parque Lezama has high-quality tango and *folklore* and ATRODEN hosts all manner of performances from tango to *zamba* and *murgas*.

Cinema
BA has a strong cine culture. The most recent generation of directors have been working in the wake of the economic crisis of 2001. Some of Argentina's best-known directors are Lucrecia Martel *(La Cienega),* Juan José Campanella *(Los Secretos de Sus Ojos),* Pablo Trapero *(El Clan),* Damián Szifron *(Relatos Salvajes)* and stylistic newcomer, Luis Ortega (*El Jockey* and *El Angel*). In commercial hits, you're more than likely to spot Ricardo Darín, Argentina's most beloved actor.

There's nothing quite seeing a film on the silver screen in a city that still loves cinema. Catch a *trasnoche* (late-night showings, midnight or later on Friday and Saturday nights) and settle in. Films are mostly shown in their original language with Spanish subtitles. For art-house films, visit the wonderful Cine Cosmos in Av Corrientes and check out the regular film program at MALBA (p168).

La Noche de los Museos
For one night in November, many city museums stay open until the wee hours of the morning. With a packed schedule of cultural events, music and activities (including the chance to enter some buildings that don't normally open to the public), it is a festive evening packed with fun. Perfect for anyone who ever dreamed of sleeping over at the museum.

FROM LEFT: QUIGGYT4/SHUTTERSTOCK, MILTON EKMAN/SHUTTERSTOCK

Feria Plaza Serrano (p170)

SHOP

Buenos Aires shopping offers hip fashion, artisanal crafts, unique art and antiques. And everything you buy supports the local market.

Shopping in Buenos Aires is a vibrant experience that reflects the city's rich culture and craftsmanship. With a strong emphasis on local businesses due to import restrictions, you'll find a diverse array of specialty shops – from charming hat stores to tailors, bespoke shoemakers and more. Shopping malls offer a mix of high street and international brands, but often at a premium. Weekend markets bring the streets alive, with lively fairs like San Telmo's showcasing art, crafts and antiques, while Feria de Mataderos (p184) offers a taste of gaucho culture. Hidden designer showrooms provide a treasure hunt for unique fashion pieces, guided by local experts. Leather goods are a highlight, with numerous shops offering everything from custom jackets to colorful bags and belts.

Art and graphic works abound, and book lovers can easily lose themselves in the city's many bookstores. Don't miss out on delicious local souvenirs like *dulce de leche* and fine Argentine wines. There's something for everyone when it comes to shopping in BA.

Best Independent Shops

MAIDANA
Specialty handcrafted hats worn by Carlos Gardel and Rod Stewart.

FACÓN
Chacarita shop with unique artisanal pieces from across Argentina.

CASA LÓPEZ
Leather goods handmade by local artisans: handbags, belts and shoes.

EL BOYERO
For *mates*, leather belts, knives and ponchos in Calle Florida.

Home-Grown Scene

Due to import restrictions, stores in Buenos Aires are primarily locally owned and operated with their manufacturing base in Argentina. And without the competition of online behemoths like Amazon or big discount stores, the city is full of surviving specialty stores, like 112-year-old Maidana (p73) for hats and Don Mundo, a shop that only sells exquisite world globes. In San Telmo, you'll find the studio/showroom of Juan Carlos Pallarols, the gold and silversmith who has made every presidential baton since 1983 and Pope Francis' papal chalice.

Where to Shop

While there are some lovely malls and shopping arcades in historic buildings, often shopping complexes are reserved for high street labels and a spattering of multinationals. They tend to be slick and modern. Also, beware, international brands can be more expensive than at home. Some have children's playgrounds and games for rainy days like Abasto Shopping (p182) and Alcorta Shopping (p169) near MALBA in Palermo (it also has an incredible outdoor terrace food court on level 3). In the center, pop into beaux arts building, Galerías Pacífico (p67).

In Buenos Aires a lot of interesting things are hidden from view, and this extends to shopping as well. Many artisans and designers don't have street-facing stores but rather show their wares in hard-to-stumble-upon *puertas cerradas* (closed door) stores and showrooms. Some are more visible – like the hip art and design store Casa Social (p152) in Colegiales – while for others it's best to contact one of the local expert guides who specialize in shopping tours.

Markets

The weekends are alive in Buenos Aires with every barrio having its own brand of *feria* (market). On Sundays, choose between San Telmo's sprawling art, collectables and craft fair (p100), which runs for over half a mile along Defensa and has an atmosphere second to none, or Feria de Mataderos (p184), a country-comes-to-the-city market filled with gaucho wear, silver and leatherwork, with folklore music and dance performances.

For art and crafts in a park setting, head to Feria de Artesanos de Plaza Francia (p141) in Recoleta (just outside the cemetery) or Feria Palermo Viejo (p170) held in Palermo Soho's Plaza Armenia. Both have wonderful selections from local artists and makers including silver knives and jewelry, *mate* and football paraphernalia, hand-crafted children's toys and knitwear.

Antiques & Vintage

On Sundays, the section of the Feria de San Telmo that surrounds Plaza Dorrego is chock full of dealers selling ceramics, glass and antiques of every description.

Galería Patio del Liceo (p165)

GALERIA PATIO DEL LICEO
Hidden complex of artist and design studios on Av Santa Fe.

JOFRÉ ART GALLERY
Artist Roberto Jofré's studio and shop, located in Caminito.

BOLAZO
Hip women's line with a uniquely Argentine spin on gaucho wear.

GALERÍA MAR DULCE
Palermo art gallery with small works by local artists.

Many have their shops along Defensa and you can visit during the week (often closed Mondays) but there are certainly not as many as pre-pandemic. Also try Mercado de las Pulgas (p183), an indoor market mostly focused on furniture.

For spectacular vintage and collectables, visit the long-standing GIL Antigüedades (p101) on Plaza Dorrego. Ring the bell and don't miss the basement museum-like collection. For those who love a rummage, the second-hand clothing markets at Parque Centenario (p179) and Parque Rivadavia (p183) in Caballito are top spots. Be prepared to spend some time here; there are gems, but you have to sift through. Along the park you'll also find second-hand bookstands with plenty of paper ephemera and books.

Leather

With all that beef, there's a bustling leather market in Argentina and locals know how to craft fine belts, boots, bags, shoes, jackets and horse gear. There are leather stores all over the city but for the best prices head to Calle Murillo between Acevedo and Scalabrini Ortiz in Villa Crespo. There are two blocks of leather stores so compare and *comprar* (buy).

In the center, you'll find leather shops on Calle Florida (use a critical eye as quality varies – try Sylvia y Mario) where you can also buy bespoke leather jackets. If you're looking for leather through a hip lens, try local women's label Las Pepas (colured disco jackets are their trademark; they have several stores across BA including in Palermo), Jessica Kessel for unique designer shoes and NIMES (p169) for the softest vegetable tanned bags and jackets.

Indigenous & Folklore Crafts & Textiles

For bright wool *mantas* (shawls and blankets) from Northern Argentina head to La Buena Tierra (p141) in Recoleta. Looking for authentic gaucho attire like *boinas* (knitted berets)? Visit El Galope (p141) in Recoleta or Feria de Mataderos (p184). Shop for *fileteado* art at La Filetería (p107) or at the markets in San Telmo.

For quality wool rug design and fair trade options, check out Facón (p180) and Elementos Argentinos (p165). Nativo Argentino (p101) in San Telmo has incredible vintage rugs, at a price. Facón also has stunning hand-painted flags and unique hand-crafted works, not seen elsewhere in the city.

ANNE HUNECKE/SHUTTERSTOCK

Gaucho attire, Feria de San Telmo (p100)

NEED TO KNOW

Etiquette
Bargaining is not accepted in Argentina. At markets, remember the person working the stall is quite often the artist or designer.

Payments
Cards are widely accepted, but foreign cards may have issues. Shops often offer a 10% discount for paying in cash. Take cash for markets.

Hours
Usually from 10am until 8pm (some close Sundays) although in Palermo shops don't open until noon. Specialty stores in Buenos Aires often have a ticket system for service.

SHOPPING BY NEIGHBORHOOD	
San Telmo	Flea market finds, antiques and collectables, and *fileteado* signs.
Palermo	Local brands, hip designers, bookstores and art galleries.
Puerto Madero	Upmarket art and design by the river.
La Boca	Art and souvenirs related to tango, football and the colorful streets of Caminito.
Retiro	Quality leather stores in calle Florida and beaux arts beauty, Galerías Pacífico.
Centro Histórico	Rummage for new and second-hand books on Av Corrientes and shop 100-year-old specialty stores.
Recoleta	Bustling high street and Patio del Liceo on Av Santa Fe with small specialty and luxury stores in the residential streets.
South of Palermo	Hidden independent design shops mixed with everyday retail and weekend second-hand markets in Parque Centenario and Rivadavia.

Graphic Art & Books

There's a healthy print and illustrator community in BA – check out the studios in Galería Patio del Liceo (p165), Quorum (p101) in San Telmo or Punc (p180) in Villa Crespo to take a poster or comic home. Galería Mar Dulce (p165) in Palermo also has a great selection of works on paper and small art pieces from local artists. The store in MALBA (p168) is another favorite with locally designed pieces and posters.

BA has hundreds of bookstores – you'll see them everywhere. For the bibliophile, it's a dream to wander a city in love with the printed word and many have weekly events and talks for their local community. Obviously, most stores cater for *porteños* and books are in Spanish. For first editions try La Librería de Ávila (p66), the oldest bookstore in BA founded in 1785.

For English books, head to KEL Ediciones (p152) in Belgrano R for the biggest range of English titles in the city. Walrus Books (p101) in San Telmo specializes in second-hand English books. There's also an English section at El Ateneo Grand Splendid (p142) housed in an opulent former theater. Keep an eye out for Argentine titles that have been translated into English under the Charco Press editorial.

Food & Drink

Food items that make great gifts are *dulce de leche* (caramel spread) and *alfajores* (bite-sized cookie sandwiches dipped in chocolate or meringue); pick up a box of the latter in the branches of Havanna (p90) scattered around the city, or Cachafaz Caminito (p117). If you want to take a taste of the city back home, purchase a bottle or two of one of Argentina's fine wines, or aperitifs like vermouth or the bitter Fernet-Branca. The ubiquitous *pinguinos* (penguin jugs) used to serve table wine in BA are also a popular souvenir.

K OF CHINA
ALVEAR ICON

BUENOS AIRES

THE GUIDE

Chapters in this section are organized by neighborhood. Neighborhoods are delineated by a specific local character or identity, where you'll find unique experiences, local insights, insider tips and expert recommendations.

Puerto Madero (p82)
DMITRII MOCHENOV/SHUTTERSTOCK

Belgrano, Núñez & Costanera Norte (p148)

Residential and peaceful parts of the city fast becoming foodie hot spots. Costanera Norte for river walks and parks.

Palermo (p160)

Palermo is for parties! Nightlife abounds and lazy days are for strolling BA's largest barrio's parks, museums and shops.

South of Palermo (p174)

Villa Crespo, Chacarita, Almagro, Abasto and Caballito: barrios away from the spotlight but nevertheless hip.

NEIGHBORHOODS AT A GLANCE

Find the places that tick all your boxes.

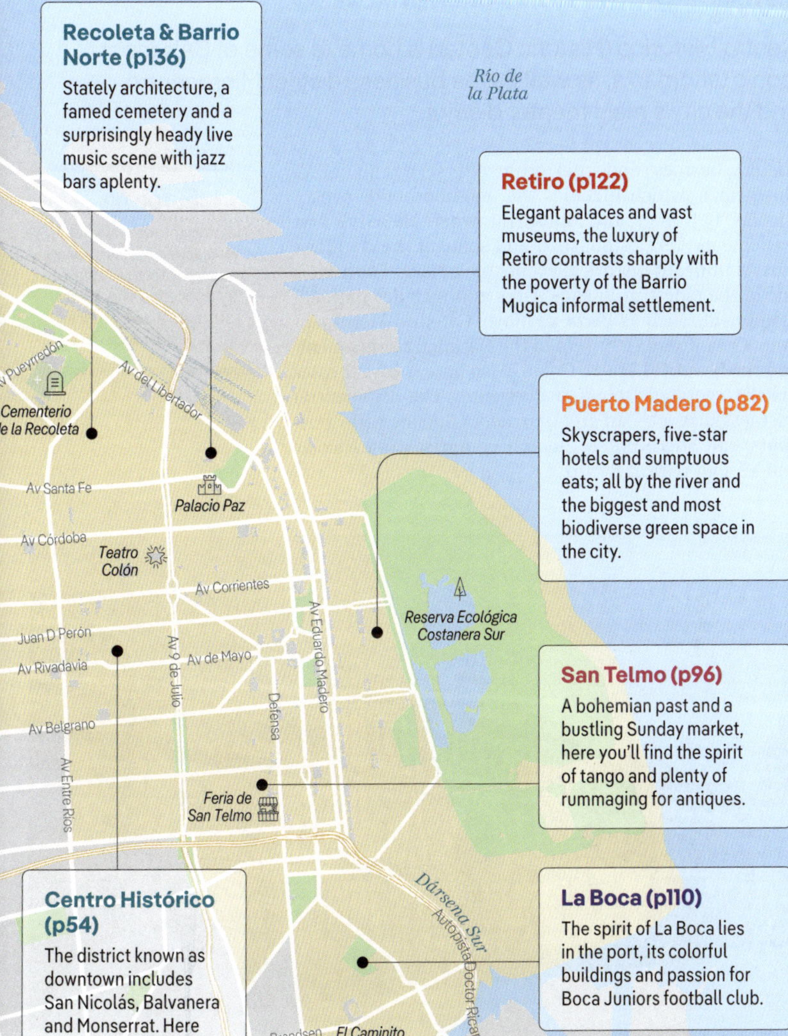

Recoleta & Barrio Norte (p136)
Stately architecture, a famed cemetery and a surprisingly heady live music scene with jazz bars aplenty.

Retiro (p122)
Elegant palaces and vast museums, the luxury of Retiro contrasts sharply with the poverty of the Barrio Mugica informal settlement.

Puerto Madero (p82)
Skyscrapers, five-star hotels and sumptuous eats; all by the river and the biggest and most biodiverse green space in the city.

San Telmo (p96)
A bohemian past and a bustling Sunday market, here you'll find the spirit of tango and plenty of rummaging for antiques.

Centro Histórico (p54)
The district known as downtown includes San Nicolás, Balvanera and Monserrat. Here you'll find the Obelisco, Plaza de Mayo and the beautiful Teatro Colón.

La Boca (p110)
The spirit of La Boca lies in the port, its colorful buildings and passion for Boca Juniors football club.

Researched by Diego Jemio

CENTRO HISTÓRICO

HISTORIC DOWNTOWN AND MONUMENTAL AREA

Centro Histórico (Historic Center) is home to some of BA's most iconic landmarks, as well as the business district Microcentro and the city's main theater district.

History, business and entertainment is served up in BA's 'downtown' which includes the neighborhoods of San Nicolás, Balvanera and Monserrat, where the city's first settlements were established and some of the country's most significant historical events took place. The area is one of the oldest in Buenos Aires and includes national monuments such as Plaza de Mayo, Catedral Metropolitana, Casa Rosada (the seat of the National Government) and the beautiful Teatro Colon. Also here is BA's theater district, centered around Av Corrientes. The city's central business district – an area *porteños* (Buenos Aires residents) call Microcentro – mostly comprises San Nicolás and a small part of Retiro.

TOP TIP

Many downtown restaurants offer *menús ejecutivos* (lunch specials) all for a reasonable, fixed price. It's a good way to try out otherwise pricey restaurants.

DOTMILLER1986/SHUTTERSTOCK

Casa Rosada (p59)

See page 197 for places to stay in Centro Histórico

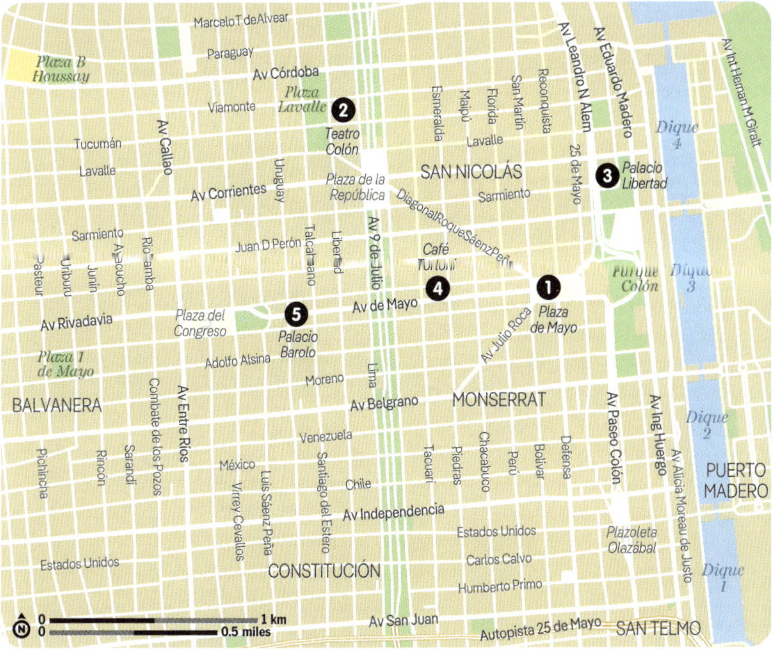

Highlights

❶ Plaza de Mayo ▶
Stand in the city's oldest square around which are some of the city's most historic buildings, including the Casa Rosada. **p58**

LEONARDO ALE ROCHA/SHUTTERSTOCK

❷ Teatro Colón
Marvel at the architecture and beauty of one of the most important opera houses in the world. **p61**

❸ Palacio Libertad
Visit the most significant cultural center in Latin America, built on the site of the former central post office. **p60**

❹ Café Tortoni
Have a coffee in this historic bar, founded in 1858, where great personalities of art and politics have passed through. **p62**

❺ Palacio Barolo
Climb the dome of the office building whose design was inspired by Dante Alighieri's *Divine Comedy*. **p76**

Getting Around

Walking
Touring the Centro Histórico on foot allows you to avoid the traffic and see some of its magnificent buildings.

Subte
Líneas A, B, C and D connect you to the main points of interest in the Centro Histórico.

Bus
Take bus 37 or 67 from Palermo, bus 86 from La Boca or bus 17 from Recoleta.

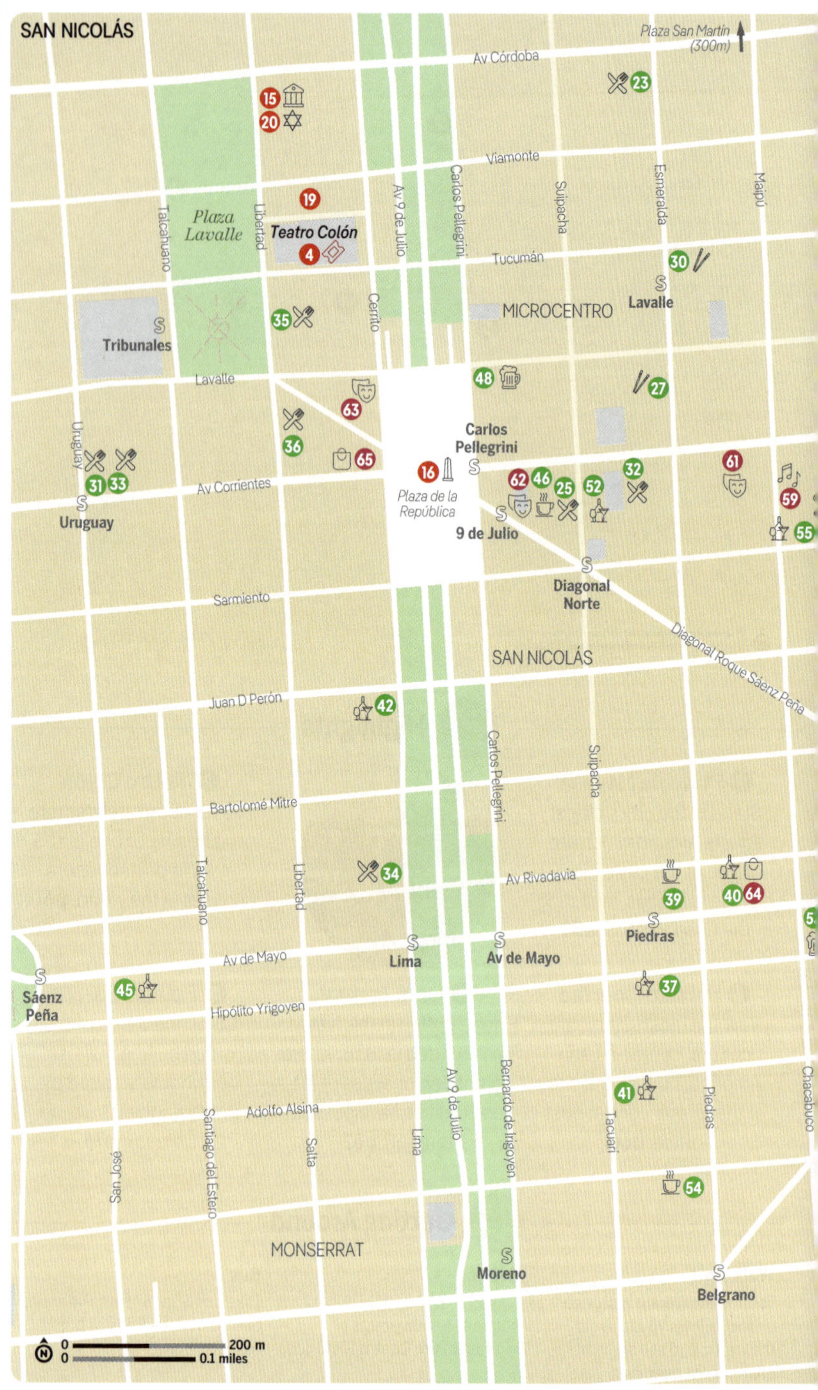
SAN NICOLÁS
Plaza San Martín (300m)
Av Córdoba
Viamonte
Tucumán
Lavalle
Av Corrientes
Sarmiento
Juan D Perón
Bartolomé Mitre
Av Rivadavia
Av de Mayo
Hipólito Yrigoyen
Adolfo Alsina
Talcahuano
Libertad
Cerrito
Av 9 de Julio
Carlos Pellegrini
Suipacha
Esmeralda
Maipú
Uruguay
Plaza Lavalle
Teatro Colón
Tribunales
MICROCENTRO
Lavalle
Carlos Pellegrini
Plaza de la República
9 de Julio
Diagonal Norte
Diagonal Roque Sáenz Peña
SAN NICOLÁS
Uruguay
Lima
Av de Mayo
Piedras
Sáenz Peña
San José
Santiago del Estero
Salta
Lima
Bernardo de Irigoyen
Tacuarí
Piedras
Chacabuco
MONSERRAT
Moreno
Belgrano
0 200 m
0 0.1 miles
15
20
19
4
35
63
36
65
31
33
16
62
46
25
52
32
48
27
30
23
61
59
55
42
34
39
40
64
37
45
41
54

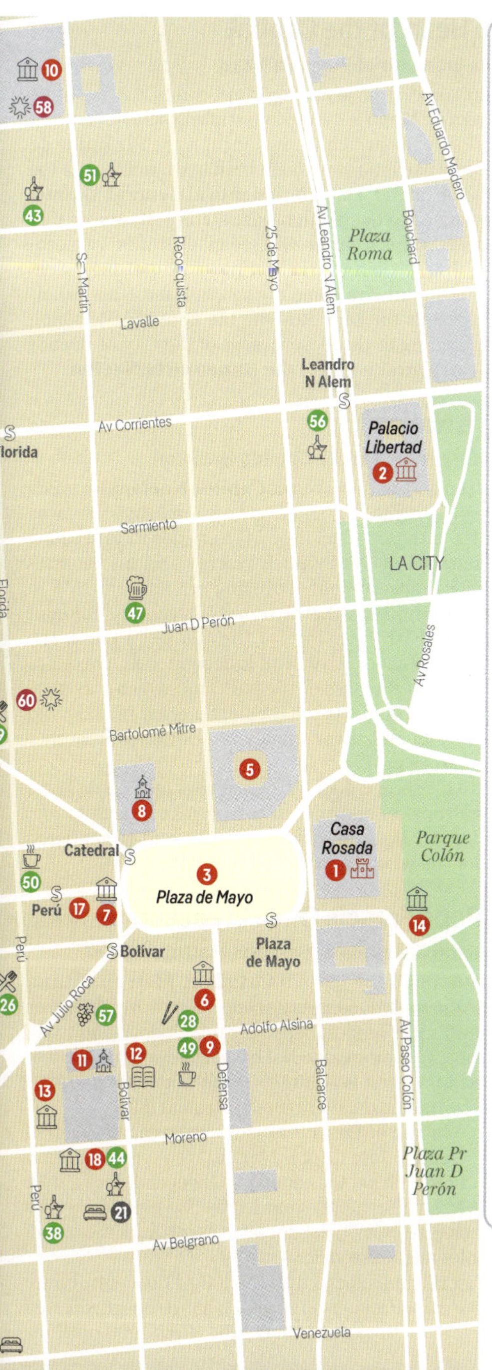

HIGHLIGHTS
1 Casa Rosada
2 Palacio Libertad
3 Plaza de Mayo
4 Teatro Colón

SIGHTS
5 Banco de la Nación
6 Buenos Aires Museo
7 Cabildo Nacional
8 Catedral Metropolitana
9 Farmacia de la Estrella
see 60 Galería Güemes
10 Galerías Pacífico
11 Iglesia San Ignacio de Loyola
12 La Librería de Avila
13 Manzana de las Luces
14 Museo Casa Rosada
15 Museo Judío de Buenos Aires
16 Obelisco
17 Pasaje Roverano
18 Paseo de la Cisterna
see 16 Plaza de la República
19 Plaza del Vaticano
20 Templo Libertad

SLEEPING
21 Cassa Lepage
22 Viajero Hostel Buenos Aires

EATING
23 Broccolino
24 Café Paulin
25 Confitería La Ideal
26 D'Oro
27 Fabric Sushi
28 Furaibo
29 Green Eat
30 In & Out Sushi
31 La Americana
32 Las Cuartetas
33 Los Inmortales
34 Museo del Jamón
35 Petit Colón
36 Zum Edelweiss

DRINKING & NIGHTLIFE
37 Abra Cultural
38 Bar El Colonial
39 Café Tortoni
40 Che Malbec
41 Cichaus
42 Cielo Sky Bar
43 Claridge Hotel
44 Cohiba Atmosphere
45 Dome Rooftop Bar
see 60 Florida 165
46 Gontran Cherrier
47 Growlers
48 Keller
49 La Puerto Rico
50 London City
51 Nivel Dios
52 Partners Coffee & Wine
53 Patagonia
54 Santa Café
55 The New Brighton
56 Trade Sky Bar
57 Vinoteca Winenot

ENTERTAINMENT
58 Centro Cultural Borges
59 Salón Marabú
60 Teatro Ástor Piazzolla
61 Teatro Astros
62 Teatro El Nacional
63 Tickets Buenos Aires

SHOPPING
see 17 Lagomarsino
64 Librería El Túnel
65 Librería Kafka

BUDGET CENTRO HISTÓRICO

Cine Gaumont (MAP p70): Cinema with low-cost admission, featuring Argentine and Latin American films.

Terraza Teatro Bar (MAP p70): Theater with low-priced or free comedy and stand-up performances.

Casa de la Provincia de Buenos Aires (MAP p70): Throughout the year, they organize concerts, art exhibitions and lectures with free admission.

Sala Leopoldo Lugones (MAP p70): An iconic picture house in Buenos Aires offering the best of world cinema since 1967.

Centro Cultural Ricardo Rojas (MAP p70): Offers a diverse artistic program with a multidisciplinary approach. Its shows are affordably priced.

Historic Heart of the Capital

MAP p56

Admire the grandeur of Plaza de Mayo

The scene of some of the most important events in Argentina's history, **Plaza de Mayo** is the obvious starting point for touring Centro Histórico. Its principal monument is the **Pirámide de Mayo**, the first patriotic monument built to commemorate the May Revolution of 1810. The **Monumento al General Manuel Belgrano**, a sizable equestrian bronze statue, also stands out. In recent years, at his feet, you will see many stones with people's names. It is a tribute to the victims of COVID-19.

Around the square are some of the city's most important buildings, such as the Casa Rosada, the Catedral Metropolitana, the building of the Government of the City of Buenos Aires and the central house of the **Banco de la Nación**.

Birth of a Nation

MAP p56

Take a history lesson at the Cabildo Nacional

At the west end of Plaza de Mayo, the **Cabildo Nacional** *(cabildo nacional.cultura.gob.ar; free; 10:30am-6pm Wed-Sun)* was the epicenter of the Revolución de Mayo, which in 1810 ended with the removal of the Spanish viceroy and his replacement by a local government. Covering events from 1766 to 1823, the museum tells the history of Argentine colonial society, the English invasions of the Río de la Plata, the construction of Buenos Aires and independence. There are also details about the uses of the building, which was once the city's jail, and objects such as art works, medals, old clothes, and gold and silver shields are exhibited, together with explanatory posters.

Head up to the second floor for a great view of Plaza de Mayo from the balcony. In addition to the permanent exhibition, there are temporary exhibits and musical and recreational activities for the whole family.

Where Pope Francis Once Preached

MAP p56

Stand beneath the dome of Catedral Metropolitana

Finished in 1827, the grand **Catedral Metropolitana** *(catedralprimadabue.wixsite.com/buenosaires)* began as a much more modest construction of adobe and wood walls. Today the cathedral has a 41m-high dome, a mosaic floor and 14 paintings of the Stations of the Cross by Italian artist Francesco Domenighini.

In one of the lateral naves is the mausoleum of General José de San Martín, the revered military hero who led the country to independence in 1816. It is permanently guarded by two grenadiers who change every two hours, but sometimes the schedules are not so strict.

In the halls located to the left of the central nave is the cathedral museum, which has a room dedicated to Pope Francis; as Jorge Bergoglio, from 1998 until his

THE GENERAL'S RETURN

In the chaos that followed Argentina's independence, General José de San Martín chose exile in France. His remains were brought to Buenos Aires in 1880, 30 years after his death. You can see a statue of the general in **Plaza San Martín** (p126).

DIEGO JEMIO/LONELY PLANET

Museo Casa Rosada

consecration as Supreme Pontiff, he was Archbishop of Buenos Aires. Admission to the cathedral is free, but you must pay to visit the museum.

Mural at Casa Rosada

MAP p56

Visit the museum of the pink-hued palace

Named for its distinctive color, **Casa Rosada** is the seat of the national government and houses the office of the president. It is closed to the public. The building occupies the site where colonial riverbank fortifications once stood; today, however, after repeated landfills, Casa Rosada stands more than 1km inland.

Located behind the palace is the interesting **Museo Casa Rosada** *(casarosada.gob.ar; free; 11:00am-6:00pm Wed-Sun)*, which covers over 200 years of Argentina's history. More than 10,000 historical pieces are exhibited, such as furniture and paintings, the great Cadillac of Juan Domingo Perón, and personal belongings of the people who shaped this country.

MADRES DE PLAZA DE MAYO

Porteños are famous for their propensity to take to the streets in protest. The best-known voices of dissent are the Madres de la Plaza de Mayo (Mothers of Plaza de Mayo). On April 30, 1977, 14 mothers whose children had disappeared under the military dictatorship gathered in the Plaza de Mayo and demanded to know what had happened to their missing children. The military government dismissed them, claiming that their children had simply moved abroad, but the women continued to march in their iconic white handkerchiefs every Thursday. Together with the Abuelas de la Plaza de Mayo (p157), they played an essential historical role as the first groups to openly oppose the military junta and open the doors for later protests.

EATING IN CENTRO HISTÓRICO: OUR PICKS

MAP p70

Helueni: A family restaurant with a small, unpretentious dining room, serving excellent Arab and Jewish food. *9am-7pm Mon-Fri, 10am-4pm Sun* $$

El Tropezón: Argentine and Spanish dishes since 1896. Try *puchero de gallina* (chicken and veg casserole). *8am-1am Mon-Fri, noon-1am Sat & Sun* $$$

Maria Fedele: Trattoria located in a 19th-century building offering good value four-course menu. Famous for its *tiramisu*. *8pm-11pm Wed-Sat, 12:30pm-3pm Sun* $$

Centro Vasco Francés: Offers traditional dishes of Basque cuisine. One of their specialties is stuffed peppers. *noon-3:30pm, 8pm-midnight* $$$

A CONTROVERSIAL NAME CHANGE

Argentines are passionate not only about soccer but also about politics. When Javier Milei became Argentina's president in 2023, he decided to rename the Néstor Kirchner Cultural Center – originally named after the former Peronist president – as Palacio Libertad, reflecting his well-known opposition to that political movement and his desire to erase its legacy. Despite the change, many locals still refer to it by its former name, Centro Cultural Kirchner (or CCK), out of habit or political affinity. Regardless of political preferences, be sure to visit and enjoy its free activities, exhibitions, and impressive architecture.

Perhaps the most beautiful object in the museum is the mural *Ejercicio Plástico* (Plastic Exercise) created in 1933 by a team formed of the famous Mexican muralist David Alfaro Siqueiros and the Argentine painters Lino Enea Spilimbergo, Antonio Berni and Juan Carlos Castagnino, together with the Uruguayan set designer Enrique Lázaro. Guided tours, lasting 45 minutes, take place on Fridays, Saturdays and Sundays at 4pm.

Beautiful Former Post Office

MAP p56

Tour Palacio Libertad

The vast beaux arts **Palacio Libertad** *(palaciolibertad.gob.ar; free; 2-8pm Wed-Sun),* formerly known as the Centro Cultural Kirchner, is Latin America's most important cultural center. Inaugurated in 2015, the building had previously housed the central post office since 1928. The magnificent restoration has managed to keep the spirit of the old building while incorporating six auditoriums and an immersive hall.

The night tour (which starts at 7pm and lasts 80 minutes) is a good opportunity to learn the history of the building and enjoy panoramic views of the city from its dome. The enthusiastic guide explains every detail of the mailbox room, original floors, old post office counters and the inkwells that were used to write and send letters. He also talks about the construction of modern facilities, such as the National Auditorium, which the locals nickname 'the whale' because it is shaped like that great animal. The guided tour ends on the ninth floor of the building, on the large terrace next to the dome. This outdoor terrace wraps around the base of the dome and offers panoramic views of the city.

A Theatrical Cafe

MAP p56

Visit Petit Colón for a pre-performance snack

A few meters from the Teatro Colón is a café called **Petit Colón** *(@petitcolonba; 7am-midnight),* popular with theatergoers before performances. Chandeliers, wooden floors and colored marble create an aesthetic that emulates the Teatro Colón. The basement tearoom is decorated with photographs of some of the stars who have performed at the theater including Mikhail Baryshnikov, Enrico Caruso, Plácido Domingo, Luciano Pavarotti, Maria Callas and Arturo Toscanini.

EATING IN CENTRO HISTÓRICO: BEST PERUVIAN

MAP p70

La Conga: Long-running family business, popular for its *ceviches* and dishes to share. Always full, but worth the wait. *11:45am-11:45pm Thu-Tue* $$

Asu Mare: A traditional Peruvian restaurant with several branches in the city. Its specialty is *ceviche. noon-11:30pm* $$

Status: A pioneer in popularizing Peruvian food in BA. Traditional dishes include *chicharrón* and different types of rice. *noon-3pm & 8pm-12:30am* $$

Chan Chan: Traditional Peruvian cuisine with coastal dishes. *noon-4pm & 8pm-midnight Tue-Sun* $$

TOP EXPERIENCE

Teatro Colón

MAP p56

Sinking into a red velvet seat for a performance at **Teatro Colón** *(teatrocolon.org.ar)* is a magical experience. This is one of the world's greatest opera houses, and you can discover it for yourself by attending a performance here or taking a behind-the-scenes tour.

Architecture & Architects

This vast theater can seat 2500 spectators with standing room for another 500. Italian Francesco Tamburini was the main architect, but after his death in 1891 his partner Vittorio Meano (who designed the Palacio del Congreso; p77) was put in charge. After Meano was murdered (possibly due to a love triangle), Belgian Jules Dormal took over and added some French elements to the theater. The stunning main hall is renowned for its acoustics thanks to its architectural proportions and the quality of its materials, which enhance its exceptional sound quality.

Take the Tour

To learn more about the theater's construction and architecture, join one of the regular daily tours. Tours in Spanish depart every 15 minutes; tours in Portuguese and English are only available at three specific times per day. There's time to take photos in the foyer, the Galería de los Bustos, the Salón Dorado and the main hall.

Theater fans will also enjoy a visit to Colón Fábrica (p113) a warehouse in La Boca, where past production scenery and costumes are on display.

TOP TIPS

- On tours between 10am and 11am there are fewer people.
- A secret passageway inside the theater leads to a cafe called **Pasaje de los Carruajes**, which serves pastries and dishes inspired by great works of classical music.

PRACTICALITIES

Scan this QR code for details on performances and tours.

THE BEATING HEART OF BUENOS AIRES

Some *porteños* call it Av Corrientes while others refer to it as Calle Corrientes. Why the confusion?

Corrientes runs for 69 blocks, from Av Eduardo Madero in the east to Av Federico Lacroze in the west, crossing the neighborhoods of San Nicolás, Balvanera, Almagro, Villa Crespo and Chacarita. Its most popular section passes through the financial and commercial heart of San Nicolás.

Until 1936, the road was known as Calle Corrientes. In that year a decision was made to widen it and officially turn it into an avenue. At the same time a new city icon was inaugurated: Obelisco (p77), standing 67.5m high.

DIONISIO IEMMA/SHUTTERSTOCK

Café Tortoni

Where Gardel & Borges Drank Coffee

MAP p56

Soak up the atmosphere of Café Tortoni

Calling **Café Tortoni** *(cafetortoni.com.ar; 8am-9pm)* just a bar is unfair. Inaugurated in 1858, it is not only the oldest still-functioning bar in the city but also a meeting place for men and women who helped shape Buenos Aires' history. National figures like tango singer Carlos Gardel, painter Benito Quinquela Martin (p113) and writer Jorge Luis Borges, have sat at its tables.

The cafe retains a bohemian atmosphere, and its lounge with large columns has all the elegance of Buenos Aires at the end of the 19th century. The original wood furniture, marble tables and stained glass windows are all from that period. On its walls, the Tortoni also showcases a collection of more than 100 works of art donated by their artists. Café Tortoni offers

EATING IN CENTRO HISTÓRICO: INTERNATIONAL FLAVORS

MAP p56, p70

Tucson: An American-style steakhouse and bar. Rib eye steaks are its star cut of meat. Be sure to try the house's special barbecue sauce. *hours vary* $$

Lalo de Buenos Aires: A traditional city restaurant specializing in pasta and meats, known for its generous portions. *11:30am-1am* $$

Pippo: A classic city center restaurant, known for its pasta. The house pesto sauce is famous, as is the homemade flan with *dulce de leche*. *hours vary* $$

Los Inmortales: Since 1952, this cafe has been serving stone-baked pizzas. The most popular are mozzarella, Neapolitan, and ham and peppers. *10am-1am* $

a good selection of coffees and a varied gastronomic menu, which includes sweets and typical dishes of the region. Its specialty is chocolate with churros.

Refuge for Artists & Writers

MAP p56

Visit historic bar London City

London City *(londoncity.com.ar; 6am-10pm)* is a bar with large windows overlooking Avenida de Mayo, one of the most beautiful avenues in Buenos Aires. Dating from 1954, it has an antique wall clock, old tables, vintage photos of Buenos Aires and a checkerboard floor. At one of the tables facing the avenue is a statue of Julio Cortázar, the famous writer who used to frequent this bar, along with other intellectuals, artists and politicians. Cortázar visited so often that he made the bar a kind of protagonist in his first novel *Los Premios*, published in 1960. Cakes are the bar's specialty.

Historic Complex Built By Jesuits

MAP p56

Explore Manzana de las Luces above and underground

Dating to colonial times, **Manzana de las Luces** *(manzana delasluces.cultura.gob.ar; free; noon-7pm Wed-Sun)* was Buenos Aires' most important center of culture and learning, and today this historic block still symbolizes education and enlightenment. Tours in Spanish are given at 3:15pm Wednesday to Friday, but you can go inside and see the main patio area without taking a tour. A cultural center also offers workshops and music, film and theater events - see the website for details.

The Jesuits built several structures here including the Procuraduría (1730; administrative headquarters), part of which still survives today, and **Iglesia San Ignacio de Loyola** *(sanignaciodeloyola.org.ar)* the oldest in church in the city, completed in 1722. Guided tours of the church include the cloister of the old Colegio San Carlos, the towers that serve as a viewpoint and the ancient tunnels that run beneath the site. These tunnels were designed as defence networks and allow you to see the old bowelrs of the city.

The Jesuits were expelled from Argentina in 1767 by the King of Spain. Along with housing offices, these buildings hosted converted indigenous people from the provinces. Later, during the 19th century, they were home to various museums, legislative offices, schools and universities.

REVITALIZING THE MICROCENTRO

Microcentro, the city's central business district, is full of banks, offices, and stores. During the COVID pandemic and with the rise of remote work, the area suffered from deterioration and insecurity problems. In recent years, the city government has been working to improve the area with new pedestrian zones, more greenery, and other urban planning measures. Some preferential loans have also been introduced for those purchasing homes in the downtown area. The plan aims to promote development and investment in the region through housing incentives and tax benefits for strategic activities.

EATING IN CENTRO HISTÓRICO: BEST ITALIAN

MAP p56, p70

D'Oro: Restaurant specializing in pasta. Its menu includes a wide variety of wines. *hours vary* $$$

Prosciutto: Restaurant specialized in pasta. The signature dish of the house is lasagna prosciutto. *8am-midnight* $$

Mazacote: Since 1982, the restaurant has been famous in the neighborhood for its pizza *al molde* and *a la piedra* (stone-baked pizza). *hours vary* $

Il Vero Arturito: Known for its large portions, especially pasta and seafood dishes. *12:15-3:45pm Tue-Sun* $$

BEST OUTDOOR SPACES IN CENTRO HISTÓRICO

Plaza Lavalle (MAP p70): Ideal place to relax. Teatro Colón and Palacio de Justicia are nearby.

Plaza de la República (MAP p56): Next to Obelisco and famous for its lights. A popular spot for taking photos.

Plaza Primero de Mayo (MAP p70): This square dedicated to the workers was once a cemetery. In the center is a monument depicting a middle-aged man carrying a heavy load on his shoulder.

Parque de la Estación: This public park was built on the site of a former railroad station and shed.

Plaza del Vaticano (MAP p56): This plaza beside Teatro Colón is used for open-air theater performances.

Story of the City

MAP p56

View thousands of photographs at Buenos Aires Museo

The **Buenos Aires Museo** *(@buenosairesmuseo; entry free on Wed; 11am-7pm Mon & Wed-Fri, to 8pm Sat & Sun)* has an ambitious goal: to tell the city's history from its beginnings to the present day. Through interactive elements, its permanent exhibition tells the story of the significant transformations of the city and how Buenos Aires became cosmopolitan. There are exhibits on the first settlers, the houses and historical and cultural landmarks of the city and a space dedicated to the role played by radio, television and sports (particularly soccer) in the lives of *porteños*. A highlight is its photographic archive of over 8000 images of the city and its inhabitants, plus about 35,000 negatives from collections of renowned photographers.

EATING IN CENTRO HISTÓRICO: BEST FOR SUSHI

MAP p56, p70

Tataki: The restaurant combines Peruvian Nikkei and sushi cuisine on its menu and is located close to the theater district. *hours vary* $$$

In & Out Sushi: A delicious variety of rolls parades along the bar at BA's first revolving sushi train restaurant. *hours vary* $$$

Furaibo: The menu features ramen, sushi, *gyoza* (dumplings), *katsu* (breadcrumbed meats), and a tea house. *noon-11pm* $$$

Fabric Sushi: It specializes in sushi and other Japanese dishes like *gyoza* and *harumaki* (spring rolls). Also offers delivery and takeout. *hours vary* $$$

HEMIS/ALAMY

Farmacia de la Estrella

The museum is located in an old mansion with two floors and rooms that converge in a central courtyard. Go up to the second floor, where there is a terrace with a good view of the Basilica San Francisco de Asis and the old Farmacia de la Estrella.

The City's Oldest Pharmacy

MAP p56

Time travel at Farmacia de la Estrella

Even if you don't have a headache, it's worth dropping by **Farmacia de la Estrella** *(farmaciadelaestrella.ba; 8am-6pm Mon-Fri)*, which first opened its doors in 1834. As soon as you enter, you encounter the Buenos Aires of the 19th century when the city's population was just 40,000. The details of the building and its decoration are exquisite. The

BEST TOURS

Hampa Tours: Nahuel Gallotta and Mariano Vidal, journalists and acclaimed authors of crime-related books, are the guides for fascinating true crime walking tours of the city. Book through @hampatours.

Mama Antula Tour: Walking tour focusing on the life and work of Mama Antula, Argentina's first female saint, canonized in 2024 by Pope Francis. Book online through civitatis.com.

Buenos Aires Pizza Tour: Ariel Santillán runs this thematic tour in an old Volkswagen Microbus model 83 with stops to try slices at some of the city's best pizzerias. Find all the information about their routes and schedules at @buepizzatour.

DRINKING IN CENTRO HISTÓRICO: BEST ROOFTOP BARS

MAP p56, p70

Olympo Sky Bar: On the 31st floor of a modern building this bar offers a diverse menu of drinks and food focused on meats, pastas and tapas. *6pm-1am Mon-Sat*

Dome Rooftop Bar: A hotel bar and restaurant offering a sky-high view of the domes of the historic buildings along Avenida de Mayo. *5pm-midnight Tue-Sat*

Florida 165: Inside the beautiful Galería Güemes, this bar offers great views. Antoine de Saint-Exupéry lived in the building in 1929. *hours vary*

Cielo Sky Bar: On the rooftop of the Hotel Grand Brizo Buenos Aires and offering a varied menu of drinks and signature tapas. *6pm-midnight Wed-Sat*

BEST BOOKSTORES IN CENTRO HISTÓRICO

Zivals (MAP p70): Spacious bookstore with a wide variety of titles in a traditional city corner. They also sell vinyl records.

Librería El Túnel (MAP p56): This bookstore, located in a historic building very close to Café Tortoni, specializes in antique, collectible and used books.

Librería Hernández (MAP p70): Operating for more than half a century, with an excellent selection of titles. They organize events with authors.

De la Mancha (MAP p70): This famous bookstore takes its name from the renowned novel by Miguel de Cervantes Saavedra.

Galerna (MAP p70): A well-known Argentine publishing house with a chain of bookstores and a distribution company.

walnut cabinets were brought from Italy, and the Murano glass, Carrara marble and Venetian floors stand out. A mural on the ceiling shows figures of women representing health, illness and pharmacopoeia.

Speedy Sandwich Service

MAP p56

Join lunching office workers at Café Paulin

The city center is full of charming little bars and restaurants. **Café Paulin** *(paulin.com.ar; 8am-8pm Mon-Fri, 8am-4pm Sat),* founded in 1988, is one of them. Specializing in sandwiches, this long, narrow cafe, which feels a bit like an old train carriage, has a long wood and marble bar, seating 38 people. What's most surprising is how they deliver their dishes by sliding them over the bar. The idea started to speed up service because office workers had little time for lunch. At Paulin, you arrive, eat and return to work as quickly as possible after receiving a flying sandwich. The *peceto* (round steak) sandwich is the most famous, complete with melted Gruyère cheese, fresh tomato, red bell pepper and hot sauce. The sandwiches are enormous, so you can order them to share. Expect to wait for a seat if you go at noon.

BA's Oldest Bookstore

MAP p56

Browse the shelves of Librería de Ávila

Buenos Aires is, among other things, a city of bookstores. According to studies by the World Cities Culture Forum, Buenos Aires is one of the cities with the most bookstores per capita in the world. Many of them are concentrated in the historic center. **La Librería de Ávila** *(@libreriadeavila; 9am-6pm Mon-Fri, 10am-2.30pm Sat)* is the oldest bookstore in Buenos Aires, founded in 1785. It remains as vibrant as ever on the corner of Alsina and Bolívar streets, close to the famous Colegio Nacional Buenos Aires, where many of the country's presidents studied. The bookstore has two floors and a stock of 150,000 books. There are books highly sought after by South American readers, such as first editions of Jorge Luis Borges, Julio Cortázar, Ezequiel Martínez Estrada and Manuel Puig. If you are lucky, you can meet Miguel Avila, its owner, who is something of a legend in BA's book world.

DRINKING IN CENTRO HISTÓRICO: AFTERNOON TEA MAP p56, p70

Gontran Cherrier: Coffee, tea and pastries with a French touch. *11am-8pm Mon-Fri, 9am-2pm Sat*

La Panera Rosa: Inside Palacio Barolo, this cafe offers a wide selection of tea and coffee, along with light meals throughout the day. *9am-midnight*

Café Mar Azul: Old bar where customers spend hours chatting and reading the newspaper. Specializes in coffee and sandwiches. *8am-8pm Mon-Sat*

Confitería La Ópera: A bar situated in a historic corner of Buenos Aires, offering a wide variety of coffee, tea and Argentine cuisine. *hours vary*

CECILIAMP/SHUTTERSTOCK

Galerías Pacífico

Historic Mall With Mural Dome

MAP p56

Look up at Galerías Pacífico

Galerías Pacífico *(galeriaspacifico.com.ar; 10am-9pm)* is one of the best-known shopping malls in the city. Designed by architects Emilio Agrelo and Raúl Le Levacher in 1889, the original idea was to house the Au Bon Marché department store, but it was never used for its original purpose. However, the most exciting thing is not the mall's range of stores but its dome of 450 sq meters decorated with murals from the mid-1940s by the outstanding Argentine painters Antonio Berni, Lino Enea Spilimbergo, Demetrio Urruchúa, Juan Carlos Castagnino and the Spaniard Manuel Colmeiro. The artwork, which bears each artist's signature, is an ode to life in the city and the birth of the great modern cities, and celebrates the idea of progress.

BOOKLOVERS' CITY

Across the city, you'll come across dozens of bookstores – offering new and used books – some of them true architectural gems, like El Ateneo Grand Splendid (p142) in Recoleta. Within this rich literary landscape, the San Nicolás neighborhood, in the heart of the historic center, boasts the highest concentration of bookstores. Every year, the city celebrates its passion for books with **La Noche de las Librerías**, a vibrant event that brings literature, writers, readers and bookstores onto the streets around Av Corrientes.

EATING IN CENTRO HISTÓRICO: BEST PIZZA PLACES

MAP p56, p70

Güerrín: Founded in 1932 and famous for its *pizza al molde* and stuffed *fugazzeta* filled with cheese and topped with sweet onions. *11am-1am* $

La Americana: Sells crispy pizzas and baked and fried *empanadas*. One of the most requested pizza toppings is anchovy. *7am-2am* $

Banchero: La Boca's classic pizzeria has branches downtown. The house specialty is the *fugazza* (onion pizza) with cheese. *11am-1am* $

Las Cuartetas: A legendary pizza place in the city's theater district. They specialize in mozzarella pizza and traditional stuffed *fugazzeta. hours vary* $

THE ART OF INVITING SOMEONE TO TANGO

Although *milongas* are becoming increasingly diverse, some practices from earlier days are still in force in Buenos Aires. One of them is the *cabeceo*. It's a subtle head movement with which you invite a person to dance instead of approaching them directly. The sequence is as follows. First, you look for someone you are interested in asking to dance. You look at that person and make a *cabeceo*. If that person holds your gaze and nods, you have succeeded and can approach. Otherwise, if they look away, they decline your invitation. Then you should look for someone else.

FOTO ARENA LTDA ALAMY

Centro Cultural Borges

Inside the shopping mall, on the corner facing Viamonte and San Martín streets, is the **Centro Cultural Borges**, which offers a wide range of art, theater and music programs.

Resurgence of a Tango Temple

MAP p56

Enjoy music and dance at Salón Marabú

It would be hard to find a place that has witnessed as many characters and events in the history of Buenos Aires as **Salón Marabú** (*tangomarabu.com; closed Wed*). The *milonga* opened its doors in 1935. Two years later, the orchestra of Aníbal Troilo, one of the most extraordinary tango musicians, debuted there. It operated until the mid-1980s. After many years of being closed, it recently reopened thanks to the support of an expat English businessman and tango lover based in the

DRINKING IN CENTRO HISTÓRICO: COFFEE SPOTS

MAP p56, p70

Café Thibon: Founded in the 1930s and known for its good coffee and tea. You can also buy spices, wines and condiments. *8am-6pm Mon-Fri*

La Puerto Rico: Beautiful art deco-style bar, famous in the city center. It specializes in coffee and you should also try their *medialunas. hours vary*

The Shelter Coffee: A specialty coffee shop with industrial decor and Chesterfield armchairs, offering cakes, sandwiches and pastries. *8:30am-8pm Mon-Sat*

Santa Café: Cozy space with good service and wide variety of specialty coffees, primarily sourced from Colombia and roasted daily. *8am-7pm Mon-Fri & 9am-6pm Sat*

US. If you go there, you will find daily tango classes, *milongas* and live orchestra performances, just like in the old days. The restoration of the place, located in the basement of an old palace, recovered the stained glass ceiling and its art deco essence. Maribú also has an online radio that broadcasts tango music all day long.

Iconic Building With a Rooftop Bar

MAP p56

Take in the view from Trade Sky Bar

Trade Sky Bar *(tradeskybar.com; 6pm-1am Sun-Thu, 6pm-2am Fri & Sat)* is located on the upper floors of the Comega building, a rationalist concrete building from the 1930s. You can go for a drink and tapas from 6pm or for dinner from 8pm. The menu has meats, risotto, fish, pasta, sushi and a wide choice of signature drinks, classics and wines, mainly Argentine. From the 19th and 20th floors, you will get an exceptional view of the buildings of Puerto Madero, such as the Puente de la Mujer and the Rio de la Plata. The best view is from the 22nd-floor outdoor terrace, which offers a 360-degree panorama including the lights of Av Corrientes with the Obelisco in the background. The terrace often features a live DJ. A good plan is to have a leisurely dinner on the 19th or 20th floor and then a drink on the terrace. Reserve in advance to secure a table with a good view.

A Bar for Selfies

MAP p56

Strike a pose at Nivel Dios

Travel and selfies are often compatible activities. **Nivel Dios** *(niveldios.ar; 8:30am-1:00am Mon-Thu, to 2am Fri, to 3am Sat, noon-9pm Sun)* calls itself the first selfie bar in Buenos Aires. You will find many rooms with different settings and photographic sets, such as the seat of an aeroplane, the presidential chair, and the movie *Up*. You can fantasize about being on the cover of *Vogue* and, since you are in Argentina, you can also take a selfie with soccer stars Diego Maradona and Lionel Messi. The menu is simple, with hamburgers, pizzas, sandwiches and other quick dishes, and they have a wide variety of drinks. An employee shows how to pose in each spot so that the photos come out great. In the basement, there is a small virtual reality playground.

THEATER TICKET DISCOUNTS

Buenos Aires has more than 280 theaters, with many located on Av Corrientes between Callao and the Obelisco. Except for some blockbuster shows, you should have no problem getting tickets at the box offices. Also be sure to visit **Tickets Buenos Aires** (MAP p70; *1-7pm Tue-Sat*), which sells vouchers to see plays for a discount. You have to go to their point of sale at Diagonal Norte and Cerrito. After buying the voucher, go to the box office of the theater, and you will pay only 50% of the ticket price. Discounts may vary according to the plays.

DRINKING IN CENTRO HISTÓRICO: WINE BARS

MAP p56

Che Malbec: A wine bar focused on Argentine producers. They organize tastings and offer a selection of tapas. *hours vary*

Vinoteca Winenot: Wine shop that regularly hosts tastings in an intimate setting. The hosts speak English. *10:30am-8:30pm*

Cichaus: Cocktails, beers (with more than 12 on tap), and wines, all served with personalized attention. *5pm-1am Tue-Fri & 6pm-1am Sat*

Partners Coffee & Wine: A comfortable spot in the middle of the bustling downtown to enjoy a coffee or a glass of wine. *hours vary*

BALVANERA & MONSERRAT
Charcas
José Uriburu
Plaza Monseñor de Andrea
Av Córdoba
Paraguay
Larrea
Junín
Ayacucho
Riobamba
Córdoba
Plaza B Houssay
Facultad de Medicina
Av Anchorena
Jean Jaurés
Ecuador
Av Pueyrredón
Azcuénaga
Zelaya
Museo Casa Carlos Gardel
Tucumán
Lavalle
BALVANERA
Corrientes
Pueyrredón
Av Corrientes
Pasteur
Valentín Gómez
Sarmiento
ONCE
Castelli
Paso
Pasteur
Uriburu
Junín
Ayacucho
Parque de la Estación (140m)
Juan D Perón
Estación Once
Once
Bartolomé Mitre
Av Rivadavia
Pasco
Alberti
Plaza Miserere
Plaza 1 de Mayo
Hipólito Yrigoyen
Pichincha
Rincón
Adolfo Alsina
Pasco
La Rioja
Av Jujuy
Moreno
0 500 m
0 0.25 miles
Rodríguez Peña
Montevideo
Paraná
Uruguay
Talcahuano
Libertad
Av Corrientes
Uruguay
0 200 m
0 0.1 miles

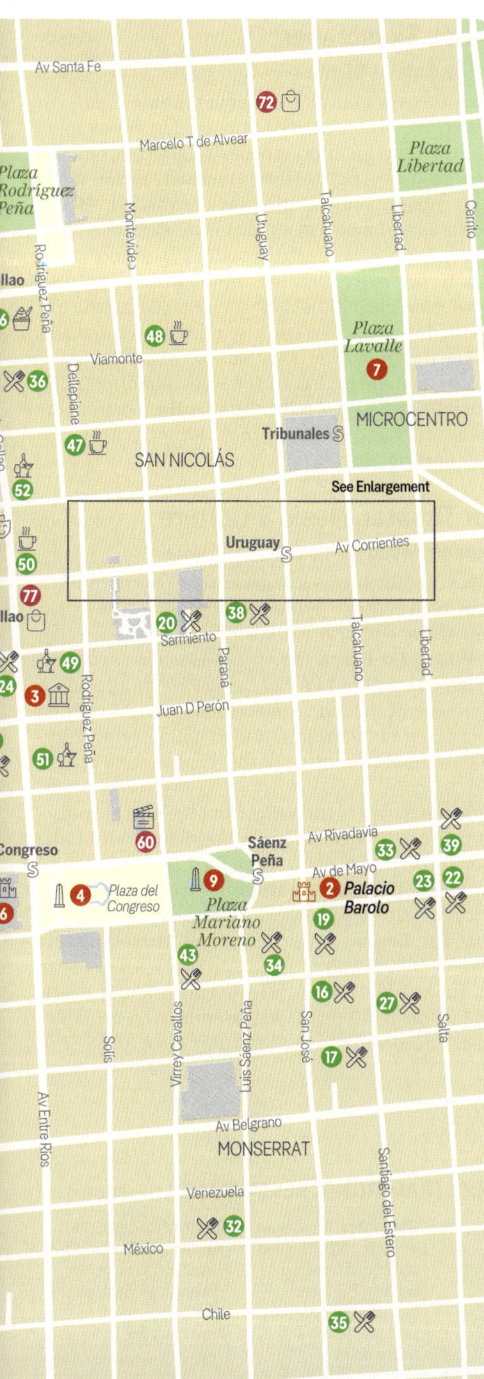

HIGHLIGHTS
1 Museo Casa Carlos Gardel
2 Palacio Barolo

SIGHTS
3 Casa de la Provincia de Buenos Aires
4 Monumento a los Dos Congresos
see 63 Museo Beatle
see 5 Museo del Agua y de la Historia Sanitaria
5 Palacio de Aguas Corrientes
6 Palacio del Congreso
7 Plaza Lavalle
8 Plaza Primero de Mayo
9 The Thinker

EATING
10 ¡Oy Vey!
11 Asu Mare
12 Bali
13 Banchero
14 Buenos Aires Grill
15 Cadore
16 Casa de Galicia
17 Centro Vasco Francés
18 Cervantes
19 Chan Chan
20 Chiquilín
21 El Gato Negro
22 El Globo
23 El Imparcial
24 El Tropezón
25 Freddo
26 Güerrín
27 Helueni
28 IL Vero Arturito
29 La Conga
30 La Giralda
31 La Gran Taberna
see 2 La Panera Rosa
see 63 Lalo de Buenos Aires
32 Lo Rafael
33 Los 36 Billares
see 63 Los Platitos
see 63 Manduca
34 Maria Fedele
35 Mazacote
36 Parrilla Peña
37 Pepito
38 Pippo
39 Plaza Asturias
40 Prosciutto
41 Puny
42 Sattva
43 Status
44 Tataki
45 Tucson
46 Via Maggiore

DRINKING & NIGHTLIFE
47 Café Mar Azul
48 Café Thibon
49 Celta Bar
see 63 Cervelar
50 Confitería La Ópera
51 Lobby Bar Imperio
52 Los Galgos
53 Olympo Sky Bar
54 Roma
see 2 Salón 1923
55 Sifón
see 63 Terraza Teatro Bar
56 The Shelter Coffee

ENTERTAINMENT
57 Café de los Angelitos
see 63 The Cavern Buenos Aires
58 Centro Cultural de la Cooperación
59 Centro Cultural Ricardo Rojas
60 Cine Gaumont
61 El Beso
62 Multiteatro
63 Paseo La Plaza
see 67 Sala Leopoldo Lugones
64 Teatro Lola Membrives
65 Teatro Picadero
66 Teatro Presidente Alvear
67 Teatro San Martín

SHOPPING
68 De la Mancha
69 Dickens
70 Edipo
71 El Ateneo Grand Splendid
72 Galerna
73 Librería Hernández
74 Librería Lucas
75 Losada
76 Maidana
77 Zivals

ICONIC THEATER OF DEMOCRACY

Buenos Aires is home to many theaters and a vibrant theatrical scene. However, one stands out as a symbol of resistance and the fight against the dictatorship that ruled the country between 1976 and 1983.

Teatro Picadero (MAP p70; *teatro picadero.com.ar*), at Pasaje Santos Discépolo 1857, hosted a festival called Teatro Abierto in the early 1980s, a response to the silence imposed by the military regime. In retaliation, the authorities ordered the theater to be burned down. It remained closed for several years until it was reopened in 2012. Today, it offers a wide variety of theater performances and stand-up shows.

Art Nouveau Skyscraper

MAP p56

Be charmed by Galería Güemes

At 87m high, the art nouveau **Galería Güemes** *(galeria guemes.com.ar)* is considered one of the earliest skyscrapers in Buenos Aires. It has an interior pedestrian arcade of more than 100m that connects Calles Florida and San Martín. Walking along this arcade, you will discover the vaulted ceiling, bronze sculptures and modernist lights from the time it was built in 1915.

In addition to browsing the shops in the arcade, you can see downtown from the building's observation deck, which is accessed on the 14th floor. You can also relax with a drink at **Florida 165** *(@rooftopflorida165; 4pm-1am Mon-Thu, 4pm-3am Fri & Sat)*, a high-rise bar in the same building (p65). In the basement is **Teatro Ástor Piazzolla** *(teatroastor piazzolla.com; dinner from 8pm, show 10pm)*, with tango dinner shows every night.

Space for Theater, Music & Culture

MAP p70

Wander through Paseo La Plaza

Mercado Nuevo Modelo was a market that operated until the end of the 19th century in the neighborhood now called San Nicolás. At the end of the 1980s, the market was redeveloped as **Paseo La Plaza** *(paseolaplaza.com.ar; 10am-1am Mon-Wed, 10am-3am Thu-Sat, noon-1am Sun)*, a space that includes several theaters, concert halls and **Manduca** *(paseolaplaza.com.ar/manduca)* a food hall offering Peruvian and Asian food, Argentine barbecue, beer and coffee, and more

The promenade feels a world away from the outside noise, thanks to a passage that connects Av Corrientes with Calle Montevideo. You can see plays, comedies, stand-ups, and music concerts at **The Cavern Buenos Aires** *(thecavern.com.ar; 3:30pm-midnight)*, a performance space and bar dedicated to The Beatles. Attached is the **Museo Beatle** (*10am-midnight Mon-Sat, 2pm-midnight Sun*) where you can see some of the world's largest private collection of Beatle memorabilia (some 8500 pieces amassed by Argentine Rodolfo Vázquez), according to the *Guinness Book of Records*.

EATING IN CENTRO HISTÓRICO: TRADITIONAL RESTAURANTS — MAP p56, p70

Lo Rafael: Specializing in seafood and Mediterranean cuisine like paella and pasta, with a variety of meat dishes also available. *11am-4pm, 7pm-midnight* $$

Green Eat: A restaurant serving vegan and vegetarian dishes, with a second-floor view overlooking the city skyline. *hours vary* $

Cervantes: Famous for its large portions, good prices and reserved waiters. The menu includes grilled meats, seafood, salads and pasta. *hours vary* $

Teatro Picadero: The theater's restaurant offers tapas and sandwiches, making it an ideal spot to visit before a performance. *hours vary* $$

LONGJON/SHUTTERSTOCK

Teatro Ástor Piazzolla

A Colonial-Era Archaeological Site

MAP p56

Paseo de la Cisterna

The archaeological site **Paseo de la Cisterna** *(paseodelacisterna.com.ar; free; 1-6pm Wed-Sun)* displays the remains of the largest colonia-era cistern discovered in Buenos Aires. The 3m high, 8m diameter cistern was uncovered in 2016 by a construction company commissioned to build a residential complex in the historic center. Formerly, the site was the residence of the family of Encarnación Ezcurra (1785–1838), the wife of Juan Manuel de Rosas, the powerful governor of the province of Buenos Aires. In the museum here you can also see other objects discovered at the site that portray daily colonial life, such as pottery, jugs, French perfume bottles, personal care and hygiene items, ornaments and toys.

CLASSIC HAT SHOPS

Dotted throughout Centro Histórico are beautiful indoor arcades dating from the beginning of the 20th century. One is the **Pasaje Roverano** (MAP p56), a few meters from Plaza de Mayo in Monserrat. It was built in 1918 and retains much of its original architecture and style, with iron columns and reinforced concrete.

Lagomarsino (MAP p56), the first store in the arcade, is a city classic. It sells hats made of cotton, leather and llama felt. In addition, some old shop objects, which are more than 125 years old, are exhibited, such as sewing machines, scissors and tools for making hats.

Another venerable hat shop is **Maidana** (MAP p70), founded in 1913. It's a city institution known for its handmade hats, each of which takes at least four days to produce.

EATING IN CENTRO HISTÓRICO: BEST STEAKHOUSES

MAP p70

Pepito: Classic restaurant specializing in grilled meat and homemade pasta, plus an extensive list of Argentine wines. *noon-1pm* **$$**

Parrilla Peña: This steak restaurant has been downtown for over 40 years. Its fried *empanadas* and *asado* are very tasty. *noon-4pm & 7pm-midnight Mon-Sat* **$$**

Los Platitos: Branch of a classic grill in the Costanera Norte area. Offers different types of meat and chorizo sandwiches. *noon-midnight Tue-Sun* **$$**

Chiquilín: A classic restaurant of Buenos Aires nightlife. Try their *bife de chorizo* and pasta. *noon-2am* **$$$**

WHY I LOVE THE CENTRO HISTÓRICO

Pablo Gabriel Fernández, Professor at the University of Buenos Aires.

Buenos Aries' architecture remains so rich and diverse that you can still find real gems with stories worth documenting in every neighborhood. Casa Viacava in Almagro (a work by architect Virginio Colombo) and the Farmacia Podestá in Constitución (by the same author) are examples of this. I wish these jewels were protected, as they are part of our identity, and it is a real shame to see them in poor condition. The city needs a policy on which properties should be preserved for their historical value so as not to lose these valuable buildings due to lack of care and the inevitable passage of time.

A Famous Tailor's Shop in Reborn

MAP p56

Dine or watch a musical show at The New Brighton

At the beginning of the 20th century The Brighton was an exclusive English-style tailor's shop in Buenos Aires. Argentine presidents and Spanish royalty used to buy their suits at this temple of elegance until it closed in the mid-1970s. The tailor's shop has regained its splendor as **The New Brighton** *(brightonbuenosaires.com.ar; 8am-midnight Mon-Fri)*, a restaurant and stage for musical shows. The place is enormous, occupying almost 450 sq meters. As soon as you enter, you feel like you are in the Buenos Aires of another era. The interior is impressive for its details: a reddish wood bar, the stools, the cedar boiserie on the walls, the mirrors and an imposing piano. There are still some posters that belonged to the tailor's shop. The restaurant's menu features pasta, fish, risotto and, of course, meat. At night, The New Brighton also has jazz, *bolero* and tango concerts.

EATING IN CENTRO HISTÓRICO: ITALIAN & SPANISH

MAP p56, p70

Broccolino: Traditional Italian cuisine, with standout dishes including fish, seafood and pizza. *noon-11pm* $$

Buenos Aires Grill: Traditional Argentine *asado* in the heart of the city's theater district. *hours vary* $$

El Imparcial: Traditional Spanish restaurant. The most popular dishes are the black rice with calamari and the paella a la Valenciana. *noon-4pm & 8pm-12:30am* $$$

Casa de Galicia: Homemade dishes that capture the spirit of Galician cuisine. *hours vary* $$$

The New Brighton

Cigar Lounge

MAP p56

Take a puff at Cohiba Atmosphere Buenos Aires

Buenos Aires is an almost 100% smoke-free city. Among the small number of shelters for tobacco lovers is **Cohiba Atmosphere Buenos Aires** *(facebook.com/cohiba.bsas; 10am-7pm Mon-Fri)* a bar, restaurant and cigar lounge. The place is divided into three sectors: the smoking-free restaurant, where meat, pasta and fish are served; a room where cigars are kept and which doubles as a wine cellar; and a smoking area with tables, armchairs and air purifiers, where you can smoke your cigarettes and have a drink. The place is licensed to sell Cuba's most renowned cigar brands, such as Coiba, Montecristo and Romeo y Julieta.

PORTEÑOS' CRAZE FOR PIZZA

Buenos Aires, and especially Centro Histórico, is filled with pizzerias. Pizza is, without a doubt, one of the favourite dishes of *porteños*. Argentina is among the countries with the highest pizza consumption in the world, mainly due to the massive Italian immigration wave at the end of the 19th century.

By the 1930s, pizza had become a cultural icon of Buenos Aires, with some of the most popular pizzerias emerging during that time, such as Güerrín (p67). The most characteristic style of Argentine pizza is *pizza al molde*, distinguished by its thick, spongy base and raised, bread-like crust. It is topped with generous amounts of cheese and is often accompanied by *fainá*, a baked pancake made from chickpea flour.

EATING IN CENTRO HISTÓRICO: BEST SPANISH

MAP p56, p70

Plaza Asturias: Specialties here include the *fabada* (bean stew) and *mondongo a la Española* (Spanish-style tripe). *11:30am-5pm & 7pm-1am* $$$

El Globo: One of BA's oldest restaurants; try their *puchero* (a stew made with meat, vegetables and beans). *noon-3pm, 8pm-midnight Wed-Mon* $$$

La Gran Taberna: Abundant and tasty food, with its most famous dishes being fish and seafood. *noon-4pm & 7:30pm-1am* $$

Museo del Jamón: Traditional Spanish dishes, with an emphasis on Iberian ham and sausages. *noon-midnight* $$$

BA'S TIMELESS BOULEVARD

Av de Mayo was the first boulevard in Buenos Aires, inspired by the grand avenues of Paris – some refer to it as the Champs-Élysées of Latin America. Inaugurated in 1894, its golden age spanned from 1910 to 1930, when it became a vibrant hub of cultural and social life. Over time, it took on a distinctly Spanish character, filled with theaters, cafes, and hotels owned by Spanish immigrants – some of which still stand today. When visitors say that Buenos Aires reminds them of Madrid, they are likely comparing Gran Vía, the Spanish capital's central avenue, to Avenida de Mayo, the heart of the Argentine capital.

SAIKO3P/SHUTTERSTOCK

Palacio del Congreso

Building Inspired by Dante's Poem

MAP p70

Catch *Divine Comedy* references at Palacio Barolo

'Welcome to hell,' says the tour guide at **Palacio Barolo** *(palaciobarolo.com.ar; daily tours, book online)*. This office building, completed in 1923 and financed by businessman Luigi Barolo. is uniquely beautiful in Buenos Aires. Its design by architect Mario Palanti includes numerous references to Dante's narrative poem *Divine Comedy*.

The building features three distinct and uniquely designed levels, symbolizing Hell, Purgatory and Paradise. The tour begins on the first floor (Hell), which stands out for its columns with dragons and Gothic floors. As you ascend, the concrete construction becomes simpler until you reach the ascetic Heaven. The guide explains the life of Barolo, the exquisite construction details of the building, and the Masonic world. From the 14th floor, it's a climb of six flights of stairs to the 20th-floor observation deck for views of the city and, on clear days, the coast of Uruguay.

DRINKING IN CENTRO HISTÓRICO: COCKTAIL BARS

MAP p56, p70

Bar El Colonial: An old bar in the city, with coffee and traditional drinks. Specialties include sandwiches and grilled meats. *7am-8pm Mon-Fri, 8am-1pm Sat*

Celta Bar: A traditional bar and restaurant with an extensive wine, drinks and cider menu. The Pineral Julep (mint, grapefruit and soda) is a house classic. *8am-2am*

Sifón: In the Paseo La Plaza complex, this informal bar specializes in vermouth. There's a second branch in the Chacarita neighborhood. *noon-1am*

Los Galgos: Authentic *porteño* café by day, with cocktails in the evening. Don't miss their potato omelet and crispy chard fritters. *hours vary*

Two more floors up, at the top of the building, a large lighthouse illuminates the city from 100m high. This last climb is very narrow and may not be suitable for everyone. At the end of the 90-minute tour, a glass of wine is served on the 7th floor where there's a museum about the building. Daytime tours are good for seeing the Río de la Plata, while night tours offers more beautiful city views.

Salón 1923 *(salon1923.com)*, on the building's 16th floor, offers good views of the Obelisco and Avenida de Mayo, to be enjoyed with tapas and cocktails. Check their website for opening hours.

A Controversial Monument

MAP p56

Weigh in on the debate about the Obelisco

Since its construction began in 1936 for the fourth centenary of the founding of Buenos Aires, *porteños* have loved and hated the **Obelisco** in equal measure. Some say it's an eyesore, a foreign body that landed in a town trying to become cosmopolitan. Others celebrate the 67.5m monument, which has become an undisputed icon of the city.

In front of the base of the Obelisco is the **Plaza de la República**, where you can see the coats of arms of each of Argentina's provinces. The place is usually filled with tourists snapping souvenir photographs. On Cerrito and Diagonal Norte, just in front of the Obelisco, there are stairs for a better view of the monument, with free admission.

In 2025, work finished on an elevator to take visitors to the top of the monument. At time of writing, the attraction with still in a pilot phase with limited access, and there was no confirmed date for opening to the general public.

Insights into Argentine Politics

MAP p70

Tour Palacio del Congreso de la Nación

The guided visit to the **Palacio del Congreso** *(congreso.gob.ar/palacio.php; free tours 11am, 1pm, 3pm & 5pm Mon-Fri)* allows visitors to see inside this beautiful building that is a National Historic and Artistic Monument. It's also a chance to understand how legislative power in Argentina is exercised through the Congreso Nacional, which is composed of the Chamber of Deputies and the Senate. The 90-minute tour includes visits to the senators' chamber and the Eva Perón Hall, which displays the shroud that covered her dead body. Aspects of the palace's construction are explained, such as

THEATER, LIGHTS, SAFETY!

The theater district is usually crowded, especially on weekends when Av Corrientes is partially turned into a pedestrian street, creating a vibrant and dynamic atmosphere. The area is filled with restaurants, theaters, bookstores, and souvenir shops. Street performers entertain passersby, adding to the lively ambience created by the shows in theaters and concert halls. Since it's a busy area, be mindful of pickpockets, which often target cell phones and wallets. It's also advisable to stay alert, particularly at night, around Peatonal Florida, Lavalle, and Plaza de Mayo, where tourists and locals frequently gather.

EATING IN CENTRO HISTÓRICO: BEST ICE CREAM

MAP p70

Cadore: Founded in 1957, Cadore is a beloved institution, especially for its iconic *dulce de leche* and pistachio flavors. *hours vary* $

Via Maggiore: It is famous for its sabayon, which many consider one of the best in Buenos Aires. *noon-midnight* $

Freddo: An Italian-style ice cream shop whose strong presence in the city is a testament to tradition. Its classic *dulce de leche* has remained unchanged since 1969. *11am-12:30am* $

Bali: Specializing in vegan and kosher ice cream. Their chocolate flavor is delicious. *hours vary* $

BEST THEATERS ON AVENIDA CORRIENTES

Multiteatro (MAP p70): Complex of four theaters offering plays mostly by Argentine artists.

Teatro Astros (MAP p56): Traditional theater, renovated in 2022 with a new design and updated equipment.

Teatro Lola Membrives (MAP p70): Focused on comedy and musicals, featuring a facade in the Italian neo-Renaissance style.

Centro Cultural de la Cooperación (MAP p70): In addition to plays, the venue hosts music recitals, film screenings and art exhibitions.

Teatro El Nacional (MAP p56): The theater opened in 1906 and has the tradition of staging at least one major musical comedy each year.

the architect's attempt to replicate the opulence of European palaces using oak panelling, stained glass windows and the enormous dome, which can be seen from the outside and is a symbol of the city. At the end of the visit, you exit through the main staircase of the palace, something you can only do by taking this tour. You will be asked for your personal information at the entrance for security reasons.

Sculptures on the Square

MAP p70

Ponder the monuments on Plaza del Congreso

The **Plaza del Congreso** was inaugurated for the centennial of the Revolución de Mayo of 1810 and designed by French landscape designer Carlos Thays, who also created other iconic public spaces like Plaza San Martín and Parque Tres de Febrero. Dominating the plaza is the neoclassical **Monumento a los dos Congresos** by Belgium artists Jules Lagae and Eugenio D'Huicque, which features bronze figures representing the Assembly of 1813 and the Tucumán Congress of 1816. Its fountain symbolizes the Río de la Plata and its tributaries.

East of Plaza del Congresco is Plaza Mariano Moreno, where you can view one of few surviving original bronze casts of Auguste Rodin's **The Thinker**, brought to BA from Paris in 1907. Its pedestal was recently raised for better appreciation. Sadly, both plazas are frequently vandalized during marches and protests.

Behind the Theatrical Scenes

MAP p70

Tour the prestigious Teatro San Martín

Although not as famous as Teatro Colón (p61), the **Teatro San Martín** *(complejoteatral.gob.ar)* is one of the city's most prestigious performing arts venues. The tour takes you through the three sections of this 1960s modernist-style building, designed to prevent vibrations from the nearby subway from reaching the halls. The regular tour, lasting 90 minutes, takes in the complex's three theaters, dressing rooms and main halls. On the weekend the itinerary includes the large scenery workshops, tailoring, sculpture and carpentry areas, not accessible during weekday tours due to internal logistics. Alejandro García and María Espósito are the weekend guides, always ready to share the history of the place.

As well as its theaters, Teatro San Martín also has a cinema and a trade school where students and professionals work side

EATING IN CENTRO HISTÓRICO: NEAR AV CORRIENTES

MAP p56, p70

Sattva: Offers a vegetarian menu with options for celiacs and vegans, including pastas, meatless burgers and pizzas. *hours vary* **$$**

Zum Edelweiss: For over a century this restaurant has served traditional German cuisine. *noon-4pm & 7pm-1am Mon-Sat, 7pm-1am Sun* **$$$**

Puny: Italian cuisine dishes, mainly pasta, risottos and antipasti. The space is decorated with photos of iconic Argentine artists. *11am-1am Sun-Thu, 11am-2am Fri-Sat* **$$**

¡Oy Vey!: Deli Recipes from the Jewish kitchen. Be sure to try their pastrami sandwich. *hours vary* **$$**

Museo Casa Carlos Gardel

by side. You can also visit **Teatro Presidente Alvear**, another city-run theater located just across the street. Founded in 1942, it was mostly rebuilt after a fire in 2018. Check the website for the performance schedule.

Where a Tango Legend Lived

MAP p70

Visit the Museo Casa Carlos Gardel

The **Museo Casa Carlos Gardel** *(buenosaires.gob.ar/cultura; 11am-7pm Mon, Wed-Fri, 11am-8pm Sat & Sun)* is a museum in the house in the Abasto market area that the iconic tango singer bought for his mother in 1927. The exhibition begins with Gardel's arrival in Argentina from Toulouse, his French hometown, when he was two years old. It's possible to listen to some of his 893 recordings by headphones. There is also a room dedicated to his international success, as well as

SECONDHAND BOOKSTORES IN CENTRO HISTÓRICO

Centro Histórico has many secondhand bookstores. These are some of the best.

Losada (MAP p70): One of the oldest and largest on Av Corrientes. Sells new and used books.

Dickens (MAP p70): In addition to used books, the place also offers DVDs of movies and vinyl records.

Edipo (MAP p70): Rummaging through its shelves, you can find everything from the complete works of Freud to comics and books by Jorge Luis Borges.

Librería Kafka (MAP p56): Used books of all genres, with a special emphasis on art and history.

Librería Lucas (MAP p70): Used books of all genres at very good prices.

EATING IN CENTRO HISTÓRICO: HISTORIC SPOTS

MAP p56, p70

El Gato Negro: This elegant cafe and spice store dates to the late 1920s. Serves specialty coffees, gourmet teas and light meals. *hours vary* $$

La Giralda: Located in the theater district, this 1932 bar is famous for its chocolate with *churros*, said to be the best in the city. *7am-1am Sun-Thu, 24 hours Fri-Sat* $$

Confitería La Ideal: 1912 cafe with beautiful stained glass windows and mouldings. Try their chocolates and sandwiches. *7am-midnight* $$

Los 36 Billares: Traditional cafe-bar from 1894 known for its basement with pool tables. House specialties are stone-baked pizza and *fugazzeta*. *9am-11:30pm* $

CARLOS GARDEL

There's no better place to dive into tango than through the music of the genre's most legendary performer, singer Carlos Gardel. Many of Gardel's tangos, like *Volver* and *Por una Cabeza*, have been re-recorded throughout the years by artists from diverse genres and have become national treasures. If you see any tango show in the city, at some point in the evening, they will include one of his songs.

In Gardel's short life, he was an international figure who made movies in Hollywood. His death in a plane crash in 1935, at the peak of his career, sealed his status. He's buried in Cementerio de la Chacarita (p178) but local tango lovers say he still sings better every day.

QUIGGYT4/SHUTTERSTOCK

Museo del Agua y de la Historia Sanitaria

Gardel's filmography as a movie star. On display are photographs, some objects that belonged to him, documents and instruments. Check the museum's schedule online as it usually has a varied agenda of tango shows with performances by singers and dancers. On Wednesdays, admission is free.

Historic Tango Cafe

MAP p70

Soak up the atmosphere of Café de los Angelitos

Inaugurated in 1890, **Café de los Angelitos** *(cafedelosangelitos.com; 9am-7pm)* is one of the emblematic bars of the city, and its history is linked to tango. Carlos Gardel frequently went there, signed his contracts at the bar's tables and even dedicated a tango to the place. Following its closure in the 1990s, and threatened demolition due to structural problems, the cafe has recovered and today enjoys good health. The atmosphere

DRINKING IN CENTRO HISTÓRICO: BEST BEER

MAP p56, p70

Patagonia: This local beer brand produces rare types of beer for Argentina, such as its Bohemian Pilsener and Weisse. *6pm-10pm Mon-Thu, noon-10pm Fri-Sun*

Growlers: Branch of a local craft brewery with a stylish street aesthetic. Its wide selection of house beers include some that are gluten-free. *hours vary*

Keller: Tavern-style bar, part of a small chain, offering a wide variety of beers including IPAs and stouts. *hours vary*

Cervelar: German-style sausages and beer are the trademark of this city wide operation with a branch in Paseo La Plaza. *5pm-1am*

captures Buenos Aires of the 1920s and 1930s, with walls full of photographs of characters and events of those decades. Tango shows are scheduled daily from 8pm. During the day, it functions as a bar and restaurant. Many go for its *Angelitos* cake with *dulce de leche* mousse, whipped cream and bitter chocolate frosting.

Old Style Milonga

MAP p70

Watch traditional tango at El Beso

Meaning The Kiss, **El Beso** (*elbeso.com.ar; noon-2am*) is more than a *milonga*. Part of BA's cultural heritage, this place preserves a traditional style. Its attendees always dance with a close and intimate embrace, which is very different from the incredible acrobatics of theatrical tango shows. With tables surrounding the room, here the important thing is the dancing. There are tango classes, practices and *milongas* every night. Sometimes live musicians play, but always as accompaniment to the dance. The *milongas* have different daily organizers, each giving it a different stamp.

A Monument to Tap Water

MAP p70

Visit a museum dedicated to water and sanitation

Along Av Córdoba in the Balvanera neighborhood is the **Palacio de Aguas Corrientes** with exuberant touches of eclectic architecture. This 1894 building, covered in terracotta and glazed bricks imported from the UK, hides massive water distribution tanks from the late 19th century. On the building's 1st floor is the **Museo del Agua y de la Historia Sanitaria** (*aysa.com.ar/culturayeducacion; 9am-1pm & 2-4pm Mon-Fri*). In the first room, you will learn about the history of the building through its construction plans and topographical models. There are also photos of the period, the old supply system and a sample of some of the terracotta pieces used to cover the palace's facade. The second and third rooms cover the creation of the company that provides water to the country and furniture and instruments of the time. The most surprising room is named after architect Jorge Tartarini, which hides the heart of the great reservoir with huge iron tanks.

JEWISH BUENOS AIRES

Buenos Aires has the largest Jewish population in Latin America, numbering around 159,000 people. The city's oldest synagogue, **Templo Libertad** (MAP p56; *templolibertad.org.ar*) can accommodate 1000 worshipers and dates to 1897. It has a Roman-Byzantine style and a facade with two rounded arches, sculptural mouldings, the Star of David and a mosaic depicting two hands with outspread fingers, representing the way that the priests of Jerusalem made blessings.

Attached to the synagogue is the small **Museo Judío de Buenos Aires**, which traces the history of Jewish immigration to Argentina and displays items relating to Jewish culture and religious practices. Bring photo ID for admission.

For deeper dives into BA's Jewish heritage, contact Lunfarda Travel (p108).

DRINKING IN CENTRO HISTÓRICO: HOTEL BARS

MAP p56, p70

Abra Cultural: Combining art and Italian cuisine, this bar is famous for its pizzas and menu of drinks and wines. *8am-midnight Mon-Fri, 9am-2am Sat*

Roma: A classic in Balvanera since 1927, this bar is known for its vermouth-focused menu. *9am-1am Mon-Fri, noon-1am Sat & Sun*

Claridge Hotel: The hotel's club-like bar has comfy green leather seats, dark wood panelling, beamed ceiling and decorative windows. *11am-10pm*

Lobby Bar Imperio: The bar's sculptures and ornamental details evoke the elegance of the belle epoque; an ideal spot for coffee, tea, or cocktails. *9am-8pm*

Researched by Diego Jemio

PUERTO MADERO

OLD PORT TURNED UPSCALE NEIGHBORHOOD

Puerto Madero offers stunning views of the Río de la Plata and a fantastic selection of restaurants. Additionally, the Reserva Ecológica Costanera Sur boasts the city's highest biodiversity.

At the end of the 19th century, when Argentina was a thriving agro-exporting country, the authorities looked for a better alternative to the port already in La Boca. That new port was built in what is now Puerto Madero. Over time, the port became obsolete and turned into a hazardous quagmire. In the early 1990s, then-president Carlos Saúl Menem promoted an urban development project to found what is now BA's youngest neighborhood. It began as a gastronomic center, then came offices and housing. Today, it is an ideal spot to walk along the river and enjoy nature, and it has a good selection of museums, bars and restaurants.

TOP TIP

For excellent sunset views over the Río de la Plata, take a boat tour of the inner harbor.

MARCELO SOMMA/SHUTTERSTOCK

See page 199 for places to stay in Puerto Madero

Dársena Norte
0 — 1 km
0 — 0.5 miles
Marcelo T de Alvear
Av Eduardo Madero
Av Leandro N Alem
Cecilia Grierson
Av Córdoba
2 Colección de Arte Amalia Lacroze de Fortabat
Suipacha
Esmeralda
San Martín
Dique 4
Juana Manso
Av de los Italianos
Río de la Plata
Av Corrientes
Laguna de las Gaviotas
Juan D Perón
LA CITY
Puente de la Mujer
MICROCENTRO
Plaza de Mayo
Parque Colón
3
Museo de la Imaginación y el Juego
4
1
Reserva Ecológica Costanera Sur
Av de Mayo
Gorriti
5 Crystal Bar
Av Julio Roca
Tacuarí
Laguna de los Patos
Av Belgrano
Laguna de los Coipos
Av 9 de Julio
MONSERRAT
Defensa
Av Paseo Colón
Dique 2
PUERTO MADERO
Chile
Av Independencia
Av Ing Huergo
Carlos Calvo
Humberto Primo
Dique 1
Rawson de Dellapiane
Av San Juan
Autopista 25 de Mayo

Highlights

MARTIN SC PHOTO/SHUTTERSTOCK

◀ 1 Reserva Ecológica Costanera Sur

Stroll the city's green lung – its forests, lagoons and pastures are excellent for bird watching. **p88**

2 Colección de Arte Amalia Lacroze de Fortabat

View one of the most important collections of Argentine art. **p86**

3 Puente de la Mujer

Admire architect Santiago Calatrava's design made of steel and concrete, a city emblem symbolizing a couple dancing tango. **p87**

4 Museo de la Imaginación y el Juego

Discover a playful, immersive museum designed especially for children under 12. **p87**

5 Crystal Bar

Take in the panoramic city views from this bar and restaurant on the 32nd floor of a hotel and apartment complex. **p89**

Getting Around

Walking

Puerto Madero is a small neighborhood. It is ideal for walking with wide sidewalks, quiet streets and river views.

Subte

The nearest station is Catalinas on Línea E. You can also use the Correo Central station on Línea E and Alem on Línea B.

Bus

Take bus 59 from Recoleta and Palermo; bus 29 from La Boca, Plaza de Mayo and Palermo.

HIGHLIGHTS

1 Reserva Ecológica Costanera Sur

SIGHTS

2 Colección de Arte Amalia Lacroze de Fortabat
3 Fuente de las Nereidas
4 Monumento al Tango
5 Museo de la Cárcova
6 Museo de la Imaginación y el Juego
7 Pabellón de las Bellas Artes
8 Parque Micaela Bastidas
9 Puente de la Mujer
10 Sin título (No podés vivir sin nosotras)

ACTIVITIES

11 Sunset Río de la Plata
12 Yacht Club Argentino

SLEEPING

13 Alvear Icon
14 Believe Madero Hotel
15 City Madero
16 Faena Hotel
17 Hotel Madero

EATING

18 Cabaña Las Lilas
19 Cauce de los Fuegos
20 Frenessì
21 Happening
see 16 Italpast
22 La Cabaña
23 La Parolaccia
24 Lupita
25 Mare by Fran
26 Mizuki
27 Museo del Jamón
28 Norimōto
29 Osaka
30 ParriVip350
31 Paru Inkas
32 Qué Parrillón!
33 Rodizio Madero
34 Shawarma Al Árabe
35 Sorrento
36 Sushi Club
37 Villegas Resto & Grill

DRINKING & NIGHTLIFE
38 Alberto Lobby Bar
39 Café Martínez
see 2 Croque Madame
see 13 Crystal Bar
40 El Boleo
41 Havanna
42 Johnny B Good
43 Kraken Bar
see 16 Library Lounge
see 31 Lobo Café
44 Negroni
45 Ol' Days – Coffee & Kitchen Madero
46 Osten
47 Peñón del Águila
see 40 Puente Gran Bar
48 Temple Craft

ENTERTAINMENT
see 16 Rojo Tango

SHOPPING
49 Beluno Design
50 Giorgio Redaelli
51 I Love Gifts
see 51 Isadora
52 Llama Violeta

NOTABLE ARGENTINE ARTISTS

Antonio Berni (1905–81) would sometimes visit shantytowns and collect materials to use in his works. Various versions of his theme *Juanito Laguna Bañándose* (Juanito Laguna Bathing) – a protest against social and economic inequality – have commanded wallet-busting prices at auctions. A mural by Berni and other renowned Argentine artists can be seen at Galerías Pacífico (p67) shopping center.

Other famous Argentine artists of this era include the realist and figurative painter Juan Carlos Castagnino (1908–72); and Emilio Pettoruti (1892–1971), who shocked Buenos Aires with his 1924 cubist exhibition.

DANIEL GUSTAVO BUENO/SHUTTERSTOCK

Colección de Arte Amalia Lacroze de Fortabat

An Exquisite Collection of Argentine Art

Visit the Colección de Arte Amalia Lacroze de Fortabat

'I have decided to share my collection of Argentine art. An exquisite collection to be combined with works by foreign artists,' said Amalia Lacroze de Fortabat in an interview, which is reproduced at the entrance of **Colección de Arte Amalia Lacroze de Fortabat** *(coleccionfortabat.org.ar; noon-8pm Tue-Sun)* The businesswoman and philanthropist, who died in 2012, inaugurated her museum, also known as Colección AMALITA, in 2008 on the fourth dock in Puerto Madero. If you walk by distractedly, you may not notice it. In its halls are international works ranging from Brueghel, Chagall and Turner to Dalí, Rodin and Warhol.

However, the museum is most notable for its large collection of Argentine art, mainly from the 20th century, including

EATING IN PUERTO MADERO: OUR PICKS

Mare by Fran: Seasonal dishes incorporating rice, pasta, fish and seafood. The chef is Fran Rosat, who has great experience in seafood cuisine. *noon-midnight* $$$

Italpast: Restaurant specializing in pasta and run by Italian chef Pedro Picciau. Nonna's lasagna dish is the specialty. *hours vary* $$$

Osaka: A neighborhood classic that combines Japanese food and technique with the flavors of Peru. *12:30-4pm & 7:30pm-midnight* $$$

La Parolaccia: Trattoria offering Italian cuisine, with a focus on pasta and Mediterranean dishes. *noon-4pm & 8-11pm* $$$

works by significant local artists, such as Antonio Berni, Juan Carlos Castagnino and Emilio Pettoruti.

The City's Most Iconic Bridge

Walk across the Puente de la Mujer

The **Puente de la Mujer** (Women's Bridge) is a modern urban icon, perhaps one of the most representative of the city after the Obelisco (p77). According to its creator, the renowned Spanish architect Santiago Calatrava, the 170m bridge represents a couple dancing tango. Of course, you need some imagination to see what he sees. The mast represents the man, while the central curvature, supported by ropes, symbolizes the woman.

The pedestrian bridge is rotating, and if you are lucky, you can see it move 90 degrees to let sailboats and other vessels pass. Inaugurated in 2001, the bridge's components were manufactured in Spain and transferred to Buenos Aires to be assembled here. In 2022, it underwent a complete remodeling. You can walk across it from Av Alicia Moreau de Justo to Olga Cossettini, from west to east of the neighborhood. You can also enjoy the view of the bridge at night from some of the bars and restaurants in the area.

Kids' Play Space in Historic Brewery

Have fun at Museo de la Imaginación y el Juego

The **Museo de la Imaginación y el Juego** *(@miju.ba; visits by reservation)*, a playful space designed for children up to 12 years old. The visits are guided (about 45 minutes) through three rooms, according to age – up to three years old, four to seven years old and eight to 12 years old. Games and activities such as puzzles invite kids to explore touch, sight, hearing, smell, motor skills and the world of digital games. There is also a 360-degree audiovisual room and a letter box where children can share their experience through drawings on a postcard. After the museum visit, the family can spend time in the outdoor playground.

The museum is housed in the former Munich Brewery, an eclectic-style building that was a meeting place for *porteños* (Buenos Aires residents) during their walks along the river during the first half of the 20th century.

WOMEN OF BUENOS AIRES

Buenos Aires is a beacon of feminism in Latin America. In addition to the famous Puente de la Mujer, the neighborhood pays tribute to remarkable women through its street names.

One of them is Juana Manso (1819-75), who fought for inclusive education. Another is Julieta Lanteri (1873-1932), a doctor and a pioneer in the fight for equal rights in Argentina and Latin America. Manuela Sáenz (1897-56), an Ecuadorian revolutionary heroine who fought for South America's independence, also has a street named after her.

The neighborhood is also home to **Parque Mujeres Argentinas**, a green space that honors these women. Guide **Eugenia Calcarami** *(@paseos buenosaires)* offers a tour in Puerto Madero focused on the country's most iconic women.

EATING IN PUERTO MADERO: BEST STEAKHOUSES

Cabaña Las Lilas: A classic in Puerto Madero, the restaurant raises its own cattle for its steaks and offers an extensive wine list. *noon-midnight* **$$$**

Cauce de los Fuegos: Excellent service and high-quality meats. One of its specialties is the *Asado Emperador Cauce*, which takes 14 hours to cook. *hours vary* **$$$**

Villegas Resto & Grill: Specializing in grilled meats, with an excellent wine list divided by regions of the country. *noon-1am* **$$$**

Rodizio Madero: Restaurant featuring a menu of meats paired with a cold buffet. A plus is its views of the Puente de la Mujer. *noon-2am* **$$$**

TOP EXPERIENCE

Reserva Ecológica Costanera Sur

This ecological reserve, the city's largest green lung, spans 350 hectares and includes forests, pastures, lagoons and marshes. In addition, the place offers the best natural viewpoint of the Rio de la Plata and is an excellent spot for bird-watching. Guided tours are organized regularly, or you can visit it on your own using well-marked trails.

JL. LAGO/SHUTTERSTOCK

TOP TIPS

- The reserve is busy on weekends. Visit weekdays to enjoy nature calmly and observe more birds.
- Apply mosquito repellent before your visit.
- Bike rentals are available at the entrances; quality varies – take a good look before pedalling away.

PRACTICALITIES

The reserve is open 8am to 6pm, Tuesday to Sunday. For more information see @reservaecologicasur.

Interpretive Center & Tours

Enter the reserve either at the north or the south. Step inside the interpretive center at the south entrance to learn about the reserve and its trails which range from 2km to almost 8km long.

Free guided tours are offered on Tuesdays, Wednesdays, Thursdays and Sundays at 2pm. The tour, which starts at the north entrance, is a leisurely three-hour walk led by friendly guides who explain the reserve's history, ecology and wildlife. Monthly full-moon tours are available – check online for the latest schedule.

Birdspotting Hot Spot

Bring binoculars if you're a birder – ducks, swans, woodpeckers, parakeets, hawks, flycatchers and cardinals are just a few of some 300 species of birds that can be spotted here.

The reserve's nursery, with over 100 species of native plants, can be visited with a guide.

Further in at the reserve's eastern shoreline you can get a close-up view of the Río de la Plata's muddy waters – a rare sight in Buenos Aires.

Homage to the Bandonéon

Search out the Monumento al Tango

Puerto Madero is not the neighborhood with the strongest tango tradition in Buenos Aires. Nevertheless it's here that you will see **Monumento al Tango**, a metallic sculpture dedicated to this music. Facing the Río de la Plata, on a concrete pedestal of almost 2m and standing 3.5m tall, this abstract work represents the *bandoneón*, an essential instrument in all tango orchestras. The piece was created by sculptor Estela Trebino and engineer Alejandro Coria. Its location facing the river is no coincidence – the instrument arrived with German immigrants. Later, Buenos Aires appropriated its sound and gave it the distinctive stamp it has today in tango. The monument has a replica in Medellín (Colombia), where Carlos Gardel, the great tango singer, died.

Artwork on the Silos

View a giant mural with a feminist theme

Puerto Madero preserves some elements of its old port era, such as the old grain silos. In 2018 a block of these silos at Dock 3, in front of the Puente de la Mujer, was transformed into a giant work of art. Created by the American artist Barbara Kruger, this large-scale mural is officially untitled but is generally referred to by some of the words in its design: **No Podés Vivir Sin Nosotras** (You Can't Live Without Us). Partly painted in the colors of the Argentine flag, the mural has a feminist theme with other words translating as 'power, pleasure, property, equality, empathy, independence, doubt, belief and women.'

Puerto Madero's Most Stunning View

Have a drink at the high-rise Crystal Bar

Puerto Madero offers the perfect setting for a stroll along the river. However, **Crystal Bar** *(alvearicon.com; 6pm-1:30am Tue-Sat)* provides the most impressive aerial view of the area and is one of the city's best-positioned sky bars. On the 32nd floor of the Alvear Icon Hotel & Residences this luxury spot overlooks the neighborhood with the highest-priced real estate in Buenos Aires. Although its minimum spend is somewhat higher than other BA sky bars, having a drink or a bite to eat here is worth the experience. Below, you'll spot the Puente de

EDUARDO MADERO'S VISION

Puerto Madero is named after Eduardo Madero (1833–94), a wealthy exporter. He proposed transforming BA's mudflats into a series of modern basins and harbors. This happened, but not quite as he had planned.

By the time of its completion in 1898 (four years after Madero's death), Puerto Madero had exceeded its budget. Madero had come under scrutiny for his attempts to buy up all the landfill in the area and from his links to politicians who had also acquired nearby lands likely to increase in value. By 1910 the amount of cargo was already too great for the new port, and poor access to the rail terminus at Plaza Once made things even worse.

EATING IN PUERTO MADERO: FINE DINING

Osten: Pasture-raised meats, pasta and signature dishes. It also offers a wide variety of cocktails. *8pm-midnight Tue-Sat* **$$$**

Frenessì: Technology (like lighting and projections) blend with taste for this concept restaurant's menu featuring mainly meats and fish, with a carefully curated wine list. *hours vary* **$$$**

Happening: A classic steakhouse overlooking the river, known for its standout dishes like lamb, sirloin and rib-eye steak. *hours vary* **$$$**

El Mercado: Blends the inspiration of European markets with the charm of Buenos Aires' legendary *cantinas*. Dishes use natural ingredients and seasonal fruits. *hours vary* **$$$**

PUERTO MADERO'S GASTRONOMIC SCENE

Carla Barbera, Executive Chef at La Cabaña shares her favorite places in Puerto Madero.

Puerto Madero's architecture never ceases to amaze me with its blend of modern and port-era structures. But what especially interests me is the gastronomic scene with many restaurants serving Argentine and global cuisines. You can find smaller specialty cafes and some with a great river view. There are inexpensive alternatives, such as the street food of Costanera Sur. For an afternoon drink, I enjoy visiting the bar **Negroni**. I also like Peñón del Águila (p93), a floating bar with a great view. Sometimes, I linger over a coffee at **Havanna**, viewing the Puente de la Mujer.

la Mujer (p87), the Palacio Libertad (p60) and the grasslands of the Reserva Ecológica Costanera Sur (p88).

The menu includes a sushi bar, snacks and mains, such as iron-grilled *bife de chorizo,* strip steak with a spicy sauce and fries. The house cocktail is the rum-based Crystal Mai Tai. If you plan to watch the sunset from the bar, note that reservations are not taken and seats are on a first-come, first-served basis.

Learn to Cook Asado

Take a hands-on class at a traditional *parrilla*

The *asado* is not only a barbecue and a cultural tradition, it is also a source of great pride for Argentinians. **La Cabaña** *(lacabana.com.ar; 11:30am-midnight)* serves top-quality meats and offers barbecue classes taught by chef Diego Moyano. The classes begin with the delivery of a cooking apron and basic notions on how to handle charcoal and fire. Students are oriented on the different cuts of meat, how to cook them and, finally, practice with loin, one of the most traditional cuts. Once the experience is over, the students can return to their table to enjoy their cooking or eat directly from the barbecue grill. A tasting of Malbec wine, Argentina's emblematic grape variety, is recommended with the meat. In the end, you will receive a participation diploma. With that, you can say with pride, and certification, that you know how to make Argentine *asado*. The restaurant also organizes wine tastings.

Casts of Sculptural Masterpieces

View 400 years of art history at Museo de la Cárcova

Filled with large windows overlooking a garden, **Museo de la Cárcova** *(museodelacarcova.una.edu.ar; free; 10am-5pm Tue-Sun)* condenses more than 4000 years of art history through its collection of plaster casts of sculptural masterpieces, found in museums such as the Louvre in Paris, the British Museum in London and Florence's Academy.

Upon entering you will surely be impressed by the reproduction of Michelangelo's *David*. In addition to that room dedicated to the Renaissance, there are others with works of art from ancient Egypt, Greece and Rome, as well as Mesoamerican and Andean art. The museum also exhibits works

EATING IN PUERTO MADERO: BEST SUSHI

Sushi Club: This Argentine restaurant offers sushi adapted to local tastes, along with other Asian dishes. There's a dedicated vegetarian section on the menu. *hours vary* $$$

Norimōto: Japanese restaurant specializing in hand-rolled sushi. Customers sit at a bar and can choose the ingredients for their sushi from the chef. *hours vary* $$$

Paru Inkas: Offers a wide variety of sushi, Nikkei (Japanese-Peruvian) flavors, and cocktails. Specialties are *tiraditos* and *ceviches*, highlighting textures and contrasts. *noon-midnight* $$$

Mizuki: As well as sushi, Mizuki serves noodles, tempura and meat prepared on a *teppan* (griddle) in front of the guests. *noon-3pm & 7pm-midnight* $$$

STEFAN LAMBAUER/SHUTTERSTOCK

Fuente de las Nereidas

by Ernesto de la Cárcova, the artist after whom the institution is named and the first director of the Academia Superior de Bellas Artes de la Nación.

Art in an Old Port Building

See what's on at Pabellón de las Bellas Artes

The **Pabellón de las Bellas Artes** *(uca.edu.ar/es/pabellon-de-bellas-artes; free; 11am-7pm Tue-Sun)* is a center dedicated to artistic experimentation at the Universidad Católica Argentina (UCA), one of the most prestigious private universities in the country. Here you can view temporary exhibitions of photography, painting, installations and design by Argentine and international artists. The museum is located in one of the loading docks of the old port and preserves its exposed brick and cast iron beams.

A CONTROVERSIAL FOUNTAIN

The beautiful Carrara marble fountain **Fuente de las Nereidas** made by Lola Mora in 1903, is very close to the south entrance of the Reserva Ecológica Costanera Sur. Years after the work was finished, the authorities proposed placing it in the Plaza de Mayo, close to Catedral Metropolitana. This sparked outrage among the upper classes and bourgeoisie due to the sculpture's nudity, depicting nereids attending the goddess Venus' birth.

Finally, it was decided to move the fountain to the city's outskirts, which was the southern waterfront in those years. The conservatives of the time saw this decision as a triumph. Because of this sculpture and her advocacy for women's rights, the sculptor Lola Mora is considered one of the pioneers of feminism in the country.

DRINKING IN PUERTO MADERO: BEST CAFES

Croque Madame: Specialty coffee and some delicacies such as scones, croissants and *alfajores* (cookies sandwiching *dulce de leche*). *8am-8pm*

Lobo Café: Great variety of specialty coffee, juices, smoothies and dishes throughout the day. *8am-1am Fri-Sat & 8am-midnight Sun-Thu*

Ol' Days – Coffee & Kitchen Madero: All-day brunch, plant-based dishes, and specialty coffee at this local chain cafe. *8am-9:30pm*

Café Martínez: This spot offers a variety of ground coffees, including decaffeinated, Italian, Brazilian, mocha, mild, intense and select blends. *7am-5pm Mon-Fri*

EL GRAN ÁSTOR

Ástor Piazzolla (1921–92) was a composer and *bandoneón* (small accordion) virtuoso, who played in the leading Aníbal Troilo orchestra in the late 1930s and early 1940s. Argentines like to call him *El Gran Ástor* (the Great Ástor), as he revolutionized traditional tango by infusing it with elements of jazz and classical music such as counterpoints, fugues and various harmonies.

This new style, known as *nuevo tango*, became an international hit in Europe (Piazzolla lived on and off in Italy and France) and North America. In his native land, however, it initially encountered considerable resistance. It took years for Piazzolla's controversial new style to be accepted, and he even received death threats for his break with tradition.

Intimate Luxurious Tango Show

Get close to the artists at Rojo Tango

Buenos Aires offers tango shows at all hours across many neighborhoods. **Rojo Tango** *(rojotango.com; dinner from 7:30pm, performance from 9:15 pm)* is one of the best-known and most luxurious. It takes place in a lounge with a cabaret atmosphere at the exclusive Faena Hotel. Unlike other tango shows, there is an atmosphere of intimacy and closeness with the artists. The show begins in the 1920s when tango gained popularity and penetrated all social classes, especially the upper ones, influenced by European trends. The 90-minute show ends with modern works by Ástor Piazzolla, perhaps the most performed Argentine musician in the world. A quintet performs the live music while the couples energize the stage with their dynamic choreography. You can pay for dinner and the show or just to see the show.

DRINKING IN PUERTO MADERO: OUR PICKS

Puente Gran Bar: Offering cocktails, beers and street food with a great view of the Puente de la Mujer. *hours vary*

Library Lounge: Intimate bar in the Faena Hotel with leather sofas, richly decorated rugs and crystal chandeliers. Has an extensive wine list. *9am-12:30am*

Temple Craft: Known for its craft beers, this spot features live DJs, a happy hour and a great selection of IPAs. *11am–2am*

Alberto Lobby Bar: Boasts one of the city's most diverse menus of classic cocktails and exclusive, special-edition drinks. *9am-1:30am*

MARK GREEN /ALAMY

Rojo Tango

The Choripán Route

Savor street food along Costanera Sur

Costanera Sur is an old seaside promenade that served as a seaside resort until the 1970s. A few meters away from the elegant restaurants of Puerto Madero, the place is a great spot for street food lovers. There are dozens of food trucks offering hamburgers, *bondiola* (pork sandwiches) and, of course, the street food star of Argentina: *choripán* (chorizo sausage sandwiches). Eating a *choripán* overlooking the river grasslands is a favorite activity for many locals on Sundays. The food trucks are open daily from 11am to midnight. **ParriVip350** and **Qué Parrillón** are two of the best known.

BEST SHOPS IN PUERTO MADERO

I Love Gifts: Souvenir store selling T-shirts, mugs, suitcases, *mate* gourds, and other items inspired by Argentina's landscapes and characters.

Isadora: This fashion brand is dedicated to the design, manufacture and sale of accessories for women.

Llama Violeta: Women's clothing brand offering a wide range of T-shirts, tank tops and vests, along with various items and accessories.

Beluno Design: Glass and porcelain household items, such as plates, dishes and soup tureens.

Giorgio Redaelli: It's a two-generation family business specializing in men's clothing with an Italian style.

DRINKING IN PUERTO MADERO: OUR PICKS

Peñón del Águila: Floating bar where you can taste over 14 styles of draft beer and 12 canned options, ranging from German classics to sour, hoppy, and fruity varieties. *hours vary*

El Boleo: This bar offers a wide variety of craft beers and has a good view of the Puente de la Mujer. They offer red, lager and stout beers, including some sweeter varieties. *10am-2am*

Kraken Bar: Serving craft beers – mainly blonde, red, and dark varieties – along with cocktails and simple dishes like burgers and fries. *10am-2am*

Johnny B Good: They offer both mass-produced Argentine beers and craft brews from small producers, along with a wide variety of drinks and spirits. *hours vary*

RECOVERING FROM A MURKY PAST

During the military dictatorship of 1976 to 1983, access to the Buenos Aires waterfront was limited, as the area was diked and filled with sediments dredged from the Río de la Plata. While plans for a new satellite city across from the port stalled, trees, grasses, birds and rodents took advantage and colonized this low-lying, 350-hectare area that mimics the ecology of the Delta del Paraná.

Today, a walk along the waterfront and through the Reserva Ecológica Costanera Sur can show you up to around 2000 animal species, including mammals, amphibians and reptiles. The area also features native vegetation such as grasslands and alder forests. Particularly notable is the bird population, with over 340 species recorded in the reserve.

Sunset Views & an Open Bar

Experience the city from the river

One of the main attractions of Puerto Madero is enjoying the river. **Sunset Río de la Plata** *(humbertom.com)* offers the chance to watch the sunset aboard a boat as it sails through the waters of the Río de la Plata. The two-hour cruise includes an open bar, electronic music, and sometimes, a small, improvised dance floor.

You'll spend the first hour enjoying the boat while it's moored and the second with navigation through the Port of Buenos Aires interior. During the tour, before enjoying the sunset, you can see from the river the old Hotel de Inmigrantes (p130), the cruise terminal and the rationalist building of the traditional **Yacht Club Argentino** *(yca.org.ar)*. Cruises are subject to weather conditions, with days and times varying according to the seasons. It has a capacity of 120 passengers.

Picnic in the Park

Stroll through Parque Micaela Bastidas

Covering 5.4 hectares, **Parque Micaela Bastidas** spans the eastern sector of Dock 2 in Puerto Madero. It was inaugurated in 2003 with the idea of providing new green areas to the youngest neighborhood of the city. Its structure is uneven, with several stone staircases like other parks in the city. It has more than 2500 trees of local species, such as poplars, tipas, jacarandas and ash. There is a rose garden, three squares and an area reserved for children's games. Overlooking the area's renovated red brick buildings, port cranes and modern skyscrapers, it is a lovely place to read a book on a summer day or enjoy a picnic.

The park is named after Micaela Bastidas Puyucahua, a hero of Spanish-American independence and the wife of Túpac Amaru II (born José Gabriel Condorcanqui), a Peruvian indigenous leader and military leader.

EATING IN PUERTO MADERO: INTERNATIONAL FLAVORS

Lupita: Restaurant offering *fajitas*, *quesadillas*, *burritos* and other Mexican specialties, along with a diverse cocktail menu. *10am-2am* **$$**

Museo del Jamón: Serving specialties of traditional Spanish cuisine. It also sells hams and sausages to take away. *hours vary* **$$$**

Shawarma Al Árabe: Arabic street-food spot. Its most renowned dishes are falafel, *baba ganoush* and *shawarmas*. *noon-midnight Tue-Sun* **$**

Sorrento: The dishes here are inspired by Mediterranean cuisine, with an emphasis on pasta, fish and seafood. *noon-1am* **$$$**

PUERTO MADERO WALKING TOUR

Follow this route, or join tour guide Eugenia Calcarami *(@paseosbuenosaires)*, to learn about important women from Argentine history.

START	END	LENGTH
Museo de la Inmigración	Blvd Macacha Güemes	2.1km; 3 hours

From the ❶ **Museo de la Inmigración** (p130) at the southern end of Retiro, walk south along Av Antártida Argentina to ❷ **Cecilia Grierson** at edge of the Río Dique – Grierson was the first woman to receive a medical degree in Argentina.

Have a look around ❸ **Colección de Arte Amalia Lacroze de Fortabat** (p86) then continue south to ❹ **Emma de la Barra** commemorating the Argentine writer who adopted the pen name of César Duayen.

Further south ❺ **Victoria Ocampo** is named after the writer, philanthropist and key intellectual of 20th century Argentina, while ❻ **Trinidad Guevara** is dedicated to a great Uruguayan actress whose career blossomed in Argentina.

❼ **Pierina Dealessi** is named in honor of the popular Italian actress. Pause for refreshments at ❽ **Ol' Days – Coffee & Kitchen Madero** (p91) then backtrack to cross ❾ **Puente de la Mujer** (p87) – Puerto Madero's iconic bridge, designed by Santiago Calatrava, symbolizes a woman in motion. Finish at ❿ **Blvd Macacha Güemes**, named after the key woman in the struggle for Argentine independence.

Immigrants to Argentina were once processed through the building that is now home to the **Museo de la Inmigración**.

Emma de la Barra published under a male pseudonym because of the societal prejudices of her era against women intellectuals.

Pierina Dealessi became a nationalized Argentine citizen with a great career in theater, cinema and circus.

Researched by
Rachel Tolosa Paz

SAN TELMO

BOHEMIAN SPIRIT AND FLEA MARKET FINDS

Plaza Dorrego is the heart of San Telmo, perfect for people-watching. Come Sundays, San Telmo is alive with its famous street market running the length of Calle Defensa.

San Telmo is a vibrant Buenos Aires neighborhood known for its centuries-old colonial architecture, antique dealers, lively street market and bohemian feel. One of the city's oldest barrios, there are layers of history here, so make sure you head down every cobblestone street to stumble upon hidden gems. While it is indeed a mecca for tourists, who flock to Defensa and the historic indoor produce market, Mercado de San Telmo, you only have to step away from the main drag to find some relative calm. The spirit of tango is alive and well in San Telmo and some of the city's best shows – both intimate and spectacular – are found here.

TOP TIP

San Telmo is not the most pram- or wheelchair-friendly spot, with narrow footpaths, cobblestone streets and heavy crowds on Sundays.

OLIVERDELAHAYE/SHUTTERSTOCK

Feria de San Telmo (p100)

See page 197 for places to stay in San Telmo

Highlights

❶ Feria de San Telmo

Soak up the atmosphere and hunt down souvenirs and old treasures at this lively Sunday street market. **p100**

❷ El Zanjón de Granados

Explore mysterious underground tunnels at this historic complex hidden in plain sight. **p102**

GIANFRANCO VIVI/SHUTTERSTOCK

❸ Museo Histórico Nacional

Peek into José de San Martín's re-created bedroom at this fascinating museum about Argentine independence. **p102**

❹ Museo de Arte Moderno de Buenos Aires

Tour this excellent modern art gallery with a quiet cafe, kids' activities and BA's oldest house in the basement. **p105**

▲ ❺ Shopping in San Telmo

Pick up an antique camera, rustle through second-hand bookstores and marvel at vintage beauties. **p101**

Getting Around

Walking

A compact *barrio*, your best option to see the sights is to pound the pavements.

Subte

Línea C connects the western edge of San Telmo with downtown and Retiro.

Bus

Take bus 59 from Recoleta and Palermo; bus 29 from La Boca, Plaza de Mayo and Palermo.

HIGHLIGHTS
1 El Zanjón de Granados
2 Feria de San Telmo
3 Mercado de San Telmo
4 Museo de Arte Moderno de Buenos Aires

SIGHTS
5 Casa Mínima
6 Centro Cultural Torquato Tasso
7 Colección Histórica del Traje Argentino
8 Iglesia Ortodoxa Rusa
9 La Scala de San Telmo
10 Mafalda
11 Museo de Arte Contemporáneo Buenos Aires
12 Museo Histórico Nacional
13 Museo Penitenciarío Argentino Antonio Ballvé
14 Parque Lezama
15 Pista Urbana
16 Sótano de San Telmo
17 Teatro Margarita Xirgu

SLEEPING
18 Cassa Lepage
19 Circus Hostel & Hotel
20 Hostel América del Sur
21 Hotel Anselmo Buenos Aires
22 L'Adresse Hotel Boutique
23 Loft Osteria by Sagardi
24 Viajero Hostel Buenos Aires

EATING
25 Alfonso
26 Bar El Federal
see 3 Beba Cocina
27 Bulevar
28 Café San Juan
29 Café Z
30 El Desnivel
31 El Fundador
see 56 El Gauchito
32 Grandes Carnicerías del Plata
33 Hierbabuena
34 La Brigada

35 La Poesia	**52** Bar Sur
see 3 Lo de Freddy	**53** Bilongón
36 Napoles	**54** El Viejo Almacén
37 Nikkai Shokudo	**see 51** Maldita Milonga
38 Obrador	**55** Todo Mundo
39 Origen Café	**SHOPPING**
40 PES	**56** Antique Cameras
41 Pirilo	**57** Eureka Records
42 The Pizza Only True Love	**see 3** Flecharte
43 Pulpería Quilapán	**58** Galería Solar de French
44 PUNTO	**59** Gil Antiguedades
45 Somos Virgen	**60** Jessica Kessel
DRINKING & NIGHTLIFE	**61** La Filetería
46 Atis Bar	**62** Nativo Argentino
47 Bar Británico	**63** Patio Ezeiza
see 29 Doppel-gänger	**64** Quorum
48 Gibraltar	**65** Taller Galería DAWA
49 La Puerta Roja	**66** Walrus Books
see 3 Nilson	**see 3** WI-PO
50 Turvina	**INFORMATION**
ENTERTAINMENT	**67** Lunfarda Travel
51 ATRODEN	

TOP EXPERIENCE

Feria de San Telmo

On Sundays, San Telmo's main drag is closed to traffic and the street is a sea of both locals and tourists browsing market stalls and soaking up the atmosphere of San Telmo's biggest day of the week. There's music, street performers, hundreds of stallholders and plenty of spots to stop for snacks and people-watching along the way.

©VICTORIA/SHUTTERSTOCK

TOP TIPS

- Watch your bag carefully, it is very crowded and petty crime does happen.
- The market is a great spot to pick up hand-painted *fileteado* (p107) signs.
- Plaza Dorrego's antique dealers start packing up around 5pm; start at that end if you want time to rummage.

PRACTICALITIES

Open 10am to 6pm Sundays; free to enter.

The Market

It started in 1970 as an antiques fair, but today you'll find all manner of items, mostly focussed on hand-crafted objects. There's everything from art and crafts to souvenirs, jewelry, leather pieces and vintage clothing – plan to spend the day because it is 1.5km of road to stroll and shop. The antique and collectable stallholders are centered around Plaza Dorrego. You'll find other arms of the market that lead off from Defensa like the artists market on Humberto Primero and the indigenous crafts market on the other side of Av San Juan.

Plaza Dorrego

Plaza Dorrego is the city's second-oldest plaza and was originally a pit stop for caravans bringing supplies into the city from around Argentina. At the turn of the 19th century, it became a public square surrounding by colonial buildings which survive to this day. During the week it is a peaceful and shady spot with plenty of seating (for the surrounding restaurants) so you can sit and enjoy the atmosphere. There are often tango students dancing here for tips and a few hippie street vendors which only adds to the relaxed vibe.

A Famed Indoor Produce Market

Browse the stalls at Mercado de San Telmo

The grand old indoor produce market, **Mercado de San Telmo** *(mercadosantelmo.com.ar; 9am-8pm)*, opened in 1897 to cater to European immigrants and has had several incarnations over the last century. In recent decades, it has been home to second-hand and collectable dealers but as with many tourist-defined sites, the pandemic (and a subsequent renovation) caused a mass exodus resulting in today's offering as a dining spot filled with eateries.

The market is certainly a little shinier than it used to be but, in the process, it has also lost a bit of its charm. It's still worth a visit but be prepared to squeeze your way between the hoards waiting in line for the toilet (bring tissues) or milling about for the same *empanada*. There are gems to be found like Beba Cocina for classic home-style cooking and **Lo de Freddy**, which is still one of the city's top *choripán* (chorizo sandwich) spots. For shopping, rummage through the vintage posters and ephemera at **WI-PO**, the secondhand clothing stalls along the Bolivar Street entrance and the indigenous crafts at **Flecharte**. But there aren't any bargains here.

Don't visit on Sundays when it is packed to the rafters with tourists. Head here midweek or early Saturday mornings for a more local affair.

Retail Gems along Cobblestoned Streets

Shop along and around Calle Defensa

The main artery of San Telmo is Calle Defensa. Our picks along this retail strip include **Quorum**, stocking paper works by Argentine artists and illustrators; **Patio Ezeiza**, a wide variety of small shops in an old *conventillo*; **Nativo Argentino** for stunning Indigenous crafts and textiles; **Juan Carlos Pallarols**, the showroom and atelier of the internationally renowned parasol maker; and the artist studio shops in **Galería Solar de French** – yes, it's the famed shopping complex adorned with colorful umbrellas, but spare a thought for the shopkeepers, skip the selfies and spend a peso or two instead.

Duck off into the adjoining blocks to wander the cobblestones and stumble along lesser-known gems like Taller Galería DAWA for artist-made ceramics, and **GIL Antigüedades**, a packed-to-the-rafters museum-like vintage store – ring the bell and make sure you head downstairs to the basement.

BEST UNIQUE SHOPS IN SAN TELMO

Taller Galería DAWA: Ceramics studio and store with a wonderful range of ceramics made by their studio artists.

Antique Cameras: Specialist vintage and antique camera shop.

Eureka Records: Under the freeway and nestled beside the football fields you'll find this bright secondhand record shop.

Jessica Kessel: Handcrafted, colorful and unique shoe offerings from a local BA designer.

Walrus Books: Cozy English-language secondhand bookstore with a wonderful range of books on Argentina.

EATING IN SAN TELMO: CHEAP EATS

Pirilo: Blink and you miss it, but this locals' pizza joint is an institution. *1-4:30pm & 6-11pm Tue-Fri, 6pm-midnight Sat & Sun* $

El Desnivel: Firm favorite serving up cheap and cheerful *milanesas* (crumbed veal) for decades. *7pm-midnight Mon, from noon Tue-Sun* $

El Gauchito: San Telmo classic with a couple of tables and some of the city's best *empanadas* and *locro* (spicy bean and meat stew). *noon-4pm & 8-11pm Wed-Mon* $

Beba Cocina: Home-style cooking in Mercado del San Telmo; try *morcilla* (blood sausage), *empanadas* and *faina* (chickpea pizza). *11am-6pm Mon-Fri, to 8pm Sat & Sun* $$

MEMENTO MORI

The unique Memento Mori exhibition at Museo Histórico Nacional displays a lock of General José de San Martín's hair; the hat that politician Leonardo N. Alem was wearing when he shot himself in 1896; and a *peinetón*, a giant fan-like comb that was fashionable among aristocratic women in the 1830s.

One of the most intriguing exhibits is the key to the tomb of Encarnación Ezcurra (1795–1838). This polarizing figure was the wife of Juan Manuel de Rosas, leader of the Argenine Confederation in the mid 19th century. She was a powerful figure in her own right and is widely thought to have paved the way for subsequent female presidents Isabel Perón and Cristina Fernández de Kirchner.

Explore Mysterious Underground Tunnels

Take a tour of El Zanjón de Granados and Casa Mínima

A must-visit site in San Telmo, **El Zanjón de Granados** *(elzanjon.com.ar; access only by tour at 10am, 2pm & 4pm)*, is a sprawling complex that reveals much of the history of colonial settlement in Buenos Aires. In the 1980s, local businessman Jorge Eckstein bought the building with plans to build a restaurant. The house had been abandoned for over a decade and was filled with rubbish. During restoration, which took 17 years, a system of tunnels was discovered beneath the floors. Originally developed by an aristocratic family who constructed the building in the 19th century, the tunnels covered the natural waterway that ran to the nearby Río de la Plata (the river was just two blocks from here in the 1800s). On this fascinating site they also have some interesting archaeological objects on view, including pieces of a pipe from Africa.

Across the road from El Zanjón de Granados is the enigmatic tiny home **Casa Mínima**, also restored by Eckstein. Keep an eye out for the green door and look up to spot the tiny balcony. It is Buenos Aires' narrowest home, measuring just 2m wide. If you wish to visit El Zanjón and Casa Mínima on the same day, you can buy the combo promotion only at the museum ticket office. Tours only of Casa Mínima are at 1pm on weekends.

English tours are held daily. If you're short on time, the one-hour Flash Tour (of both sites) is an option, but we recommend going the whole hog, you'll find yourself wanting to linger longer if you sprint through.

Check out San Martín's Sword

Enter Parque Lezama to find the Museo Histórico Nacional

Parque Lezama is a historic park (lately used by President Javier Milei to make announcements of note) where you'll see people playing chess or wandering the small pop-up markets. It also houses the **Museo Histórico Nacional** *(museo historiconacional.cultura.gob.ar; free; 11am-7pm Wed-Sun)* which has some of the most important objects and paintings from Argentina's 19th century revolutionary and post-independence history. It's not a big museum but it is filled with many fascinating pieces (with some description labels in English), meaning it is easy to spend an hour or two here. The centerpiece is the sword of General José de San Martín (p126), a symbol of liberation for the nation that paved the way for Argentina's independence in 1816.

EATING IN SAN TELMO: OUR PICKS

Nikkai Shokudo: Authentic Japanese restaurant serving up sashimi in the Asociación Japonesa en la Argentina. *noon-3pm, 7:30-11pm Mon-Sat* $

PES: Fun hole-in-the-wall tapas with street-side seating on Calle Bolívar; great spot to people watch. *6pm-midnight Mon-Fri, noon-midnight Sat & Sun* $$

PUNTO: Specialty coffee with tasty breakfast and lunch offerings; don't miss the *chipa* (cheesy bread balls) and house-made croissants. *8am-8pm Mon-Sat* $

Alfonso: Delicious contemporary eats in this lunch-only minimalist diner, bookings essential. *noon-4:30pm Tue-Sat* $$

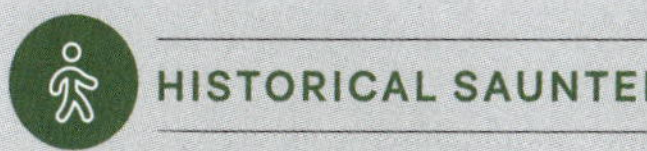

HISTORICAL SAUNTER

Wander the length of Defensa to discover underground tunnels, indoor markets and cavernous contemporary art spaces

START	END	LENGTH
Mafalda	Bar Británico	1.5km; 2½ hours

Take a selfie with ❶ **Mafalda** (p109) on the corner of Defensa and Chile. Saunter down the street to the incredible series of tunnels and brick archways of ❷ **El Zanjón de Granados**. Take a peep at ❸ **Casa Mínima**, BA's narrowest residence.

Head south on Defensa and stop at lively ❹ **El Desnivel** (p101) for a classic Argentine steak feast. Don't miss strolling through the covered ❺ **Mercado de San Telmo** (p101).

Back on Defensa you'll soon reach the heart of the *barrio*, ❻ **Plaza Dorrego** (p100). A block south, ❼ **Museo de Arte Moderno de Buenos Aires** (p105) offers cutting-edge exhibitions by Argentine artists. Next door is ❽ **Museo de Arte Contemporáneo Buenos Aires** (p105), great for abstract art.

The freeway location of the ❾ **Club Atlético Memorial** is simply awful – but so is its history. Admire the blue cupolas of ❿ **Iglesia Ortodoxa Rusa** (p104) then stroll through ⓫ **Parque Lezama** to the ⓬ **Museo Histórico Nacional** for an insight into Argentina's history. Finally, rest your tired feet at the atmospheric ⓭ **Bar Británico** (p104). Snag a prized window seat and order a drink – you deserve it.

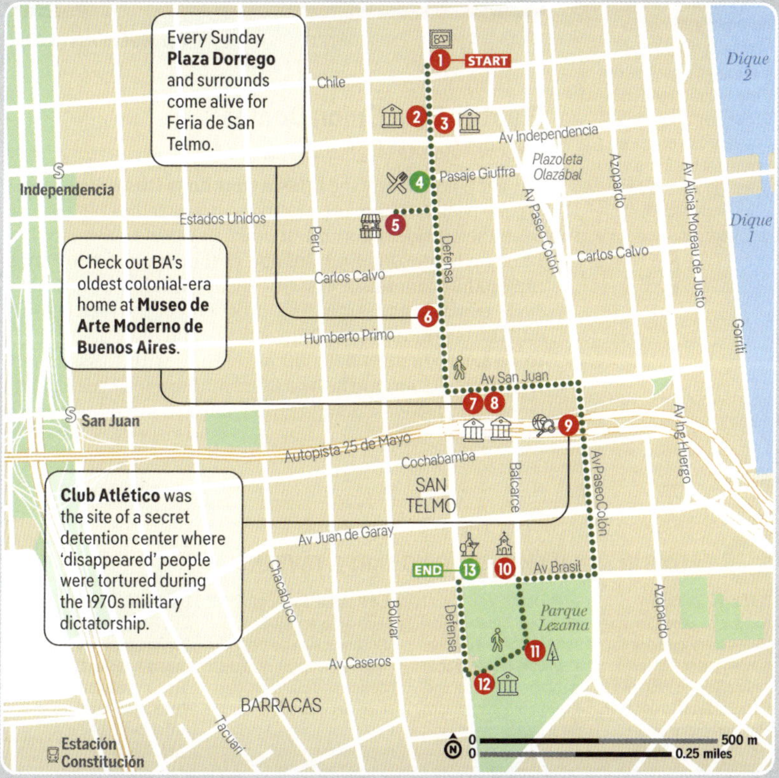

Every Sunday **Plaza Dorrego** and surrounds come alive for Feria de San Telmo.

Check out BA's oldest colonial-era home at **Museo de Arte Moderno de Buenos Aires**.

Club Atlético was the site of a secret detention center where 'disappeared' people were tortured during the 1970s military dictatorship.

HISTORIC SPOT FOR BA'S QUEER COMMUNITY

Opposite Casa Mínima (p102) is a building that is currently a Western Union and storage for various local restaurants. It is also an important landmark in Buenos Aires' lesbian cultural history. During the 1970s dictatorship, here was an underground club and cultural space for lesbians known as the **Sótano de San Telmo** (Basement of San Telmo). Today, people attempt to reclaim this history by writing messages on the building walls, but they are fairly swiftly covered over. It's a popular meeting spot prior to the start of the Pride March each November.

Parque Lezama (p102)

Electric Blue Onion Domes

Discover the site of Iglesia Ortodoxa Rusa

The five blue domes of the **Iglesia Ortodoxa Rusa** *(iglesiarusa.org.ar)* peak out from certain spots in San Telmo, but to see it from the outside in its entirety take in the view from Parque Lezama. Inside this 1901 Russian Orthodox church are stunning painted murals and stained-glass windows. Many Russians emigrated to Argentina at the end of the 19th century and the beginning of the 20th century and there are believed to be approximately 300,000 Argentines with Russian heritage. Guided tours are held on Sunday afternoon once a month (see the website for details). Alternatively, attend a mass on Sunday mornings.

EATING IN SAN TELMO: HISTORIC BARS & TAVERNS

Pulpería Quilapán: Historic *pulpería* tavern-style eatery with a great garden patio, live music and *peñas*; guaranteed to transport you to another time and place. *9am-midnight Wed-Sun* $

La Federal: Very busy *bar notable*; head early (before 8pm) to share a *picada*, a typical platter of cold meats and cheese, and a vermouth with friends. *8am-2am* $

La Poesía: *Bar notable* with a literary vibe and the bohemian heart of San Telmo; soak it up with coffee and classic Argie fare. *8am-2am* $

Bar Británico: One of San Telmo's great corner *bar notables* on Parque Lezama; expect to wait during peak periods but there's excellent people watching to be done. *7am-3am* $

San Telmo's Art Museums

Enjoy modern and contemporary art collections

Originally founded in 1956 and focussed on Argentine and international art from the 20th century, **Museo de Arte Moderno de Buenos Aires** *(museomoderno.org; free entrance Wed; 11am-7pm Mon, Wed-Fri, 11am-8pm Sat & Sun)* is commonly referred to as Museo Moderno. Since 2018, it has been housed in an historic tobacco factory on Av San Juan. Spot the decorative number 43 on the museum's upper façade which was a well-known Argentine brand of cigarettes.

The multi-story museum has an excellent permanent collection and rotating schedule of exhibitions that cover contemporary art, performance, cinema and experimental sound. They also have a great children's program on weekends. Be sure to head to the auditorium where you can view (behind glass) the remains of BA's oldest home, Casa de Naranjo. It was found in its entirety when work began on the renovation of the old factory for the museum and dates from the end of the 18th century.

There's a very small gift shop and a cafe serving coffee and cakes – a generally cool and quiet spot with large share tables and soaring windows – perfect on hot days if you need a pause (there's no need to pay the museum entrance fee to enter here).

A couple of doors down is **Museo de Arte Contemporáneo Buenos Aires** *(MACBA; macba.com.ar; noon-7pm Wed-Mon)* This private museum dedicated to contemporary art houses a large collection of geometric abstract works and rotating exhibitions in a contemporary building.

Tango in San Telmo

From spectacles to the street

Part of the charm of San Telmo is its heady relationship with nostalgia, so it's little wonder that the tango is also everywhere you turn. From showy spectacles to neighborhood *milongas*, you're bound to find something to suit.

El Viejo Almacen *(viejoalmacen.com.ar)* is a dinner and a show performance – you eat first and then head across the road to an historic grocery store where the tango performances have been held since 1969. For something more intimate, try **Bar Sur** *(bar-sur.com.ar)* set in an historic cafe where you can have a coffee during the day – it's an atmospheric

GET LOST IN SAN TELMO

Julian Solari is a flautist with the Orquesta Académica del Teatro Colón. *@julisolarii*

I like to describe San Telmo as an historic neighborhood with multiple urban layers. There's the touristy element but also the heritage, immigrant, bohemian and local layers. Each moment of each day reveals the different portraits of San Telmo. The massive tourist dimension is the one that generates the least interest in me, so to tour San Telmo, I always suggest getting lost through its streets and passages. Let yourself go and allow yourself to discover new places and objects. The sheer variety of curiosities would be overlooked if one only chooses a fixed destination, thinking that they know where to go.

EATING IN SAN TELMO: OUR PICKS

El Fundador: Delicious artisanal ice cream in this sweet spot in Caseros; no added sugar. *11am-midnight Sun, Tue-Thu, 11:30am-1:30am Fri & Sat* $

Café San Juan: At this beloved Spanish spot every dish bursts with flavor; bookings essential. *7.30pm-midnight Tue-Thu, 12:30pm-4pm, 7:30pm-midnight Sat, 12:30pm-4pm Sun* $$

Grandes Carnicerías del Plata: Some of the city's best meat is served by friendly waiters in this old-school space with soaring ceilings. *noon-midnight Tue-Sun* $$

La Brigada: World-renowned *parrilla* (steakhouse) famous for its perfectly grilled meats that you can eat with a spoon; bookings essential. *noon-3pm, 8pm-midnight Tue-Sun* $$$

PANDEMIC IMPACT

As an area heavily reliant on tourists and those working in offices in nearby Microcentro, San Telmo was one of the Buenos Aires *barrios* most impacted by the COVID-19 pandemic. Many long-standing antiques and collectable stores faced closures as the country had one of the toughest lockdowns in the world. In its wake, you'll find several touristy *dulce de leche* (milk caramel) shops littered along Calle Defensa, San Telmo's main shopping streets. All in all, it's harder to find treasure in San Telmo these days but perhaps that makes the search even more worthwhile. Also, note, a lot of San Telmo businesses are closed Mondays.

spot that takes you straight back in time. Bookings are essential for both these venues.

For *milongas*, on Thursdays head to the popular **Maldita Milonga** *(@malditamilonga)*. It's been going strong for nearly two decades and includes classes, performances and live music. On Fridays, head to the more recent addition, **Bilongón** *(@bilongon)* which also has a live orchestra, classes and *milonga* that goes on to the wee hours of Saturday morning.

Perhaps the most delightful tango to witness is that of the dancers in Plaza Dorrego (p100). It might seem touristy, but these dancers are usually students who, in essence, are spending hours practicing while earning some tips (be sure to pop some *pesos* in their hats). It doesn't matter if you've seen it 100 times or more, it never fails to put you under its spell.

EATING IN SAN TELMO: OUR PICKS

The Pizza Only True Love: Modern organic pizza joint with sourdough bases and creative toppings; from the owners of nearby Hierbabuena. *5pm-midnight Wed-Fri, from noon Sat & Sun* $$

Hierbabuena: Pioneering organic veg café; three cute spots including an organic deli and vegan-only joint. *9am-8pm Mon, to midnight Tue-Sun* $$

Somos Virgen: Fun Mexican stop with plenty of neon, tacos, quesadillas and cocktails. *5pm-midnight Tue-Thu & Sun, to 1am Fri & Sat* $$

Napoles: Needs to be seen to be believed; a cavernous Italian restaurant absolutely filled with cars and collectables – and it's all for sale. *8am-midnight Sun-Thu, to 1am Fri & Sat* $$

Fileteado

BA's Traditional Sign Writing

Try your hand at *fileteado*

In San Telmo, you'll find small signs for sale at the markets or at **La Filetería** *(@la.fileteria)* a women's cooperative working hard to keep this *porteño* culture alive (fewer than 200 artists form part of the official association of *fileteadores*). They offer workshops where you can try your hand at painting your own *mate* gourd and sell works made by the studio's artists.

Also, throughout the *barrio* of Boedo, west of San Telmo, there are more than 40 *fileteado* signs that were painted by Luis Zorz, one of the city's master *fileteadores*. He started working in the style from 13 years of age and Buenos Aires is home to over 200 of his pieces.

HISTORY OF FILETEADO

You can't fail to notice the distinctive fonts on signs around the city. Thought to have been inspired by Italian metal designs, the beautiful stylistic artwork known as *fileteado porteño* (or *filete*) originally appeared on early 20th century horse carts, eventually moving to BA's trucks and buses.

During the military dictatorship between 1976 to 1983, *fileteado* was banned from public transportation systems leading artists to find other creative spots for their works like newsstands and other buildings. *Fileteado* is now everywhere – from the big block letters used for political messages in the street to the intricate hand-painted signs with decorative flourishes used for transport and in some restaurants and shops.

MORE FILETEADO

There's a *fileteado* collection in the **Buenos Aires Museo** (p64). Check out the murals of Gardel in the Carlos Gardel Subte station (Línea B), too.

DRINKING IN SAN TELMO: BEST COFFEE STOPS

Bulevar: Hip coffee joint on Caseros with top-notch pastries; Sunday brunches and guest chefs. *10am-7pm Tue-Sun* $

Origen Café: Tucked away in the backstreets, cozy Origen serves great coffee and a healthy brunch spread. *8am-8pm Tue-Sun, 9am-8pm Sun* $

Café Z: Incredible coffee toasters with a low-profile; they work directly with co-ops, expect great brews. *10:30am-6.30pm Mon-Sat* $

Obrador: Cozy and chill cafe owned by locals with seasonal ingredients and veg options; best pick for breakfast in San Telmo. *8am-8:30pm Thu-Sun* $

BEST FOR LIVE MUSIC

Centro Cultural Torquato Tasso: Locals' favorite for tango and folk music; Wednesday to Sunday.

Todo Mundo: On Plaza Dorrego; live shows from rock to salsa, jazz, folk and reggae.

La Scala de San Telmo: Folk music, tango and improv in a sprawling historic home; Thursday to Sunday.

Teatro Margarita Xirgu: Indie music, plays and art in this spectacular theater.

Pista Urbana: Intimate space with tango and *folklore* (traditional folk music) every night.

ATRODEN: All manner of shows from tango to *zamba*, folk music and *murgas* (street-style dance and percussion).

From Home for Priests to Women's Prison

Tour an incredible penitentiary museum

Having undergone a major restoration project in recent years, the **Museo Penitenciarío Argentino Antonio Ballvé** *(museopenitenciarioab.ar; 11am-3pm Sun)* is an incredible site hidden in plain view, just half a block from Plaza Dorrego. It started as a home for retired Jesuit priests in the 1700s – the still-standing chapel Nuestra Señora del Carmen dates from 1734 – and operated as a women's prison from the end of the 19th century until 1974. The museum displays prison-related objects, photos and uniforms. Outside you'll see a tile embedded in the footpath in homage to the women who were detained here as political prisoners during the 1960s. Check ahead before going, because opening appears to be sporadic.

Argentina's Fashion Museum

The history of Argentina through clothes

A must for designers, researchers and students looking to connect clothing to wider historical and social contexts is **Colección Histórica del Traje Argentino** *(@museodeltrajeba; 11am-7pm Wed-Sun)* which contains over 9000 historical pieces of clothing from the 18th century to the 1980s. Housed in an historic *casona* (grand house), the collection includes pieces from *pueblos originarios* (original peoples), African-Argentines and clothing from across the range of immigrants that settled in Buenos Aires and Argentina. Other hits are the gaucho (cowboy) wear, tango suits and Eva Perón's use of Dior's New Look.

Local Guides with a Difference

Hear another side to the story with community-led tours

Lunfarda Travel *(@lunfardatravel)* is a 100% Argentine-owned and -operated tourist agency with a firm commitment to community-led storytelling. They train guides from the African Argentine, Jewish and transgender communities,

DRINKING IN SAN TELMO: OUR PICKS

La Puerta Roja: Late night sports bar popular with locals; spot the red door and head upstairs. *noon-3:30am Sun-Wed, noon-4am Thu-Sat*

Dunkel: Decorated beer hall complete with cans and bottles from around the world; fun vibe with karaoke Fri nights, *4pm-1am Tue-Thu, 4pm-4am Fri & Sat*

Plaza Dorrego: Pull up a pew at any table in the plaza (p100) to soak up the atmosphere any hour of the day. *hours vary*

Atis Bar: Head up the stairs to sip drinks in this sprawling character-filled *conventillo* (boarding house). *9am-midnight Sun-Thu, 9am-2am Fri & Sat*

JAMES BRUNKER/ALAMY

Mafalda

and are deeply passionate about giving visitors alternative perspectives of their beloved city.

One of their most popular tours is BA's first Black-centered Afro-Argentine Heritage Walking Tour in San Telmo. Alternatively, to discover more about local queer identity, join their three-hour walking tour (also starting in San Telmo) that covers several sites in the city including a guided visit to Mocha Celis, a pioneering school for transgender adults in Balvanera.

They also run Desafío Porteño, a fun three-hour immersive and interactive game where travelers hunt down clues while deep-diving into *porteño* culture.

SAY HELLO TO MAFALDA

Scattered around San Telmo and Puerto Madero there are small colorful sculptures of famous Argentine comic characters. Known as **Paseo de la Historieta** (Comic Strip Walk) this urban art project began with **Mafalda** (on the corner of Defensa and Chile) who is seated outside her creator Joaquín 'Quino' Lavado's former home.

Quino's satirical socio-political comic strip ran from 1964 to 1973 and was very popular in Latin America, Europe and, perhaps surprisingly, Quebec and Asia. Mafalda's main concerns are humanity and world peace – Umberto Eco once said that if Charlie Brown was the unheard voice of a child from the northern hemisphere, Mafalda was the unheard voice of a child from the south.

Nilson: Small bar with a mighty wine list on the edge of Mercado de San Telmo. *5pm-midnight Tue-Sat, 2pm-10pm Sun*

Turvina: Wines by the glass at this calle Caseros wine bar on the south side. *5:30pm-midnight Wed-Sat, 1pm-11:30pm Sun*

Gibraltar: Cozy English-themed bar filled with expats. Perfect if you've got a hankering for fish and chips. *noon-2am Sun-Wed, noon-3am Thu-Sat*

Doppelgänger: No wine, no beer, just superb cocktails at San Telmo's classiest bar. *7pm-1am Tue-Thu, 7pm-3:30am Fri & Sat*

Researched by Diego Jemio

LA BOCA

FAMED FOR TANGO, SOCCER AND THE CITY'S MOST COLORFUL STREET

This working-class and immigrant neighborhood keeps its past alive. In addition to the famous street El Caminito, it offers a circuit of art galleries, museums and renowned soccer club Boca Juniors.

La Boca was the original port of Buenos Aires. At the end of the 19th century, thousands of European immigrants settled here, including many Italians mainly from Genoa, who brought their customs, habits and identities. The first homes of many of these immigrants were the *conventillos* (tenement houses), which had rented rooms and shared spaces like the kitchen and bathroom. El Caminito, La Boca's most important street and one of the most photographed locations in the city, keeps part of that history alive with those buildings still standing. It is enough to walk through La Boca to feel the spirit of its people and the passion awakened by Boca Juniors, Argentina's most popular soccer club.

TOP TIP

Street performers and tango dancers will expect to be tipped by those who stop to watch or take a photograph.

CLAIRE SALVAIL PHOTOS/SHUTTERSTOCK

El Caminito (p115)

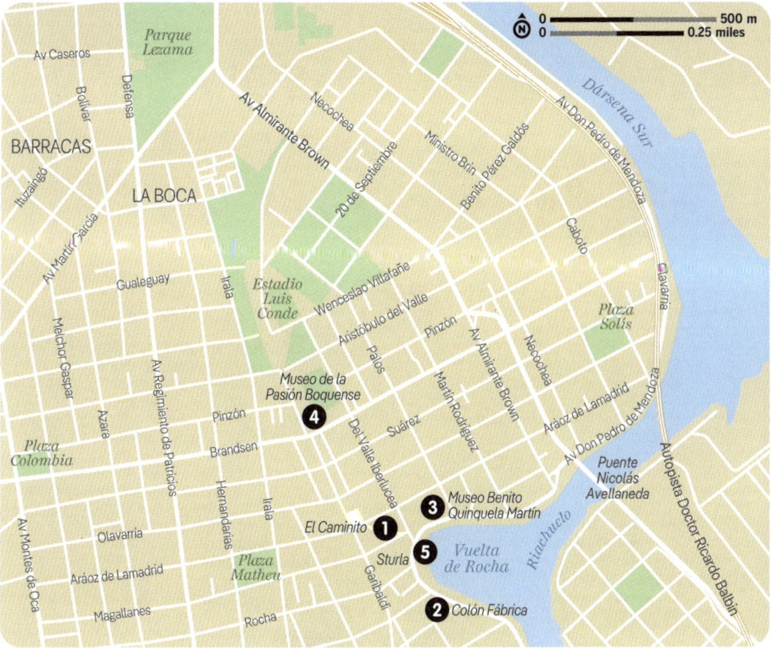

Highlights

❶ El Caminito
Walk through the country's most famous open-air museum, with its tenement houses and tango shows. **p115**

❷ Colón Fábrica
Admire the amazing set designs and costumes of the fabled opera house in its visitable warehouse. **p113**

❸ Museo Benito Quinquela Martín
Visit the old house and studio of the famous painter and one of the creators of El Caminito. **p113**

❹ Museo de la Pasión Boquense
Understand Argentina's soccer craze at the Boca Juniors museum. **p116**

❺ Sturla
Sail from La Boca to Puerto Madero on the Postales de Buenos Aires cruise enjoying views of the city from the river. **p112**

DIEGO GRANDI/SHUTTERSTOCK

Getting Around

Walking
El Caminito and surroundings are safe for walking during the day. However, don't stray far from the most touristic areas.

Subte
Although there are projects to extend the subway in the city, the service still doesn't reach La Boca.

Bus
Take bus 64 or 29 from Palermo; bus 10 from Recoleta and bus 33 from San Telmo.

HIGHLIGHTS

1 El Caminito
2 Fundación Proa
3 Museo Benito Quinquela Martín

SIGHTS

4 Barro
5 Colón Fábrica
6 Fundación Andreani
7 Galería Sendrós
8 Grupo de Teatro Catalinas Sur
9 Jofré Art Gallery
10 La Bombonera
11 La Torre del Fantasma
12 La Verdi
13 Marco
14 Martín Ron murals
15 Munar
16 Museo de la Pasión Boquense
17 Puente Transbordador
18 San Diego del Barrio de La Boca
19 Silos Arenos
20 Ungallery
21 Usina del Arte

ACTIVITIES

22 Alejandra Fenochio
23 La Otra Buenos Aires Tours

EATING

24 Banchero
25 Bodegón La Buena Medida
26 Café Roma
27 El Genovés
28 El Obrero
29 Il Matterello

DRINKING & NIGHTLIFE

30 Amberes Bier
31 Juan de Dios
32 Lo del Diego
33 Temple Craft Caminito
34 Vico
35 Vinoteca Florio

ENTERTAINMENT

36 El Conventillo de Pedro

SHOPPING

37 Almacén porteño
38 Cachafaz Caminito
39 Cueros Pampa
40 Tienda Paraíso Xeneize

TRANSPORT

41 Sturla

A Journey along the Riachuelo

Board the 'Postcards from Buenos Aires' cruise

La Boca takes its name from its location at the mouth of the Riachuelo into the Río de la Plata. To view the city from the water, board one of the cruises offered by **Sturla** *(sturlaviajes.com.ar)* called Postales de Buenos Aires (Postcards from Buenos Aires) and linking La Boca and Puerto Madero.

If you board the cruise in La Boca, it departs a few meters from El Caminito. The boat passes by the historic monument Puente Transbordador (p114) and the neighboring road bridge Puente Nicolás Avellaneda, then sails past the old shipyards of the neighborhood. You'll also see part of the Reserva Ecológica Costanera Sur (p88). On the boat, there is an audio guide in Spanish, English and Portuguese that explains details of the ecosystem of the river and the marshes, the industrial landscape, and the history of Buenos Aires. There is also a cafe on board.

The journey is approximately 40 minutes each way. Check the website for departure times for the four daily services.

The Man Who Painted La Boca

Visit the Museo Benito Quinquela Martín

The former home and studio of Benito Quinquela Martín, now a **museum in his name** *(museoquinquelamartin.geco.com.ar; book visit online)*, is an excellent opportunity to learn about the artist's work and the life of the neighborhood. Quinquela Martín's paintings feature all the characters and scenes of the neighborhood, including the port, boats and workers.

Besides being a painter, Quinquela Martín was a bohemian *porteño* (Buenos Aires resident) with a rich social life, which is also reflected in the museum's photographs and objects. There are three floors dedicated to Argentine art, figureheads (Quinquela Martín collected them) and, of course, the painter's work. On the top floor is his atelier with objects that belonged to him. From the terrace you can get a good view of El Caminito, Puente Transbordador and the river.

Opera Sets & Costumes Up Close

Explore the warehouse Colón Fábrica

Colón Fábrica *(teatrocolon.org.ar/colon-fabrica; noon-6pm Fri-Sun & holidays)* is a warehouse that exhibits the costumes, curtains, scenery and special effects of the city's fabled Teatro Colón (p61). If you've been to the grand opera house, a visit here will be a great complement to understanding how its workshops operate. And if you haven't done it yet, afterwards

CLEANING UP THE RIACHUELO

The Riachuelo, also known as the Río Matanza-Riachuelo, is the sinuous river that separates the city from the surrounding province of Buenos Aires. For decades industrial waste, general garbage and untreated sewage were dumped into the river. The pollution took its toll, and for years the abandoned port's waters around La Boca have been trapped under a thick layer of smelly, rainbow-colored sludge.

In recent years rusting boat hulks have been removed and other efforts to clean the river have taken place, but progress has been slow and the waterway remains one of the most polluted rivers in the world. A public agency called ACUMAR (Matanza Riachuelo Basin Authority) is responsible for cleaning and maintaining the watercourses, removing floating debris on a daily basis.

EATING IN LA BOCA: OUR PICKS

Il Matterello: The dishes are regional Italian cuisine. The house's specialty is lasagna bolognese stuffed with pork and beef ragu. *hours vary* $$$

Banchero: At this beloved neighborhood pizzeria, the house classic is the *fugazzeta*, a pizza stuffed with cheese and topped with onions. *hours vary* $$

Bodegón La Buena Medida: Located in front of the square where Boca Juniors was founded, this is a neighborhood standout. Try their *albóndidas* (meatballs). *hours vary* $$

1905: Argentine cuisine restaurant, located inside the Boca Juniors Stadium. The dishes come with extra spice. *10am-6pm* $$

PUENTE TRANSBORDADOR

Transporter bridges are a type of bridge on which a gondola hanging from metal cables moves from one side of a body of water to the other. Buenos Aires is one of only eight places the world with such a bridge.

Next to road bridge Puente Nicolás Avellaneda, Puente Transbordador has been a La Boca landmark since its construction in 1914. Both bridges are officially named after Avellaneda, Argentina's president from 1874 to 1880. The original 1600m iron span between two 53m towers connected La Boca with Isla Maciel in Buenos Aires Province until 1960 when it was decommissioned. Puente Transbordador was slated to be scrapped in the 1990s, until local pressure groups enabled it to be restored and conserved as a National Historic Landmark.

you'll want to rush out to see one of the most beautiful theaters in the world.

Until recently, the scenography and costumes were showcased at Teatro Colón. Since 2021, those elements have been displayed in a former French metallurgical building in La Boca, a couple of blocks from El Caminito. There are two visit options. One is a self-guided tour. Each element is accompanied by a sign detailing its origin, usage and material characteristics. Small screens also show a short video of the theatrical performance. The guided tour departs every half hour from 3pm, with a more detailed explanation of the fantasy worlds of operas such as *Turandot* and *Aida*. The tour combines elements of art, heritage and historic theatrical crafts in reasonable doses.

Industrial Buildings Transformed

Check out Barro and Usina del Arte

La Boca is home to an extensive arts district with more than 15 art galleries, artists' studios and cultural spaces. One of the most active is **Barro** *(barro.cc; noon-6pm Mon-Fri)* which occupies an industrial building from the 1930s and holds five contemporary art exhibitions a year.In addition, they develop projects with artists in Buenos Aires and prestigious institutions. The gallery's spacious layout enables it to accommodate bold and varied projects.

Another prominent arts and cultural center is **Usina del Arte** *(buenosaires.gob.ar/cultura/usina-del-arte; free; 2pm–8pm Tue-Sat, from 11am Sun),* which occupies an eclectic-style building that originally served as a power plant. After falling into abandonment, the building was restored and reopened in 2013 as this arts hub. Managed by the city of Buenos Aires, the cultural center hosts activities including live music, theater, art and spaces for children. It also hosts major festivals such as the Tango World Cup. On Saturdays and Sundays, there is a one-hour guided tour in the afternoon. It begins in the courtyard of the building and tells the history of its architecture and the modifications it has undergone throughout the years.

DRINKING IN LA BOCA: OUR PICKS

Temple Craft Caminito: Sit back and watch the world go by at this bar serving craft beers and cocktails in a great spot to take pictures in El Caminito. *11am-8pm*

Vico: Wine bar with several wine-tasting options and some finger food. They focus on wines by the glass, featuring more than 100 labels from different Argentine regions. *9am-7pm*

Vinoteca Florio: Wine bar, with tastings combining wines, cold cuts and ice cream. *10am-6pm*

Amberes Bier: Craft beer and fast food dishes, such as pizzas and hamburgers. They also serve a wide range of signature cocktails. *hours vary*

TOP EXPERIENCE

El Caminito

Multicolored El Caminito is a magnet for visitors. This open air museum is only 150 meters long but it's easy to spend hours viewing the brightly-painted tenements, now converted into restaurants, art galleries and souvenir stores. Along the street, you'll encounter tango singers, dancing couples and artisans selling handmade products.

LUIS WAR/SHUTTERSTOCK

Painting the Neighborhood

The poor immigrants who lived in La Boca's shanty buildings in the late 19th and early 20th century painted their dwellings with the leftover paint from other projects – giving the the neighborhood its distinctive multi-hued look.

In the 1950s a group of La Boca neighbors decided to turn a dark and lifeless alley into a place of pride that would tell the history of the area and its community houses. This is how El Caminito became a pedestrian open-air museum street, named after a tango composed by Juan de Dios Filiberto and Gabino Coria Peñaloza.

Enter Benito Quinquela Martín

Leading the charge to beautify El Caminito was the artist Benito Quinquela Martín. Quinquela Martín's house and studio have been turned into an excellent museum (p113), but you can get an idea of his style on El Caminito. Look for a small tiled reproduction of his *Día de Trabajo* (Day of Work) on a green wall and a much bigger one of his *Regreso de la Pesca* (Return from Fishing) at the end of the street, both by Ricardo Sánchez.

TOP TIPS

- Avoid peak crowds by arriving before 10am.
- You'll need to be patient if you want to take photos, especially at the weekend.
- The area is safe during the day, but when the vendors start to pack up, take it as your cue to get going, too.

PRACTICALITIES

Visit El Caminito from 10am and leave before it gets dark.

WHY I LOVE LA BOCA

Muriel Mahdjoubian Rebori has been dancing tango for more than 25 years. *@murielrebori*

As a teenager, I used to go to *milongas,* hiding from my parents. I knew La Boca since I was very young because my aunt had her house there. It is a very authentic neighborhood, which keeps traditions alive. I dance in a show there at **El Conventillo de Pedro**. It is the old courtyard of a house, where at the beginning of the 20th century men practiced tango, when that music was only danced among men. Pedro, its owner, is listening to tango at any time, out of the tourist circuit. I love La Boca because it still preserves the deepest soul of tango.

MORE SOCCER

The other of the two most famous clubs in Argentina is River Plate, whose stadium is **Estadio Mâs Monumental** (p157) in Nuñez.

JULIAN EDUARDO FERNANDEZ/SHUTTERSTOCK

La Bombonera

All About Boca Juniors

Museum dedicated to a beloved soccer team

A must for soccer fans is **Museo de la Pasión Boquense** *(museoboquense.com; 10am-6pm)* located under one of the stands of Estadio Alberto J Armando, better known as **La Bombonera**, the homeground of Boca Juniors. The museum reviews the legendary team's history with a gallery of the club's great heroes, a touch screen to look up the names and details of past players and a 360° 3D video that makes you feel like a player being cheered on by the fans on match day. There is also, of course, a section dedicated to Diego Armando Maradona, one of the great idols of the club and world soccer. The tour is short – about half an hour – and somewhat frustrating for fans because there is no access to the field or locker rooms, as was the case in the past. (Such access remains possible at the River Plate stadium in Nuñez.)

Tangol *(tangol.com)* organizes a tour of both La Boca and Nuñez so soccer fans can visit the Boca Juniors and River Plate stadiums on the same day.

Stories from Across the Riachuelo

Visit the Museo Comunitario Isla Maciel

Isla Maciel is a neighborhood just across the river from La Boca in Buenos Aires Province. Here a group of neighbors created a civil association to promote tourism in the area and to raise awareness of the area's culture and history. The community-run **Museo Comunitario Isla Maciel** *(@museocomunitario; 11am-3pm Wed-Sat; book in advance via Instagram)* exhibits objects donated by residents: photographs, clothes of Italian immigrants, old typewriters and statuettes of Juan Domingo Perón, three-time president.

To visit the museum, it's best to contact the staff in advance. They will kindly pick you up in La Boca and guide you through the entire tour.

Tenement Converted into a Gallery

View modern art at Fundación Andreani

Fundación Andreani *(fundacionandreani.org.ar: free; noon-7pm Wed-Sun)*, the private museum of an Argentine mail company, has temporary exhibitions throughout the year, focused on promoting diverse artistic expressions and building a bridge with new generations. There are plastic arts exhibitions, concerts and poetry recitals, among other activities.

The museum occupies an 1880 port-style Italianate building that was once a shipyard, restaurant and tenement house. Its restoration, which preserved the original building's facade and colors, was carried out by the prestigious architect Clorindo Testa. On the third floor, there is a terrace overlooking the Riachuelo.

Modern Art & Sweeping Views

Visit Fundación Proa

The cultural center and museum **Fundación Proa** *(proa.org; noon-7pm Wed-Sun)* occupies a converted old Italian house from the late 19th century with glazed walls overlooking the river. This private museum, supported by a multinational metallurgical company, is mainly dedicated to the most important artistic movements of the 20th century. Throughout the year, temporary exhibitions, concerts and film seasons are organized. On the third floor is a bar and restaurant with splendid views of La Boca.

BEST ART GALLERIES IN LA BOCA

Marco: Studios and exhibition space for contemporary artists in an art nouveau building. Also has a small cafe.

Ungallery: Contemporary art gallery, with particular emphasis on photography and video. Promotes the work of artists beyond Buenos Aires.

Galería Sendrós: Focused on launching and promoting emerging artists, this gallery stands out for its exhibitions featuring drawing, painting, photography, sculpture and installations.

Munar: Specializes in digital art, live art and installations.

La Verdi: Workshops and cultural activities on the first floor of a century-old theater.

DRINKING IN LA BOCA: BEST COFFEE SHOPS

Juan de Dios: Specialty coffee is served a few meters from the Boca Juniors stadium. The cafe has a terrace overlooking the stadium. *hours vary*

Cachafaz Caminito: Have a coffee with the statue of Messi at this famous and colorfully-painted *alfajores* shop in the most touristic part of El Caminito. *9am-7pm*

El Genovés: This cafe and restaurant serves classic Argentine dishes (mainly meat) in front of the Boca Juniors stadium. *7am-1am* $$

Café Roma: An unmissable classic, in business since 1905, the same year Boca Juniors was founded. Its specialty is coffee and pastries, such as the shell-shaped Neapolitan *sfogliatella*. *hours vary* $$

DIEGO & LIONEL

Diego Maradona is the great god of Argentine soccer, joined by Lionel Messi in recent years.

Maradona (1960–2020) played for Boca Juniors and was crowned world champion with the Argentine national team in 1986. He is remembered for his vibrant personality and for several iconic phrases that have become part of Argentina's collective imagination.

Messi (born 1987) is from Rosario, Argentina, but has spent his entire professional career in Europe and the United States. Constantly compared to Maradona, he led Argentina to triumph in the 2022 FIFA World Cup in Qatar. A quieter leader than Maradona, he is equally adored around the world.

On the second floor of Cachafaz Caminito (p117) is a giant 3D printed sculpture of soccer player Lionel Messi, lifting the World cup. Many visitors to La Boca come here to snap selfies with the Argentine soccer hero. Another Messi photo opp is the massive 35m-high **mural** of the player, created by urban artist Martín Ron on the side of a building at the corner of Bernardo de Irigoyen and Av Belgrano in the Monserrat neighborhood.

Bar Dedicated to a Soccer Legend

Get your Diego Maradona souvenirs

Lo del Diego *(@lodeldiegocaminito)* is a theme bar and souvenir store dedicated exclusively to the great Argentine soccer player Diego Maradona. On the first floor are dozens of jerseys of the clubs where Maradona played, as well as statues, caps, and replicas of his cups. On the second floor, as well as the bar, there is an interactive game about Maradona's most iconic goals.

Proud La Boca Theater Group

Check out the work of Grupo de Teatro Catalinas Sur

The **Grupo de Teatro Catalinas Sur** *(catalinasur.com.ar)* is a community theater group with over 40 years of history in La Boca. On the exterior wall of their theater is a large mural that was designed by Omar Gasparini, one of Buenos Aires' best known plastic artists, and Ana Serralta. Many neighbors and artists from the neighborhood participated in creating this vibrant 50m long mural which captures the spirit and culture of La Boca. Check the theater group's website, as they stage plays year-round (all in Spanish) and host festivals featuring international theater companies.

AGF SRL/ALAMY

Señor Tango

Tango Two Ways

Tango spectacular vs traditional *milonga*

Two very different tango shows can be seen in the Barracas neighborhood, very close to the border with La Boca.

Señor Tango *(srtango.ar)* is perhaps the city's best-known and most spectacular tango show, with several decades of experience and a Broadway-style show. This grandiloquent show is set on a circular stage in a spacious hall that accommodates 900 guests. There is a giant screen with images of the Obelisco (p77), many couples dancing and, perhaps the most excessive thing, two horses on stage. A live orchestra plays, and the singer and big figure of the night is Fernando Soler, the creator of Señor Tango. Throughout the evening, you can hear famous tangos from various historical periods, from Carlos Gardel to the modernism of Ástor Piazzolla.

They've been dancing the tango at the bar and restaurant **Los Laureles** (*loslaureles.ar*) since 1893. Its floor is worn and perhaps not the best for dancing these days, but that matters little here. They organize tango classes, *milongas* to practice, and live shows from Thursday to Sunday. On Thursdays, there is the *Peña de Cantores,* with old singers from the neighborhood and surrounding areas. If you are up for it, you can sing a tango song. There is also a *milonga* followed by a dinner show on Fridays and Saturdays.

BEST SHOPPING IN LA BOCA

Jofré Art Gallery: In El Caminito buy works of art and objects, such as bags and T-shirts, created by the artist Roberto Jofré, whose atelier is also located there.

Cueros Pampa: The store on El Caminito promenade sells garments made of cow and sheep leather.

Almacén Porteño: Pick up local gourmet delicacies, such as wines, *alfajores* (sweet cookie-type pastries) and *dulce de leche.*

Tienda Paraíso Xeneize: Boca Juniors fans can buy T-shirts, hats, mugs, and other merchandise from the country's most popular club.

Fundación Proa: This art gallery (p117) has a charming bookstore that also sells handcrafted objects.

EXPLORING URBAN ART

To discover the best La Boca murals, follow this tour yourself on foot or join one of La Bicicleta Naranja's bicycle tours (labicicletanaranja.com.ar).

START	END	LENGTH
Bienvenidos a La Boca	El Regreso de Quinquela	3.5km; 3hrs

Start at 1 **Bienvenidos a La Boca**, located opposite Parque Lezama. Omar Gasparini's mural includes caricatures of characters from the neighborhood and scenes from its history. Continue south to the 2 **Martín Ron murals** with images of Boca Juniors club idols and tango.

About 700m ahead, pause at 3 **San Diego del Barrio de La Boca**, a tribute to soccer legend Maradona, created by Alfredo 'El Pelado' Segatori, who depicts the soccer player as a saint.

Continuing south, near the river, are 4 **Silos Arenos**, which Segatori created in homage to Benito Quinquela Martín, the neighborhood's most famous painter. The next stop is 5 **El Caminito** (p115), the most photographed street in the city, ideal for contemplating the tenement houses and the spirit of the neighborhood of immigrants and workers.

Close to the Barracas neighborhood is 6 **Barraca Peña**, a historical complex of buildings dating back to 1860. Continue 2km south to reach the monumental 7 **El Regreso de Quinquela** (The Return of Quinquela), another Segatori creation which holds the title of the largest mural in the world made by a single painter with freehand aerosol paint.

The mural **Bienvenidos a La Boca** incorporates materials recovered from La Boca's *conventillos*.

Measuring 2000 sq meters, **El Regreso de Quinquela** features a portrait of Benito Quinquela Martín as its centerpiece.

One of the tracks at otherwise closed **Barraca Peña** railway station is still used for freight transport.

A Classic La Boca Restaurant

Soak up the soccer spirit at El Obrero

Founded in 1954, **El Obrero** *(@elobrero1954; 8pm-2am Tue-Sat)* has become one of the most iconic restaurants in La Boca. As soon as you enter the place, you will be surrounded by the spirit of soccer. There are jerseys of neighborhood club Boca Juniors (p116) and of dozens of clubs from Argentina and abroad. Scarves and other objects also refer to the most popular sport in this country.

It has the spirit of a workers' restaurant and is always packed with customers. The restaurant and some customers say that when US president Bill Clinton arrived with his entourage, the restaurant manager told him, 'I'm sorry, you must wait.' The menu is extensive, with several options of meat and Spanish cuisine. The house specialty is *tortilla de papas* (potato omelette) and *rabas* (crispy fried calamari). If Clinton had to wait, you probably will, too.

La Boca in Art & Culture

Sign up for tours of La Boca

On Tuesday evenings artist **Alejandra Fenochio** *(instagram.com/alejandraderrocha)* organizes drawing and painting tours to capture the vibrant colors and landmarks of La Boca. The experience begins at El Malevaje, a *milonga* and cultural space. From there, Alejandra guides the experience in groups of a maximum of 15 people. Make a a reservation via her Instagram.

Another La Boca walking tour is offered by **La Otra Buenos Aires Tours** *(@laotrabuenosairestours)*. Their two-hour walk focuses on the neighborhood's social history. Guide Nicolás Cancino shares how immigrants forged this neighborhood guided by the idea of mutual support, and why it is one of the best-known neighborhoods in Latin America. The tour visits a tourist tenement house, another where families still live, the Firemen's Square and the Boca Juniors stadium, among other places. Pop into a bakery and learn the history of the names of Argentine pastries linked to anarchism in the neighborhood.

LA BOCA'S GHOST TOWER

Completed in 1910 **La Torre del Fantasma** (closed to the public) is an emblematic La Boca building designed by the Spanish architect Guillermo Álvarez, a pioneer of modernism in the city. Its owner, a wealthy woman named María Luisa Auvert Arnaud, asked for its design to have Catalan influences.

As well as for its architecture, the building is also noted as it is believed to be haunted. The owner rented apartments here to several artists. One of them, a young woman, died when she fell or jumped from the building. 'She was pushed by the goblins who live in the tower,' claimed Auvert Arnaud.

Researched by Diego Jemio

RETIRO

LUXURIOUS PALACES AND WORKING-CLASS NEIGHBORHOODS

Retiro once had its bullring and welcomed thousands of immigrants. Today, it features elegant apartment buildings, museums and historic squares.

In the mid-19th century, yellow fever struck Buenos Aires. At that time, many wealthy families moved from the city's south to the north in search of a healthier environment. This is how they began to build their residences at a time when Argentina was a prosperous country. That history is reflected in Retiro's large mansions, many of which today are hotels and public buildings near the Plaza San Martín. On this square was once a bullring and training place for the soldiers of General José de San Martín, a hero of Argentina. The neighborhood combines art galleries, luxury buildings, exclusive boutiques and Barrio Mugica, one of the most populous informal settlements in the city. Elegant and popular, Retiro has many faces to show.

TOP TIP

Pickpockets can be a problem in Retiro. Be especially careful at night around the train station and Plaza San Martín.

NRUARG/SHUTTERSTOCK

Palacio Paz (p129)

See page 197 for places to stay in Retiro

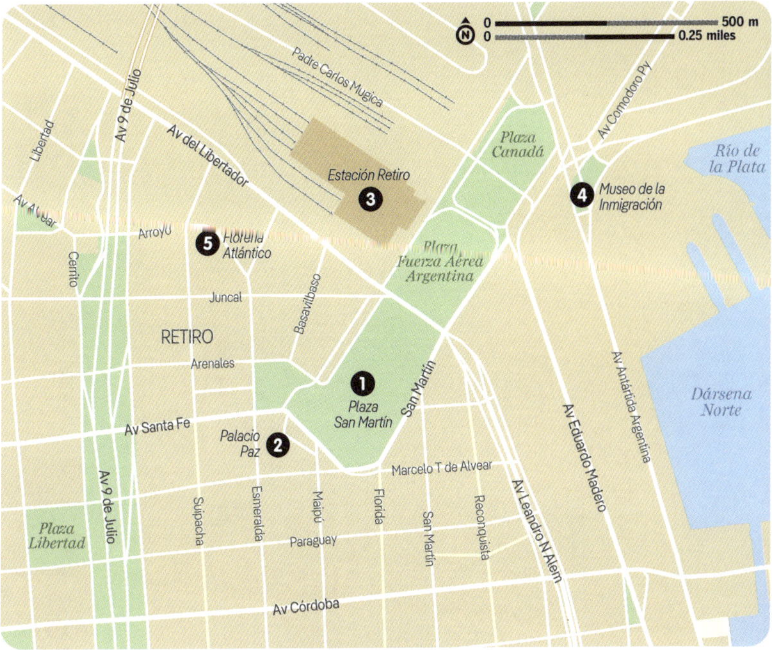

Highlights

❶ Plaza San Martín
Visit one of BA's oldest squares and the site of significant historical events in Argentine history. **p126**

❷ Palacio Paz
Book a tour of one of the city's architectural wonders or attend one of the Tango Hora Cero shows here. **p129**

▼ ❸ Estación Retiro
Visit the city's iconic train station, one of the great monuments made with pieces brought from the United Kingdom. **p128**

❹ Museo de la Inmigración
Learn the history of Argentina's immigrants with documents and photos at this museum. **p130**

❺ Florería Atlántico
Have a drink at the most award-winning bar in the country, hidden beneath a flower shop. **p131**

SANDRA MORAES/SHUTTERSTOCK

Getting Around

Walking
Retiro is a relatively small neighborhood. Walk around it to best appreciate its large palaces and other grand architecture.

Subte
Líneas C and E connect Retiro with downtown and many of the city's tourist areas.

Bus
Take bus 152 from Palermo; bus 130 from La Boca and bus 93 from Recoleta.

Av del Libertador
Av Alvear
Montevideo
Parera
Cerrito
Plazoleta Carlos Pellegrini
Libertad
Av 9 de Julio
Carlos Pellegrini
Arroyo
Suipacha
Juncal
Basavilbaso
RETIRO
Arenales
San Martín
Av Santa Fe
Marcelo T de Alvear
Plaza Libertad
Paraguay
Maipu
Av Córdoba
Uruguay
Talcahuano
Esmeralda
Viamonte
Tucumán
Lavalle

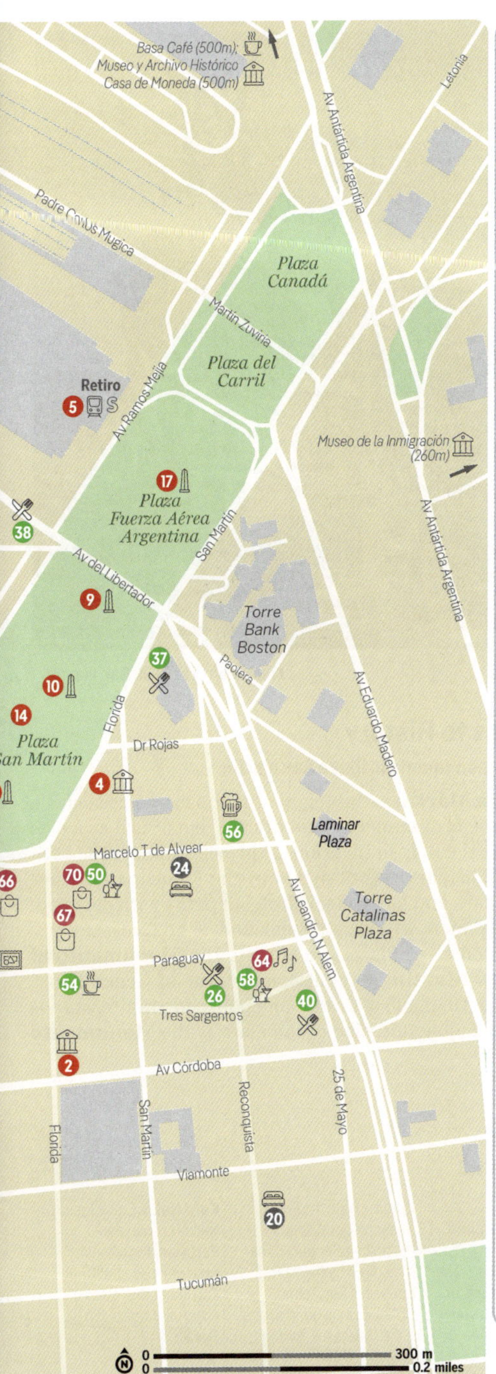

HIGHLIGHTS

1 Palacio Paz

SIGHTS

2 Centro Naval
3 De Sousa
4 Edificio Kavanagh
5 Estación Retiro
6 Galería van Riel
7 Jorge Luis Borges' Last Residence in Argentina
8 La Duda
9 Monumento a los Caídos de Malvinas
10 Monumento al Gral. San Martín
11 Museo de Arte Hispano-americano Isaac Fernández Blanco
12 Museo Nacional Ferroviario
13 Palacio San Martín
14 Plaza San Martín
15 Rolf Art
16 Teatro Nacional Cervantes
17 Torre Monumental
see 15 Vasari
18 Zurbarán

SLEEPING

19 Algodon Mansion
20 Amérian Buenos Aires Park Hotel
see 57 Casa Lucia
21 Embajador Hotel
22 Hotel Emperador
23 Palacio Duhau – Park Hyatt Buenos Aires
24 Up Retiro

EATING

25 Azul Profundo
26 Bárbaro
27 BASA
28 Boca Abajo Boca Arriba
29 Confitería Dos Escudos
30 El Correntino
31 El Cuartito
32 El Fundador
33 Elena
34 Heladería Esmeralda
35 Huacho
36 Kuro Neko
37 La Raya
38 La Torre de Retiro
39 Le Moulin De La Fleur
40 Mercado de los Carruajes
see 1 Moby Dick
41 Norte
42 Nuestras Costumbres Criollas
43 Pal Que Guste
44 Parrilla Cero5
45 Rapanui
46 Tanta

DRINKING & NIGHTLIFE

47 Barís
48 Boca de Toro
49 Café Castelar
50 Chabrés Bar
51 Farinelli
52 Felicia Bar
53 Florería Atlántico
54 Florida Garden
55 Gran Bar Danzón
56 Kilkenny
57 Le Club Bacán
58 Martineta
59 Maru Botana
60 On Tap Retiro
61 Presidente
62 Saint Moritz
63 The Shelter Coffee

ENTERTAINMENT

64 El Legado
see 1 Tango Hora Cero

SHOPPING

65 Abraxas Discos
66 Casa López
67 El Boyero
68 Galerna
69 Patio Bullrich
70 Sylvia y Mario

JOSÉ DE SAN MARTÍN

In Retiro, a street is named after José de San Martín (1778-1850) and there's a statue of the general on the neighborhood's main square. The same is true in hundreds of cities across the country.

San Martín was an Argentine military leader and politician, often nicknamed 'the liberator of Argentina, Chile and Peru' for his crucial role in freeing these nations from Spanish colonial rule. Along with Simón Bolívar, he is one of the most important figures of the Spanish-American wars of independence. Despite his legacy, he spent his final years in exile in France due to Argentina's political instability, the lack of a clear role for him in the new governments, and the intolerance of specific political sectors.

GIMAS/SHUTTERSTOCK

Monumento al Gral. San Martín

Witness to History

View the monuments in Plaza San Martín

Plaza San Martín is the neighborhood's main green space and the scene of numerous historical events, such as a battle during the British invasion at the beginning of the 19th century. The park was designed by the French landscaper Carlos Thays and has wide pedestrian paths with old specimens of linden, willow, pine, oak and ceibo trees.

In the center of Plaza San Martín, the **Monumento al Gral. San Martín**, an equestrian statue of General José de San Martín made of bronze and polished granite, stands out. On the downhill side of the Plaza is the **Monumento**

EATING IN RETIRO: OUR PICKS

Tanta: Celebrity chef Gaston Acurio's restaurant offers *ceviches* and classic Peruvian dishes. It also has a selection of gourmet sandwiches. *noon-midnight Mon-Sun* $$$

Basa: Local and Mediterranean-inspired dishes in a warm underground setting. The lamb *empanadas* are an excellent choice to start with. *hours vary* $$$

Elena: Inside the Four Seasons Hotel, this Michelin-selected space is inspired by the historic houses of San Telmo. Specializes in aged meats. *12:30-3:30pm & 7pm-midnight* $$$

Kuro Neko: Enjoy fusion Nikkei (Japanese-Peruvian) food by experienced chef Raúl Zorrilla at the 'black cat'. *noon-midnight Mon-Sat* $$

a los Caídos de Malvinas, 25 black marble plaques with the names of the 649 soldiers who died in the Falklands War (1982). Also look out for **La Duda** (The Doubt), a neoclassical marble sculpture by Charles Cordier expressing the dilemma of religious belief.

Best View of Retiro

Ride the elevator up Torre Monumental

Even though it was renamed **Torre Monumental** in 1982 following the Falklands War, many *porteños* (Buenos Aires residents) still call it by its old name, the Torre de los Ingleses (the English Tower). A gift from the British residents in Argentina in 1916 and located in the Plaza Fuerza Aerea Argentina, the red brick and carved stone clock tower stands 60m high. Ride the elevator to the sixth floor for a 360-degree view of the neighborhood and as far as BA's port.

Neocolonial Art & a Spanish Garden

Tour the Museo Fernández Blanco

The **Museo Fernández Blanco** *(@museofernandezblanco; 11am-7pm Mon, Wed-Fri, 11am-8pm Sat & Sun)* has an extensive collection of art from the time of the Viceroyalty of the Río de la Plata, the last administrative division of the Spanish in America in 1776, which included Argentina, Uruguay, Paraguay, Bolivia and part of Brazil. Exhibits range from the 16th to the 20th centuries, in addition to an essential collection of artistic and decorative objects from Argentina. Don't miss the basement, where objects of Argentine culture from the 19th and 20th centuries are exhibited, such as silver *mate* gourds, silverware sets and antique dolls.

The museum's Andalusian-style garden is a breath of fresh air in the middle of an administrative and commercial district and includes a restaurant. See the museum's Instagram for details of chamber music concerts, talks and literary meetings.

AROUND PLAZA SAN MARTÍN

The impressive art nouveau **Palacio San Martín** (1912) is actually three independent buildings around a courtyard. It was designed by Alejandro Christophersen for the powerful Anchorena family and later became the headquarters of the Foreign Ministry. Today it's used mostly for official purposes.

The handsome art deco-style apartment building **Edificio Kavanagh** was commissioned in 1934 by Corina Kavanagh, a feisty millionaire of Irish descent. On completion in 1936 it was the tallest skyscraper in Latin America. A local rumor claims that the heiress, vengeful toward another aristocratic family for scorning her daughter, had the structure built that high to block light from entering the basilica where her rivals attended Mass every Sunday.

EATING IN RETIRO: INTERNATIONAL FLAVORS

El Cuartito: You will probably have to wait in line at one of the most famous pizza restaurants in town – but it's worth it. The specialty is the *fugazzeta* pizza. *hours vary* $

Moby Dick: A restaurant that combines Argentine traditions with international style overlooking the iconic Plaza San Martín. *7:30am-11:30pm Mon-Sat, to 3pm Sun* $$

Le Moulin De La Fleur: This charming bakery offers authentic French bread and pastries. One of its signature dishes is the ham and cheese brioche. *8am-9pm Mon-Sat, 9am-8pm Sun* $$

Azul Profundo: Oriental and Mediterranean fusion food, with some dishes of Argentinean gastronomy. They serve generous portions. *hours vary* $$

HISTORIC STATION DINING ROOM

In 1900, Argentina's railroad network became one of the most extensive in the world and an example for the rest of Latin America. Unfortunately, neglect and lack of investment, mainly in the 1990s, led to the decline of the trains.

However, a glimpse of the railroad's former grandeur can be seen inside the Estación Retiro. Here is perhaps the most beautiful Burger King in the world occupying what was the station's 1930s dining room. The restoration was carefully done, and the place still preserves the magnificent panelling, marble details and stained-glass dome. From the second floor of the restaurant, there is a view outside to the Torre Monumental (p127).

A British-Influenced Train Station

Tour the Estación Retiro

British engineers and architects designed the great **Estación Retiro**, which opened in 1915 with parts manufactured in the United Kingdom. The structure is reminiscent of the great stations of the 19th century, with two parallel 250m naves and the use of iron and glass typical of the Industrial Revolution era.

Fully restored in 2018, the station remains in good condition today. The state-owned company **Trenes Argentinos** *(@trenesargentinosop)* organizes station tours on the first and third Wednesday of each month at 3pm, and on the last Saturday of each month at 1pm. Lasting one hour, the tour includes the ticket office, old carriage yard, bust commemorating General Mitre, the monitoring center and the internal balcony on the second floor (only accessible during tours) for its panoramic view of the hall and its impressive architecture. The tour is free, but you must reserve a spot through their Instagram.

Inspect a Historic Train Used by Presidents

Learn about railroad history at Museo Nacional Ferroviario

Museo Nacional Ferroviario *(argentina.gob.ar/museo-nacional-ferroviario; 10am-8pm)* showcases Argentina's railroad history by exhibiting objects like ticket machines, telephones, telegraphs, office furniture and other antique pieces. The collection of antique lanterns and hundreds of different objects from the daily life of the Argentine railroads is wonderful. The self-guided tour covers the halls distributed on two floors, with a video about an old Buenos Aires-Cordoba trip. You need to join a guided tour to access the station platform – here you can sit inside a wooden presidential car from the beginning of the 20th century and see a steam locomotive.

DRINKING IN RETIRO: BEST COFFEE

Farinelli: This cafe has an excellent ambience and seasonal products. Their brunch is famous, but they only serve it on weekends. *8am-midnight Mon-Sun*

The Shelter Coffee: Specialty coffee, good macarons and croissants in a 1950s building designed by British engineers and architects. *8:30am-8pm Mon-Sat*

Maru Botana: Pastry chef Maru Botana is a celebrity in Argentina, known for her specialty: the Rogel cake, layered with plenty of *dulce de leche. hours vary*

Basa Café: On the border between Puerto Madero and Retiro. Try their classic French-style grilled cheese and ham sandwich Croque Monsieur. *7am-6pm Mon-Fri*

TOP EXPERIENCE

Palacio Paz

Once the home of media magnate José Camilo Paz and now a private club for retired military officers, this opulent palace covers 12,000 sq meters with three wings, four floors and 140 rooms. Decorated with marble, velvet and gilt accents it's a glimpse into how rich *porteños* once lived.

José Clemente Paz

Paz was the founder of the newspaper *La Prensa,* and served as Argentina's ambassador to France. In 1902, he commissioned French architect Louis-Marie Henri Sortais to design and build this mansion. However, construction took 12 years and finished two years after Paz's death.

Nearly all of the palace's materials were shipped from France. There's a definite resemblance to the Palace of Versailles, especially in the ballroom, but other rooms show more of a Louis XVI, Renaissance or Tudor style. With seven elevators and 40 bathrooms, it remains Argentina's largest single-family home ever built.

Great Hall of Honor

The most majestic place in the Palacio Paz is the Great Hall of Honor, with its 21m high dome. A wonderful way to experience this space is to attend a **Tango Hora Cero** *(@tangohoracero)* show here. Featuring two couples of dancers and a live tango quartet, unlike other BA tango shows, this one takes the time to explain the life stories of the musicians and highlights their works. They have previously dedicated their shows to figures such as Ástor Piazzolla.

TOP TIPS

- Tango Hora Cero shows are weekly and change days and times according to the availability of the hall. The ticket includes a drink.
- Paz is buried at Cementerio de la Recoleta (p140) in his family's elaborate tomb.

PRACTICALITIES

For details of how to book a tour here, see @palacio.paz

BEST RETIRO ART GALLERIES

Rolf Art: Showcases contemporary Latin American visual arts, with an emphasis on the political dimensions of art.

De Sousa: Latin American art gallery founded in 1972. Its members serve as advisors to international collections and museums.

Galería van Riel: Founded in 1924, historic gallery currently organizes modern and contemporary art exhibitions.

Vasari: Since launching in 2005, Vasari has been dedicated to promoting the work of Argentine photographers.

Zurbarán: A gallery with a rich tradition in Argentina, focusing on showcasing local artists.

BRESTER IRINA/SHUTTERSTOCK

Museo de la Inmigración

The Immigrants' Story

Visit the Museo de la Inmigración

Immigration has been continuous in Argentina since the mid-19th century, mainly from European and Western Asian countries. The **Museo de la Inmigración** *(untref.edu.ar/muntref/es/museo-de-la-inmigracion; free; 11am-6pm Wed-Sun)* focuses on that history. The museum, on the banks of the Río de la Plata, is on the third floor of where the old Hotel de Inmigrantes once stood. Here, immigrants were received, lodged free of charge for five days, and oriented for work in the country. The museum's permanent exhibition invites visitors to learn about the immigrants' experiences through stories, photographs of the daily life of the time, documentary records and objects. The museum also holds records of the date, the ship and the trade with which immigrants arrived in the country.

DRINKING IN RETIRO: BEST HISTORIC CAFES & BARS

Florida Garden: Figures such as Diego Maradona and the writer Jorge Luis Borges visited this historic bar on busy Calle Florida. Its specialty is the cheesecake. *7am-midnight*

Café Castelar: A classic bar serving *medialunas* (the Argentine version of the croissant) and Argentine dishes like meat and pasta. *7am-9pm Mon-Sat*

Saint Moritz: This bar, frequented by notable Argentine writers like Jorge Luis Borges, is famous for its sweet pastries and sandwiches. *7am-1am*

Bárbaro: Another classic Retiro bar and restaurant frequented by artists and intellectuals, serving coffee, tapas and drinks. *hours vary*

Afternoon Tea in a Hidden Garden

Refreshments at the Hotel Emperador

At the classic **Hotel Emperador** *(hotel-emperador.com.ar)* on elegant Av Libertador, afternoon tea is served from 4pm in its expansive garden, a hidden oasis amid the city's bustle. The menu includes sweet and savory options, such as cheesecake, lemon pie, apple strudel, fresh cucumber sandwiches and cheese scones flavored with sundried tomatoes. In addition to herbal tea and coffee, they serve a glass of champagne at the end. If you don't want to order the full menu, you can opt for a coffee in the garden or one of the hotel lounges.

Hidden Bar & Restaurant

Uncover Florería Atlántico and Boca Abajo Boca Arriba

Once upon a time, **Florería Atlántico** *(floreriaatlantico.com.ar; 6pm-2am)* was a secret bar accessed through a door hidden in a flower shop. Now this multi-award-winning bar is an open secret because of its cocktails and food quality. Try the Negroni Balestrini, infused with wood embers and named in honour of 'Tato' Giovannoni, the grandfather of the bar's owner.

The cozy and intimate restaurant **Boca Abajo Boca Arriba** *(@bocabajo.bocarriba; 7:30pm-12am Mon-Sat)* hides behind the facade of a laundry. It features a diverse wine cellar with bottles from lesser-known wineries. The menu varies according to the guest chefs that pass through the place. But in general, it has a contemporary Argentine profile. Each dish is paired with a wine. One dish that is usually on the menu is the *bife de chorizo* (sirloin steak) with yeast sauce and carrots.

Drink with Rock Legends

Wine, dine and dance at Le Club Bacán

On one of the most beautiful streets in Retiro, **Le Club Bacán** *(@leclubbacan)* is located inside Hotel Casa Lucía Hotel, a recently restored 1920s building. The bar pays tribute to Argentine rock with photographs of its great musicians on the walls and drinks inspired by their songs. Try the vodka

BEST SHOPS IN RETIRO

Patio Bullrich: This shopping center, one of the oldest in BA, is in a neoclassical building and has more than 100 stores, bars and restaurants.

Casa López: Traditional store selling leather handbags, belts, shoes and accessories. handmade by local artisans.

El Boyero: Sells *mates*, leather belts, *ponchos* and other local products.

Galerna: Bookstore and publishing house featuring a diverse catalog of Argentine authors.

Mercado de los Carruajes: A gourmet market offering fresh Argentine products, including wines and cheeses.

Sylvia y Mario: Factory and sale of Argentine leather garments with a long tradition in the city.

DRINKING IN RETIRO: BEST COCKTAIL BARS

Boca de Toro: This bar in the basement of Hotel Pulitzer Buenos Aires serves classic drinks and other Spanish-inspired options. *11am-midnight Mon-Sat*

Presidente: Award-winning bar offering an extensive menu and elegant chandeliers to create an intimate atmosphere. *8pm-2am Sun, Tue & Wed, to 3:30am Thu-Sat*

Gran Bar Danzón: Elegance personified for a special night out. Renowned for its illuminated bar. Order a gin and tonic or one of their martinis. *7pm-1am Sun-Wed, to 3am Thu-Sat*

Martineta: Bar and restaurant with an extensive menu of imported and local gin. *noon-midnight Mon-Sat*

WHY I LOVE RETIRO

Tour guide **Eugenia Calcarami** offers walking tours in Retiro and other city neighborhoods. *@paseosbuenosaires*

Retiro brings back memories of my childhood, especially the shops on Calle Florida. Buenos Aires is a flat city, but Plaza San Martín is on a natural ravine, making it unique in the city. The park condenses many stories. For example, there was a bullring there with a capacity of about 10,000 people. Our great hero, General José de San Martín, trained his soldiers there. Also, at that point, the English sold and bought enslaved people during the colonial era.

Another place you cannot miss is the Estación Retiro, made by British engineers.

cocktail '11y6' in honour of a song by Fito Páez. There are over 400 different Argentine wines on the menu, along with a selection of tapas. Every evening from 8pm, they host live music, DJ sets, and vinyl record nights.

Architectural Theater Jewel

Admire the design of Teatro Nacional Cervantes

Despite being just 200m from Teatro Colón (p61), the **Teatro Nacional Cervantes** *(teatrocervantes.gob.ar; box office 10am-10pm Wed-Sun)* often goes unnoticed by tourists visiting Buenos Aires. Its construction was born out of the love of two Spanish artists, María Guerrero and Fernando Díaz de Mendoza y Aguado, who formed a theater company and commissioned this performance space, which opened in 1921.

King Alfonso XIII of Spain collaborated financially with its construction, including providing details such as red slabs from Tarragona and paintings for the ceiling frescoes from Barcelona. The theater has three halls, the largest of which seats 860 and has a classic Italian-style design. There are regular guided tours of the theater interiors – see the website for details.

A Breathtaking Front Door

Go through the entrance of Centro Naval

The first thing that grabs attention at **Centro Naval** *(centro naval.org.ar; tours by reservation)* is its grand entrance door. Gilded and majestic, it was crafted from bronze and cast iron cannons used in the Spanish American wars of independence, the battles and military campaigns in several South American countries.

This social space was created to create camaraderie among the graduates of the Naval Military School. Today, visitors on guided tours can explore the opulent building, inaugurated in 1914. The Sarmiento Hall is one of the most impressive rooms due to its extraordinary collection of paintings on naval themes, including one by Benito Quinquela Martín (p113).

EATING IN RETIRO: OUR PICKS

La Raya: The specialty at this steakhouse, with a history of over 80 years operation in BA, is *achuras* (offal). *hours vary* $$$

Norte: In a relaxed and unpretentious atmosphere, Norte specializes in meat and Spanish-inspired dishes. *8am-4pm & 8pm-midnight Mon-Sat* $$

Parrilla Cero5: Abundant dishes, mainly meat. Their menu includes a whole loin, with more than 1kg of beef. *noon-midnight Tue-Sun* $$$

Huacho: A steakhouse with Patagonian influences, cooking over a wood fire. Be sure to try their star dish, the *ojo de bife* (rib-eye steak). *noon-midnight Mon-Sat* $$$

Centro Naval

Meet an Iconic Bartender

Step into Oscar's bar

Oscar Chabrés has lived many lives. He's been a postman, caddy, waiter and, finally, a bartender, including serving at BA's famed Claridge Hotel. A legend of the local cocktail scene, Oscar is now the welcoming host at **Chabrés Bar** *(chabres bar.com.ar; 5pm-3am Tue-Fri, 7pm-3am Sat)*. The place has an old wooden door and a large bar; the 1960s furniture is intact. The atmosphere and music are relaxed. Oscar defines his cocktail bar as "classic" and invites you to try his creations such as the gin-based Zoe.

BARRIO MUGICA: A SYMBOL OF INEQUALITY

Although not an official neighborhood, **Barrio Mugica** is one of the most emblematic areas in the Retiro and Recoleta districts. This informal settlement was known as Villa 31 for many years – in Argentina, slums are called 'villas.' Over time, to avoid stigmatization, the name was changed; Barrio Mugica is named after Father Carlos Mugica, who was murdered by a vigilante group in 1974.

Its origins date back to the 1930s when the city's population began to grow due to the arrival of immigrants from the country's interior and neighboring nations. Since then, various governments have attempted to urbanize the area with limited success. Today, it covers 72 hectares, located near luxury hotels, the railway station and the bus terminal.

EATING IN RETIRO: BEST FOR DESSERT

Rapanui: Chocolate and ice cream shop from Bariloche with branches throughout Argentina. Try their milk chocolate bar with pistachios, salt and caramel. *10am-1am* $$

El Fundador: Traditional ice cream parlor in Retiro. Don't miss their pistachio and dark chocolate flavors. *hours vary* $$

Confitería Dos Escudos: An old-fashioned neighborhood bar specializing in cakes and sandwiches. *7am-8pm* $$

Heladería Esmeralda: The ice cream parlor has been in the city for several generations. Its specialty is the handmade *dulce de leche*. *2-9:30pm* $$

AVENIDA 9 DE JULIO

Av 9 de Julio, hailed as the world's widest avenue, is named after Argentina's independence day. It's only 1km long but 16 lanes wide (140m) and takes a walking pedestrian at least two traffic-light cycles to cross, via raised islands. *If* they don't dillydally.

When the widening construction started in 1935, the avenue was considered a patriotic symbol of the city's modern aspirations. Designers modeled it on Paris' Champs-Élysées, but made it twice as wide as a way to one-up its predecessor. Dozens of blocks of traditionally styled European buildings had to be demolished through the city's center, and thousands of residents displaced. Only the original French Embassy remained untouched. It still stands today, as the lanes of 9 de Julio forcefully curve around it.

SOBREVOLANDO PATAGONIA/SHUTTERSTOCK

Avenida 9 de Julio

Retiro's Popular Piano Bar

Sing along with Juan and his crowd

In 2023, **El Legado** *(legadopianobar.meitre.com; 6pm-2am Tue-Thu, 7.30pm-2am Fri & Sat)* opened on a street that is not very busy at night, and it has been making a name for itself in Retiro. Exposed brick walls, vinyl records stuck to the wall, and an upright piano with its lid open create the setting before, at around 10pm, house pianist Juan, begins to play some songs, which might be Argentine rock, *boleros* or pop. That's just the start, to get the night going. Next, the customers come up to sing, choosing from Juan's own book with more than 200 options. If it's not in the book, the pianist usually manages to play it and everyone sings together. The atmosphere is convivial and fun, and the music is complemented by a varied wine and cocktail list. 'The night at El Legado is long,' says the host, and he's right.

DRINKING IN RETIRO: BEST PUBS

Kilkenny: A favorite among downtown office workers, this Irish pub is famous not only for its beers but also for its massive parties on St Patrick's Day. *hours vary*

On Tap Retiro: Known for its craft beer and pleasant atmosphere. It serves tapas like hamburgers, *empanadas*, pizza and falafel. *5:30pm-1am Mon-Sat*

Barís: Small bar with great beers and ciders. Its hot dogs are well known, especially the sauerkraut one. *hours vary*

Felicia Bar: Modern bar with classic and signature drinks inside the five-star Sofitel hotel. Live DJs frequently play at the bar. *6-11:30pm*

Food Market in a Historic Building

Graze Mercado de los Carruajes

The building was built in 1899 at the request of the then president Julio Argentino Roca, to house the stables and carriages of the presidency. The location was ideal due to its proximity to the Casa Rosada. Since 2022, **Mercado de los Carruajes** *(mercadodeloscarruajes.com; 8:30am-10pm Mon-Wed, 8.30-midnight Thu-Sat, 8.30am-8pm Sun)* has been operating as a gourmet market, which stands out for its elegant brick facade, dome and arcades. The gastronomic offering is varied, with restaurants and small local takeaway shops. These include **San Ginés**, the Argentine branch of the famous *churro* house in Spain; **La Cabrera**, one of the most famous steakhouses in the city; and **Furio**, a Neapolitan-style pizzeria.

For Vinyl Fans

Flick through the platters at Abraxas Discos

One of the city's most legendary record stores is located in the Galería 5ta Avenida on Av Santa Fe. Founded in 1983 **Abraxas Discos** *(abraxasdiscos.com.ar; 11:30am-7:30pm Mon-Fri, noon-7pm Sat)* specializes in rock and pop and has an exquisite soul, jazz, and tango collection. Its owner, Fernando Pau, a native of Uruguay, personally attends the store and recommends records, if the customer requires advice. He remembers which record a customer bought even years later.

For Banknote Enthusiasts

Book ahead to tour this money museum

Casa de la Moneda is the Argentine institution responsible for printing banknotes and minting coins. One of its halls houses the **Museo y Archivo Histórico Casa de Moneda** *(email museo@casademoneda.gob.ar to arrange a tour)* a small museum exhibiting part of its historical collection. The history of the building, situated in the city's port area, is also narrated. The 50-minute guided tours must be booked in advance.

BORGES' LAST RESIDENCE

Many of the greatest lights of Argentine literature called Buenos Aires home, and the one that burned brightest was without doubt Jorge Luis Borges (1899–1986), one of the foremost writers of the 20th century.

Though he received numerous honors in his lifetime – including the Cervantes Prize, the Legion of Honor and an OBE – Borges was never conferred the Nobel. He joked of this in typical fashion: 'Not granting me the Nobel Prize has become a Scandinavian tradition. Since I was born they have not been granting it to me.'

Fans can head to his last residence in BA: a private apartment building near the corner of Florida and Santa Fe in Retiro. Look for a plaque on the wall.

EATING IN RETIRO: BEST EMPANADAS

Pal Que Guste: Traditional flavors from northern Argentina, with specialties like juicy meat *empanadas* and *locro* (a spicy stew of maize, beans and meats). *hours vary* $$

Nuestras Costumbres Criollas: A classic in Retiro. Don't miss their *empanada* made in the authentic style of the province of Tucumán. *11am-3pm, 7-11pm* $$

La Torre de Retiro: The restaurant specializes in pizzas and *empanadas* and serves large portions. *hours vary* $$

El Correntino: Serves pizzas, *empanadas*, and regional dishes like *locro* and sweet pastries. *11am-10pm Mon-Sat & 7pm-10pm Sun* $$

Researched by
Rachel Tolosa Paz

RECOLETA & BARRIO NORTE

A FAMOUS CEMETERY AND STATELY HOMES

Best known for its historic Cementerio de la Recoleta – a top sight on every visitor's bucket list – Recoleta also surprises and delights with locals' spots.

Recoleta and Barrio Norte are compact barrios, loosely bordered by Av Libertador in the north, Av 9 de Julio (east), Av Santa Fe (south) and Av Coronel Diaz (west). Of course, everyone comes for the cemetery and to seek out Evita's grave, but Recoleta has a bigger story to tell for those who are willing to listen. Yes, there are plenty of stately mansions and luxury hotels along Av Alvear but, if you venture out beyond the cemetery gates, there is a decidedly neighborhood vibe to Recoleta. You'll find intimate bistros, underground jazz clubs, elegant bars and everything in between.

TOP TIP

Flee the cemetery crowds and head toward Av Santa Fe into Barrio Norte, a residential area with great neighborhood bistros and a more *tranqui* (relaxed) vibe.

JAN JERMAN/SHUTTERSTOCK

See page 197 for places to stay in Recoleta & Barrio Norte

Cementerio de la Recoleta (p140)

Highlights

❶ Cementerio de la Recoleta
Wander one of the world's most ornate cemeteries and seek out Evita's grave. **p140**

❷ Biblioteca Nacional Mariano Moreno
Explore this brutalist beauty, Argentina's national library, with exhibitions showcasing the country's writers. **p141**

❸ Floralis Genérica
Wander around the iconic soaring sculpture in the center of lush lawns. **p144**

MARK GREEN/SHUTTERSTOCK

◀ ❹ Museo Nacional de Bellas Artes
Spend some time with the country's most extensive Argentine art collection. **p147**

❺ El Ateneo Grand Splendid
Marvel at one of the planet's most beautiful bookstores, housed in an opulent former theater. **p142**

Getting Around

Bus
Bus 59 heads from Palermo to San Telmo along Av Las Heras and there are plenty of buses that run along Av Santa Fe.

Subte
Línea D (green) covers the southern section of Recoleta (along Av Sante Fe). Línea H (yellow) Las Heras station is six blocks from Recoleta cemetery.

Walking
Recoleta is a safe and compact barrio to walk around – just watch out for dog poo!

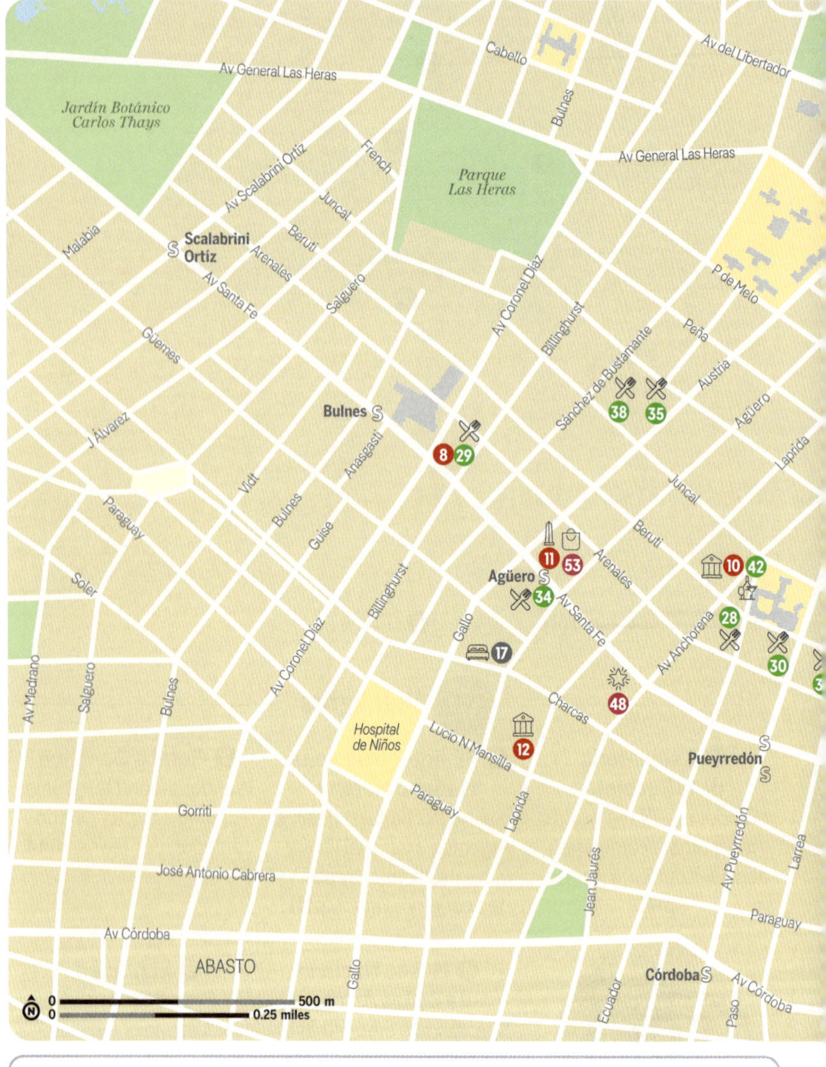

HIGHLIGHTS

1 Cementerio de la Recoleta

SIGHTS

2 Automóvil Club Argentino
3 Av Pueyrredón 2190
4 Av Quintana 222
5 Av Quintana 263
6 Biblioteca Nacional Mariano Moreno
7 Centro de Historieta y Humor Gráfico Argentinos
8 Charly García's home
9 Floralis Genérica
10 Jorge Luis Borges International Foundation
11 Memorial tile for a 'disappeared' person
12 Museo de Xul Solar
13 Museo del Libro y de la Lengua
14 Museo Nacional de Bellas Artes
15 Residencía Maguire

SLEEPING

16 Algodon Mansion
17 Attico Calas
18 Mio Buenos Aires
19 Palacio Duhau - Park Hyatt Buenos Aires
20 Poetry Building
21 SuMa Recoleta Hotel

EATING

22 Almacén 1249
23 Aramburu
24 Clorindo

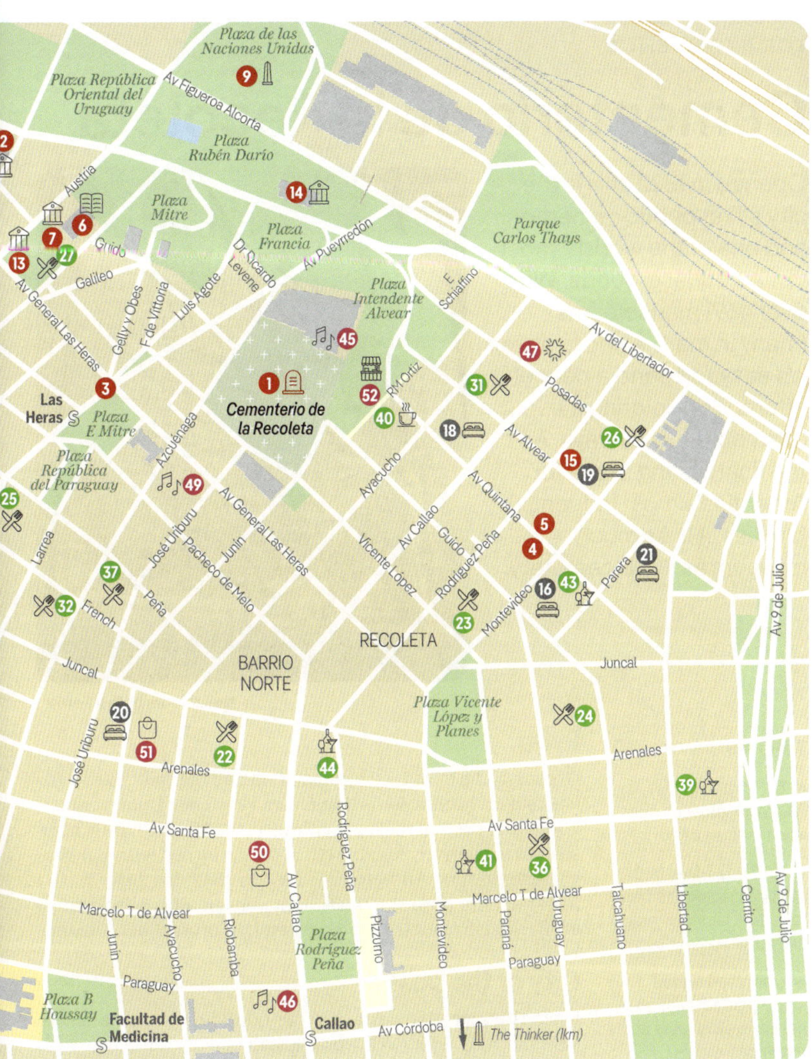

25 Confitería Caren
26 Gioia Cocina Botánica
27 Invernadero
28 Jay's
29 La Aguada
30 La Cocina
31 L'Orangerie
32 Los Pinos
see 19 Los Salones del Piano Nobile
33 Más Pastas
34 Néctar
35 Peña La Morena
36 Rondó Café
37 Roux
38 Sid Café

DRINKING & NIGHTLIFE

see 31 Alvear Roof Bar
39 Gran Bar Danzón
40 La Biela
41 Milión
see 19 Oak Bar
42 Ochava Bar
43 Presidente
44 The Shamrock Bar & Basement

ENTERTAINMENT

45 Centro Cultural Recoleta
46 Clásica y Moderna
47 Jazz Voyeur Club
48 Prez Jazz & Music Club
49 Rock & Beer

SHOPPING

50 El Ateneo Grand Splendid
51 El Galope
52 Feria de Artesanos de Plaza Francia
53 La Buena Tierra

TOP EXPERIENCE

Cementerio de la Recoleta

Opened in 1822, this is the city's first public cemetery and one of the world's most visited burial grounds. With over 4691 mausoleums (many in marble and bronze), it's easy to spend a peaceful afternoon exploring its labyrinthine alleyways. As the final resting place for Argentina's most influential families, it is as much a museum as it is a cemetery.

Mausoleum of Eva Perón

TOP TIPS

- For English guides, try Free Walks Buenos Aires who run tours daily.
- Lunfarda Travel (p108) offers engaging children's tours for children 8 years and up.
- Download a good map – printed maps are not always available at the entrance.

PRACTICALITIES

Scan the QR code for details about the cemetery's history, opening hours and tours.

Evita

Of course, the most famous inhabitant and the vault most tourists make a beeline for is that of Eva Perón nee Duarte. About 200m to the left of the main entrance, the Duarte family mausoleum is relatively humble but always adorned with bunches of fresh flowers. Although she died in 1952, her body wasn't interred here until the 1970s. Evita lies in a heavily fortified crypt some five meters underground, to protect her remains.

City of the Dead

Once the vegetable garden of the Iglesia de Nuestra Señora del Pilar next door (well worth a step inside), the cemetery is the resting place of over 20 of Argentina's former presidents (including Sarmiento and Raúl Alfonsín) alongside literary greats, such as Victoria Ocampo and Adolfo Bioy Casares, Nobel Prize winners and military commanders such as Julio Argentino Roca. Among the famous names are lesser-known figures. Look out for the mausoleum of Liliana Crociati, who died on her honeymoon. Her parents reconstructed her bedroom within her tomb and you'll spot Liliana in her wedding dress, with her beloved pet dog at her side.

National Library on the Hill

Tour the brutalist Biblioteca Nacional Mariano Moreno

Designed by Italian Argentine architect Clorindo Testa, the concrete **Biblioteca Nacional Mariano Moreno** *(bn.gov.ar)* was opened in 1992 after 20 years of stop-start construction. This fine example of Latin American brutalist architecture sits high on the hill which was originally the site of Unzué Palace, the official residence where President Juan Perón and Evita lived (it was demolished in 1958). Bring your passport to enter and go to floors 1, 3 and 5 to view temporary exhibitions and the concrete interior filled with original furniture. Head to the top floor (piso 5) to catch a glimpse of the Río de la Plata in the distance.

Guided tours in Spanish are held at noon, Monday to Friday, and Saturdays at 2pm and 4pm. In the surrounding complex, you'll find some delightful literary themed enclosed parks; the Invernadero (p146) gin and tapas garden café; **Museo del Libro y de la Lengua** *(@museolibroy lengua; 2-7pm Tue-Sun)* dedicated to books and language; and the Argentine graphic art museum **Centro de Historieta y Humor Gráfico Argentinos** *(@archivo.de.historieta.bn; 2-8pm Tue-Sun).*

Classic Car Collection

View the Automóvil Club Argentino's museum

Along Av del Libertador you'll spot a commanding rationalist beauty completed in 1942. It is the national headquarters of the **Automóvil Club Argentino** *(aca.org.ar/museo; free; 10am-5.30pm Mon-Fri)* and was designed by local architects Antonio U Vilar and Alejandro Bustillo, the latter known for his significant contribution to architecture in Argentina including the Llao Llao Hotel in Bariloche.

A working building – there's a gas station on street level and plenty of locals coming and going to carry out administration inside the ACA – it is open and accessible to walk inside and view the art deco details. If you're there for the cars, there are two impeccably restored historic cars in the lobby but head through the doors beside the elevators (towards the gas station) and you'll find an exhibition of cars, motorcycles and memorabilia related to Argentine auto history. Take the elevator or stairs to the first floor

BEST RECOLETA SHOPS

Feria de Artesanos de Plaza Francia: Sprawling weekend arts and crafts market in the lovely hillside park beside the cemetery.

El Ateneo Grand Splendid: Buy a book by an Argentine author in this beauty of a bookstore (p142).

La Buena Tierra: Indigenous crafts from across Argentina including textiles and wooden objects

El Galope: Gaucho (cowboy) wear, knives and *mates* in this tiny neighborhood space.

Néctar: Specialty BA ceramics, art and food stuffs in this *puerta cerrada* (p144). Ring the bell.

Don Mundo: Come here for exquisite world globes.

EATING & DRINKING IN RECOLETA: BEST CAFES

Sid Café: Superb coffee and friendly staff in a low-key location away from the hoards. The freshly baked croissants and yoghurt bowls are top picks. *8:30am-8pm Mon-Sat* $

Rondó Café: Specialty coffee, house-made pastries and delicious breakfast options, this pet-friendly spot is popular with locals and has some street-side seating. *8am-8pm Mon-Sat* $

Clorindo: For architect fans, visit this hidden gem nestled behind the neo-Tudor-style Biblioteca Ricardo Güiraldes; it pays homage to brutalist architect, Clorindo Testa. *9am-8pm Tue-Sun* $

La Biela: Opened in 1850 this is BA's oldest cafe – it's overrun with tourists but there's still plenty of charm. Best for coffee or aperitifs. *7am-2am* $

BORGES IN THE BARRIO

Jorge Luis Borges (p135) lived most of his adult life in Recoleta (his early childhood was in Palermo, his later years in San Telmo) where he was a regular at BA's oldest cafe, La Biela (p141). Close by the cemetery, you'll discover several of his former homes: **Av Quintana 222** and **263**; the apartment on the 5th floor of **Av Pueyrredón 2190** and the building at Anchorena 1660, which today operates as **La Fundación Internacional Jorge Luis Borges**, founded by Borge's widow, Maria Kodama. She passed away in 2023, surprisingly leaving no will and putting the future of Borges' estate in limbo.

for the official museum which has an impressive collection including Fangio's Ferrari 166, driven in 1949 in what today is known as the Formula One and an antique Daimler from the 19th century. Collection descriptions are in English and Spanish.

The World's Most Beautiful Bookstore

Browse El Ateneo Grand Splendid

El Ateneo Grand Splendid *(@elateneograndsplendid; 9am-9pm Mon-Sat, noon-9pm Sun)* is consistently ranked among the world's most beautiful bookstores. This stunning venue, housed in a lavish theater built in 1919, was once the stage for opera, ballet, and tango. The Odeon record label was based here, and singers such as Carlos Gardel (p80)

EATING IN RECOLETA: BEST TAKEAWAYS

Almacén 1249: Hands-down best baguettes in BA at this tiny deli with limited seating; don't miss the burrata and *jamon crudo. 9am-8pm Mon-Fri 9am-1pm Sat* $$

La Cocina: Character-filled hole-in-the-wall dive bar with some of BA's tastiest *empanadas;* order the *picachu*, a spicy onion and cheese specialty. *noon-4pm, 6:30pm-midnight Mon-Sat* $

Confitería Caren: Serving up *sandwiches de miga* since 1969; do as the locals do – pick up a slab of delicate sandwiches and picnic in the park. *8:30am-8pm Tue-Sun* $

Más Pastas: Pasta deli where you can pick up hot and fresh pastas with delicious house-made salsas. Try the plump *sorrentinos* (Argentine version of ravioli). *9am-2pm, 4:30-8:30pm* $

POSZTOS/SHUTTERSTOCK

El Ateneo Grand Splendid

recorded on the premises. The venue even gave birth to its own radio station, LR4 Radio Splendid, which began transmitting from the building in 1923. In the late 1920s, it became a cinema showing some of Argentina's first 'talkies'. A bookstore since 2000, today visitors can marvel at the breathtaking original ceiling frescoes by Italian Nazareno Orlandi and relax in ornate balcony boxes that have been converted into cozy reading nooks.

The basement is dedicated to children's books, where you will also find the music section filled with CDs and LPs from Argentine legends like Charly García (p146) and Ástor Piazzolla (p92). For those seeking English titles, walk towards the bookstore's cafe Havanna (located on the original stage with a striking mural backdrop) and you'll find a small selection on the upright shelves to the left.

AVENIDA ALVEAR

The grand old Av Alvear – where many of BA's aristocracy built their mansions during the late 19th century – is today a tree-lined street lined with luxury hotels and stately buildings, now mostly housing government officials. Number 1628, **Residencía Maguire** (or Ex-Duhau or Ex-Hume), is the last remaining privately owned mansion. Built in 1890 by Alexander Hume, a Scottish railway entrepreneur, many materials were imported from Scotland. Acclaimed landscape architect Carlos Thays (of Jardín Botánico (p165) and Parque 3 de Febrero (p170) fame among many others) designed the gardens which neighbor the terraced lawns of the Palacio Duhau (p197).

EATING IN RECOLETA: OUR PICKS

Jay's: Hankering for an American breakfast, pancakes, waffles or a burger? This sports-themed diner hits the spot. *9am-7pm Tue-Fri, 9am-5pm Mon & Sat* $

La Aguada: Humble home-cooking from the provinces in a cosy setting; must-try dishes are the *locro* and the *empanadas* from Tucuman. *11am-3:30pm, 7-11pm* $

Peña La Morena: Very reasonable Northern Argentine *peña* (folk music club) serving regional classics. Live folk music Thursday to Saturday. *11am-4pm, 7-midnight, until 1am Fri-Sat* $

Los Pinos: Argentine *parrilla* (steakhouse) serving up the classics; a locals' favorite with old-fashioned service, top-quality meat and flan to die for. *noon-3pm, 8-11:45pm* $$

HIDDEN IN PLAIN SIGHT

Much of what you see wandering the streets of Buenos Aires is just the tip of the iceberg. The rest is behind closed doors, up winding stairways and in tunnels and basements – it is a city that reveals its secrets slowly over time. That said, there's a little hidden history that's always visible – you just have to look down. All over BA you'll spot tiles embedded in the pavement that indicate that a 'disappeared' person lived in this neighborhood. So far over 1700 tiles have been laid in BA, and there's one on Av Santa Fe between Austria and Agüero.

An Eccentric Visionary

Visit Xul Solar's labyrinthine home and museum

The **Museo de Xul Solar** *(xulsolar.org.ar; noon-8pm Tue-Sat)* is the former home of renowned Argentine artist and eccentric visionary, Xul Solar. Born Oscar Agustín Alejandro Schulz Solari in 1887, his adopted name is *lux* backwards and combined with the word *solar* becomes 'light of the sun'. He was a pivotal figure in the Argentine avant-garde movement in the first half of the 20th century and a polymath who worked across painting, writing and sculpture. Fascinated by surrealism and symbolism, utopias, astrology, the metaphysical and spiritual, he created his own language (designed to unite the people), added a third row of keys to a piano (on view in the museum), devised a complicated chess-like board game and illustrated his own set of tarot cards.

The museum itself is a brutalist remodel of Solar's original home by local architect Pablo Tomas Beitia – it's a labyrinth of levels with hidden rooms and steps that lead to nowhere. Solar enjoys enduring popularity and influence – artists, designers, architects, and even linguists often refer to his work for inspiration. Check the museum's website for upcoming workshops that delve deeper into Solar's genius and theater and music performances held in the gallery.

Modern Icon of BA

Gaze in awe at Floralis Genérica

Nothing can quite prepare you for the immense scale of the stainless-steel flower, **Floralis Genérica**. This soaring monument, over 20m high, by Argentine architect Eduardo Catalano is located on the lush lawns of the Plaza de las Naciones Unidas (beside the **Facultad de Derecho** and **Parque Thays**), about halfway between the Museo Nacional de Bellas Artes (p147) and Museo Moderno (p105). With hydraulics and photoelectric cells, the petals were designed to automatically open during the day and fold closed at night although the piece has been damaged by severe storms in recent years. Work is underway to repair the mechanism which will allow the petals to move once again and ensure the longevity of the sculpture.

EATING IN RECOLETA: OUR PICKS

Néctar: Sporadic but sublime *puerta cerrada* (closed door restaurant) from local chef Toti Quesada; generally once a month but check dates via @nectar.casa. *hours vary* $$

Gioia Cocina Botánica: Vegetarian fine dining at the Park Hyatt. Try the mushroom *escabeche* or splurge on the tasting menu. *7am-11pm* $$$

Roux: Intimate and chic neighborhood bistro with French, Spanish and Argentinian influences; street-side seating and excellent service. *noon-3:30pm, 7pm-midnight Mon-Sat* $$$

Aramburu: BA's only two Michelin star restaurant from chef Gonzalo Aramburu; the 18-course degustation offers delights like Patagonian prawns; bookings essential. *6pm-10:30pm Tue-Sat* $$$

STROLL THE HILLS OF RECOLETA

Wander the few undulating hills of Buenos Aires, taking in exclusive residential enclaves, historic staircases, modern bridges and lush lawns.

START	END	LENGTH
Biblioteca Nacional Mariano Moreno	Museo Nacional de Bellas Artes	2.5km; 2-3 hours

Start at the 1 **Biblioteca Nacional Mariano Moreno** (p141). Take your passport to go inside this brutalist beauty and see the views from the fifth floor. Afterwards, head downstairs for a coffee at 2 **Invernadero** (p146) and wander the small elevated literary-themed 3 **Plazoleta del Lector**. Climb the stairs at Calle Guido to enter this historic residential area; pass through the park to see the 4 **Bartolomé Mitre Monument**.

Follow Guido to exit via the stairs onto Dr Luis Agote; on the left you'll notice the very modern 5 **British Embassy** and continue along the street. Cross Av Libertador to visit the 6 **Museo Nacional de Bellas Artes** (p147).

Cross through the lovely parks to gaze in awe at the soaring metal icon, 7 **Floralis Genérica**. Then loop back to climb the stairs of the city university's 8 **Facultad de Derecho** and step inside the impressive entry hall. It's a cool and peaceful spot to take a moment or two.

Walk the modernist curved pedestrian bridge, 9 **Puente de Figueroa Alcorta** (a great spot for sunset photos) and stop at the restaurants at the rear of the 10 **Museo Nacional de Bellas Artes** (on Av Figueroa Alcorta; p147) if you're getting hungry.

It's considered bad luck for students to enter the **Facultad de Derecho** via the center door until they graduate.

Look for *palo borracho* trees (literally drunk sticks!) near the **Museo Nacional de Bellas Artes**.

Spot a hopscotch in **Plazoleta del Lector**, in homage to Julio Cortázar's masterpiece.

CHARLY GARCÍA'S HOME

On the corner of Av Santa Fe and Av Coronel Diaz (opposite the shopping mall Palermo Alto) you will see a fairly non-descript apartment building door covered with handwriting. It is the home of Charly García (born 1951) – one of Argentina's most enduring rockstars and largely considered the father of *rock nacional*, Argentina's home-grown version of rock. Fans from around the world pass by his door and leave intimate messages for their hero. Go to Google Maps to view the building's rooftop painted with a giant mural of Charly's Oberheim keyboard.

JOHNNIE RIK/SHUTTERSTOCK

Merienda **(afternoon tea)**

Luxury Afternoon Teas

Take *merienda* in a mansion

Merienda (afternoon tea) in Buenos Aires is a cultural institution. Even the busiest of *porteños* take a break late afternoon, after all there are many hours between lunch and dinner and a refueling pause is a must.

In Recoleta, one opulent way to *merendar* (snack) is to take advantage of the offerings at the five-star hotels on Av Alvear. Alvear Palace Hotel has played host to many of the world's presidents, royalty and celebrities who indulge in its Louis XV-style furnishings. Snack on delicious sweets

DRINKING IN RECOLETA: OUR PICKS

The Shamrock Bar & Basement: For late night fun, this 1990s institution fits the bill; regular gigs in the basement and happy hour until 10pm. *4pm-2am Sun-Thu, 4pm-6am Fri-Sat*

Ochava Bar: Top wines with regular live music from electronic to jazz at this corner spot oozing city charm; also has a great selection of share plates. *5pm-2am Tue-Sun*

Invernadero: Gin and tapas bar nestled beneath the soaring Biblioteca Nacional; the lush and leafy patio is a welcome oasis on summer evenings. *9am-2am*

Milión: Sprawling bar set in an historic mansion with a superb garden patio area; a locals' institution for pre-late-night drinks. *8am-midnight Sun-Thu, 8am-2am Fri & Sat*

and savories at the afternoon tea served at the hotel's **L'Orangerie** between 5pm and 7pm. Alternatively, stroll on to the Palacio Duhau - Park Hyatt Buenos Aires (p197) where afternoon tea is served on the stunning terraced lawn at **Los Salones del Piano Nobile** between 4pm and 6:30pm. Book ahead for both afternoon tea services.

Argentine Art and European Masters

Explore the Museo Nacional de Bellas Artes

The **Museo Nacional de Bellas Artes** *(bellasartes.gob.ar; free; 11am-7:30pm Tue-Fri, 10am-7:30pm Sat & Sun)* has the most extensive collection of Argentine art together with one of the most impressive collections of 19th and early 20th century paintings in Latin America. Key works by Argentine artists such as Xul Solar, Eduardo Sívori and Benito Quinquela Martín and Antonio Berni are on display and there are also many paintings by European masters such as Picasso, Degas, Cézanne and van Gogh.

The museum collection also has some important works by Auguste Rodin who had an interesting relationship with BA. The museum's founder, Eduardo Schiaffino, purchased two works from Rodin in 1906, including *The Thinker* (1907) which sits in Plaza Mariano Moreno (p78). That cast was one of the few made by Rodin before he destroyed the original mold. In 1900, Rodin also created the bronze sculpture of former president Sarmiento in Parque 3 de Febrero (p170). It was the only commemorative sculpture that Rodin created outside of France and the first piece commissioned in the Americas.

The building itself is a former pump station that was used for the city's waterworks. It was later remodeled by Alejandro Bustillo, an architect known for his work both in Buenos Aires and Bariloche.

BEST MUSIC SPOTS IN RECOLETA

Clásica y Moderna: Bookstore, cafe-bar and live music venue full of history and charm.

Centro Cultural Recoleta: Cultural space with packed schedule of music, art, cinema and dance.

Rock & Beer: Legacy dive bar with a cult following. Music is on the rock and heavy metal side.

Ochava Bar: Sweet corner spot with outdoor tables, great menu and regular live music until 2am.

Prez Jazz & Music Club: Jazz and other shows in this intimate club; buy tickets online.

Jazz Voyeur Club: Shows in the basement club at Meliá Recoleta Plaza (Evita's first BA residence); book online, no cover charge Wednesdays.

DRINKING IN RECOLETA: OUR PICKS

Bimbi-Nilo: Hidden in the basement under a sushi restaurant, this intimate listening bar has an unrivalled vinyl collection and second-to-none negronis. *7pm-1am Tue, 8pm-2am Thu-Sat*

Alvear Roof Bar: One of BA's most charming roof top offerings with spectacular city views and cocktails; bookings essential and minimum spend. *7pm-11:30pm Wed-Sun*

Oak Bar: First come, first served in this intimate whisky bar, oozing old-school gentlemen club vibes; settle in among the timber-lined walls. *5pm-midnight*

Buller Bar: With an enviable position beside the park and cemetery, while away the afternoon with a craft beer and a burger. *noon-2am Sun-Wed, noon-3am Thu-Sat*

Researched by
Rachel Tolosa Paz

BELGRANO, NÚÑEZ & COSTANERA NORTE

PEACEFUL BARRIOS UNLESS IT'S MATCH DAY

There's a lot to love in the northern suburbs of Buenos Aires. It's *tranqui* (relaxed) and there is plenty of great eating to be done.

Belgrano and Núñez are areas that have significantly improved post-pandemic. Lots of *porteños* (Buenos Aires residents) seeking a bit more space and peace moved into these barrios breathing new life into the foodie scene. Nowadays, there seems to be a new bar or restaurant opening every other week and Barrio Chino (BA's compact Chinatown) has exploded, barely recognisable from a few years ago. There are delightful museum gardens to explore and open-air *milongas* to while away the nights. On the coast in Núñez and Costanera Norte, you'll find River Plate's home ground, a museum dedicated to the dictatorship, endless cycle paths and lush parks that lap at the river shore.

INCLUDES

Barrio Chino (p150)

Río de la Plata
Av General Paz
1 El Museo Sitio de Memoria ESMA
Av Int Cantilo
COSTANERA NORTE
Parque de la Memoria 4
NUÑEZ
5 Estadio Mâs Monumental
Av Guillermo Udaondo
Av Figueroa Alcorta
Av Leopoldo Lugones
Av Costanera R Obligado
Parque Norte
Av del Libertador
Ariebeños
3 de Febrero
Av Crisólogo Larralde
Av Cabildo
Iberá
Congreso
Av Monroe
BARRANCAS DE BELGRANO
Aeroparque Jorge Newbery
Echeverría
Sucre
La Pampa
Av Figueroa Alcorta
3 Barrio Chino
3 de Febrero
Cuba
Barrancas de Belgrano
Campo Municipal de Golf
Lago de Palermo
Av Ricardo Balbín
Av Monroe
Museo Larreta 2
Av V Alsina
BELGRANO
La Pampa
Mendoza
Juramento
11 de Septiembre
Av Federico Lacroze
Av del Libertador
Hipódromo Argentino
Av Cabildo
Zabala
LAS CAÑITAS
0 1 km
0 0.5 miles

Highlights

1 El Museo Sitio de Memoria ESMA
Spend some time learning about Argentina's dark past during the military dictatorship. **p155**

2 Museo Larreta
Explore this beautiful Andalusian garden and historic home filled with antiques. **p152**

3 Barrio Chino
Eat your way through BA's Chinatown packed with restaurants and specialty Asian grocers. **p150**

4 Parque de la Memoria ▶
Take a stroll in this peaceful memorial park with public art and top river views. **p157**

DIEGO GORZALCZANY/SHUTTERSTOCK

5 Estadio Mâs Monumental
Attend a River Plate match at this iconic football stadium. **p157**

Getting Around

Subte
Take Línea D to Juramento.

Train
Trains from Retiro stop at Belgrano C for Barrio Chino, Belgrano R for Belgrano R and Rivadavia and Núñez for Núñez and Costanera Norte.

Bus
Take the 29 to Barrio Chino and Núñez from Palermo and downtown. Bus 28 runs between Espacio Memoria y Derechos Humanos Ex ESMA and Costanera Norte.

Belgrano

Initially named after historic train lines, today many see Belgrano C (the north-east section) as standing in for 'Barrio Chino' and Belgrano R (the south-west section) for residential.

AVENIDA MELIÁN

If you're strolling the streets around Belgrano R, be sure to keep walking past Plaza Castelli to Av Melián (on the corner with La Pampa). This wide avenue is lined with distinctive *palo borracho* trees and a mix of English-style homes and modernist architecture apartment blocks. Interestingly, there used to be horse races here in the mid 19th century – a fact that's easy to believe once you lay eyes on the street. At Av Olazábal, turn right and you can walk back under the railway tracks where there are some bold, tiled murals on both sides of the road.

BA's Chinatown

Explore Barrio Chino

In **Barrio Chino** you'll find plenty of street-food style eateries set into the elevated train tracks of the train station, Belgrano C. There are heaps of options (mostly under the banner of 'international cuisine') but if crowds aren't your caper, aim for a late afternoon mid-week, when it is usually a little quieter. Some restaurants close on Mondays.

For a more traditional experience, walk beneath the Chinese arch at the corner of Av Juramento and Arribeños and wander the four or five blocks that make up the original part of Barrio Chino. Here you'll find old-school Chinese restaurants like **LAI-LAI** and specialty Asian grocers selling spices, ingredients and imported goods not found elsewhere in BA. Vegans can also find vegan-friendly products – try **Casa China** for decent prices.

If the bright lights of the VIAVIVA passageway (between Avs Juramento and Mendoza) are a bit too shiny try the southern end of Pasaje Echeverría (between Avs Juramento and Echeverría). It's a bit more laid-back and you'll find local favorites like Copetín (beers and tapas; p153), VINA (wine and *empanadas*) and gin specialists, Chintonería (p153) in the open-air alleyway. These spots are tiny with limited seating – but the vibe is great.

Watch Tango in the Park

Stroll through hillside Parque de Barrancas

Lush **Parque de Barrancas** is located on one of the few hillsides in Buenos Aires (let alone within the flat plains of the

EATING IN BELGRANO C: OUR PICKS

La Esquina: Popular, long-standing, street-side *parrilla* with choice *choripán*; line up with the fans on River Plate match days. *noon-3:30pm Tue-Sun* $

VINA: Delicious crispy organic *empanadas* paired with natural wines by the glass at this hole-in-the-wall; vegan pastry options. *noon-midnight Wed-Sun* $

Yatai Yatoi: Find Asian-fusion street food in Barrio Chino's Pasaje Echeverría in this hip canteen; don't miss the *baos de panceta* with cilantro and sriracha. *noon-midnight* $

Corte Charcutería: Known for its delish charcuterie; highlights include the squid ink salami and tongue terrine. *9am-9pm Mon-Sat, 9am-4pm Sun.* $$

HIGHLIGHTS
1 La Glorieta
2 Museo Larreta

SIGHTS
3 Barrio Chino
4 Parque de Barrancas

EATING
5 Anafe
6 Corte Charcutería
7 Gordo Vegano
8 La Esquina
9 La Sorellina
10 LAI-LAI
11 Mercado de Belgrano
12 Narda Comedor
13 Neko Sushi
14 Obun
see 16 Sucre
15 Treintasillas
see 3 Yatai Yatoi

DRINKING & NIGHTLIFE
see 3 Chintonería
see 3 Copetín
16 Kōnā Corner
see 3 Puerta Uno
see 3 VINA

SHOPPING
17 Casa China
18 Casa Social
19 Cocoliche
20 KEL Ediciones
see 3 Monoblock

province). The Río de la Plata lapped here until the middle of the 19th century when work began on the railway. Look out for the miniature Statue of Liberty – the little sister of New York City's iconic lady, created by the same

Obun: True Argentine Asian fusion tucked away in Paseo del Belgrano; don't miss the iconic *choribao* and kimchi *empanadas*. *11am-11:30pm* $

Sucre: Michelin-recommended *parrilla* on a park-lined street in Bajo Belgrano; steak is the specialty. *noon-4pm, 8pm-midnight Tue-Sun* $$

Neko Sushi: Great atmosphere, creative hand rolls and fresh sashimi in a romantic spot; there's another outpost in Villa Crespo. *noon-4pm, 8pm-midnight Mon-Sat* $$

Narda Comedor: Innovative dishes from top chef Narda Lepes; plenty of divine veg, vegan and gluten-free options. *8:30am-11pm Mon-Sat, 8:30am-7pm Sun* $$

BEST SHOPS IN BELGRANO

Monoblock: Exhibitions and colorful stationery including locally designed BA-themed souvenirs to take home; stores in Barrio Chino and across the city.

Casa Social: Technically in Colegiales (between Palermo and Belgrano), don't miss this well-curated art and design shop located in the front space of a residential home.

KEL Ediciones: BA's biggest English bookstore; located in a beautiful blue building on the corner of Plaza Castelli in Belgrano R.

Cocoliche: Secondhand clothing store with quality Argentine high-street brands; also trade in clothing for credit.

Casa China: Chinese supermarket in Barrio Chino; great for vegan produce and other hard-to-find ingredients.

French artist, Bartholdi. It was erected in Belgrano in 1875, 11 years prior to that of its famous US counterpart.

The park's centerpiece is the charming **La Glorieta**, an open-air decorative gazebo from 1910. On weekends, it plays host to tango classes at 5pm and *milonga* until 11pm (free; check @laglorietamilongaabierta for updates). It is a unique and authentic experience of tango in Buenos Aires where all ages and levels are welcome. A superb spot to soak up the atmosphere.

Andalusian Garden & Historic Home

Explore Museo Larreta

Museo Larreta *(@museolarreta; free Wed; 11am-7pm Mon, Wed-Fri, 11am-8pm Sat & Sun)* is a refuge in the city, a delightful home and garden where you can spend an hour or

EATING IN BELGRANO R: OUR PICKS

La Sorellina: Outpost of Argentina's best pizzeria Ti Amo (on the outskirts of BA); the airiest of crusts, arrive early to nab a table. *7pm-midnight Thu-Mon* $$

Gordo Vegano: Stylish vegan spot with Wes Anderson vibes in Belgrano R; breakfast, lunch and dinner options. *10am-11:30pm Wed-Mon* $$

Anafe: Bistro with lots of tasty vegetarian options; ex Canadian premier Justin Trudeau once dined here. *8pm-midnight Mon-Thu, noon-4pm & 8pm-midnight Fri-Sun* $$

Treintasillas: An old guard of BA's *puerta cerrada* scene; bookings essential via @treintasillas as there is very limited seating. *8pm-midnight Thu-Sat* $$$

PABLO DUCROS/SHUTTERSTOCK

Parque de Barrancas (p150)

two. Built in 1886 in neo-Spanish colonial style, the residence belonged to Enrique Larreta and his wife, Josefina Anchorena (she's buried in the Recoleta Cemetery, p140) and was gifted to them by Josefina's parents when they married. Larreta was a writer, diplomat and collector of 16th and 17th century paintings, objects and furniture, much of which is on display. Marvel at the tiled and timber gilt decorated floors, luxe textiles and the sumptuous reading room. Don't miss the tucked away bathroom with marble tub and arched shower nook (Larreta was a fan of the Alhambra in Spain).

The museum is surrounded by a deep arched portico and an Andalusian-style garden with low hedges and a variety of trees and sculptures – it's perfect for a stroll or to read a book in one of its shady corners. In summer, there are often concerts and markets here.

BARES NOTABLES

In BA, *bares notables* are more than just bars – they're living pieces of history. Officially recognized by the city's Ministry of Culture, these spots earn their status based on age (usually 50-plus years), cultural significance and architectural charm. Many were regular haunts of writers, artists or tango legends. Think old-school waiters, wood panelling and stories in every corner. Once declared notable, they receive preservation support and promotion as cultural landmarks. Visiting one is like stepping back in time – perfect for a quiet *cortado* (coffee with a dash of milk foam) or vermouth.

Each November the city celebrates the **La Noche de los Bares Notables** with events and special menus.

DRINKING IN BELGRANO C: OUR PICKS

Copetín: Chilled vibe at this tiny bar with beers and tapas; located in the hip strip of Pasaje Echeverría in Barrio Chino. *noon-midnight Tue-Sun*

Chintonería: Barrio Chino gin specialists, headed up by Argentinian cocktail pioneer Pablo Pinata; arrive early for a bar seat. *6pm-1am Tue-Fri, 1pm-1am Sat & Sun*

Puerta Uno: Hidden bar in Belgrano C, there's no sign on the door; cozy and chic, it's been serving sublime cocktails for two decades. *7:30pm-3am Tue-Sat*

Kōnā Corner: Top mixologist Inés de los Santos is behind this Japanese cocktail bar and restaurant. *7pm-midnight Mon-Thu, to 1am Fri & Sat*

WALKING THE DOG

In Buenos Aires, *paseaperros* (professional dog walkers) are a common sight, often managing a dozen leashed dogs through parks in Palermo, Recoleta, and downtown. Hired by busy apartment dwellers, these walkers handle everything from purebreds to scruffy mutts, each of their tails happily a-wagging. While charming and photo-worthy, the streets also bear the downside: dog poo is everywhere, despite cleanup laws (largely unenforced). Visitors quickly learn to watch their step. Still, the daily parade of orderly, trotting canines has become a beloved part of the city's landscape, blending urban life with a touch of delightful chaos.

PABLO DUCROS/SHUTTERSTOCK

Mercado de Belgrano

Belgrano's Food Market

Shop and graze at Mercado de Belgrano

In the heart of Belgrano, **Mercado de Belgrano** *(@mercadodebelgrano; restaurants 11am-midnight; fresh produce stalls 8:30am-8pm Mon-Sat)* is a compact neighborhood gem. Largely frequented by locals doing their daily shopping, it is the perfect spot to check out rows of eggs and piles of *milanesas* (breadcrumbed veal). It has a good balance of excellent produce shopping (from butchers, bakers, fruit and veg, seafood, kosher to gluten-free grocers) and eating options like **Ian** (Middle Eastern; try the eggplant *empanadas* and tabouli), **LAB Bistró de Cocina** (serene sustainable café with very reasonable zero-waste meals from La China Sanchez and Leandro Cristino; they also teach fermentation classes) and classic trattorias like **Pinuccío** (housemade pastas).

Take a seat at the bar at **Rienda Suelta** (run by the crew behind Palermo's wine-on-tap bar Amores Tintos, p166) and have a hotdog (all sausages and bread are made inhouse) and a glass of *vino tinto* (red wine), beer or vermouth. It's a very *tranqui* vibe and you probably won't see many tourists. Outside, there is a large outdoor terrace for warmer days.

MORE FOOD MARKETS

Other indoor food markets in Buenos Aires include **Mercado de San Telmo** (p101), **Mercado de los Carruajes** (p131) in Retiro and **Mercado del Progreso** (p183) in Caballito.

Núñez & Costanera Norte

Costanera Norte edges the shore of the Río de la Plata and borders BA's domestic airport. Núñez lies at the outer northern limits of the city of Buenos Aires where it is fast becoming a foodie hotspot.

Clandestine Torture Site

Pay witness at Ex ESMA

The former naval training school grounds, known as Ex ESMA, have become the site of **Espacio Memoria y Derechos Humanos** *(Space for Memory and Human Rights; espaciomemoria.ar; 9am-8pm Mon-Fri, 9am-9pm Sat & Sun)*. The grounds were used during the military dictatorship from 1976–1983 as a clandestine torture site where kidnapped dissidents were held and mostly killed, either by firing squad or dropped from planes into the Río de la Plata.

Around the corner from the **El Museo Sitio de Memoria ESMA** *(free; 9am-10pm)* you can see one of the original planes used during the death flights. It was discovered by a journalist in Florida, being used as a mail plane until it was returned to Buenos Aires a few years ago. The museum is a somber place, mostly empty of artifacts and furniture to give space to the remembrance of the tragic stories that took place here.

The grounds are free to enter, and guided tours (in Spanish) are held at noon every day. Ex ESMA also hosts several human rights organizations including the headquarters of the Abuelas de la Plaza de Mayo (Grandmothers of Plaza de Mayo; p157) and **Casa Por La Identidad**, a building you can enter to view photographs which tell the story of these incredible women. Next door, in a soaring warehouse, you'll also find a small café, **H.I.J.O.S**, run by a co-operative, which offers cheap eats. They also host tango *milongas* here, see @tangonautas.milonga for schedules.

NÚÑEZ: CITY LIMITS

Located on the border of the northern city limits of Buenos Aires (cross over Av Gral Paz and you're in the province of Buenos Aires), Núñez is a compact and peaceful residential barrio that is rapidly developing post-pandemic as a foodie and drinking destination with a new round cropping up each month. Although the Subte doesn't reach Núñez, the above-ground train stops at both Núñez and Rivadavia where you'll find plenty of spots to whet your appetite. Must visits are dimly lit speakeasy, Al Fondo (p159), and WIDE Cocina y Vinos (p158), for low-intervention wines and tapas.

EATING IN NÚÑEZ: OUR PICKS

No Tan Santos: Cheap and easy *parrilla* with a friendly atmosphere and popular with locals; book ahead for a table in the courtyard. *10am-midnight* $

Hola Chola Garage: Delicious vegetarian plates in a colorful setting; be prepared to line up with the crowds. *7pm-11pm Wed-Sun* $

Ruiz: Reinventing the traditional neighborhood *rotisería* with dine-in and takeout options; the *milanesas* are the house specialty. *noon-midnight* $$

Piedra Pasillo: Michelin-listed fine diner; innovative and creative dishes in an historic building with a hidden bar out the back. *8pm-midnight Mon-Sat* $$

HIGHLIGHTS
1 El Museo Sitio de Memoria ESMA
2 Parque de la Memoria

SIGHTS
3 Casa Por La Identidad
4 Espacio Memoria y Derechos Humanos
5 Estadio Mâs Monumental
6 Museo River Plate
7 Parque de Innovacion

ACTIVITIES
8 Parque Deportivo

EATING
9 Espacio García
10 Gardiner
11 H.I.J.O.S
12 Happening
13 Hola Chola Garage
14 No Tan Santos
15 Piedra Pasillo
16 Ribs al río
17 Ruiz

DRINKING & NIGHTLIFE
see 15 Al Fondo
18 CiTiO
19 El Pollo Gomez
20 Forma Café
21 Mauer
22 Oporto Almacén
23 Vereda Adentro
24 WIDE Cocina y Vinos

ENTERTAINMENT
25 Tierra Santa

River Plate's Homeground

Visit the largest stadium in Argentina

The iconic football stadium, **Estadio Mâs Monumental** *(cariverplate.com.ar)*, home to Club Atlético River Plate, officially opened in 1938 (although River Plate was founded in La Boca from 1901). It holds a prominent place in football history, having hosted Argentina's 1978 World Cup win, and it is the field of choice for Argentina's national team.

At one time, it was the largest stadium in the world, and it still retains its status as the largest stadium in Argentina and one of the largest in South America, with a seating capacity of almost 85,000. The stadium's unique architectural design features a deep bowl and tiered seating, allowing for excellent sight lines from nearly every seat. You'll be hard-pressed to nab a ticket to a match (p212) but, if you can, the atmosphere is nothing short of electrifying.

For die-hard football fans, visit one of the world's largest sports museums, **Museo River Plate** *(@museoriver; 10am-7pm)*, to learn more about the history of the football club, River Plate and for the chance to tour the grounds (but not step onto the field).

A Park for the Disappeared

Pay respects to victims of the military dictatorship

Nestled on the shore of the river, peaceful **Parque de la Memoria** *(free; open until 6pm)*, is one of BA's best kept secrets. Lush lawns cover the park, and it is impeccably maintained, in part owing to its purpose as a memorial to those who were 'disappeared' during the military dictatorship. Public art works (by Clorindo Testa, Jenny Holtzer and Dennis Oppenheim among others) jut out of the ground, framed by the stretch of water behind (and the coast of Uruguay in the distance). The somber monument in the park center has the names of the official 9000 disappeared but space for the suspected 30,000 who were kidnapped and killed. Use the park respectfully as family members visit the site to mourn, remember and leave flowers.

Riverside Promenade

Stroll or cycle Costanera Norte

Recent shoreline developments in Costanera Norte, along the river from Recoleta to Nuñez, have created lovely promenades

ABUELAS DE LA PLAZA DE MAYO

Argentina's military junta detained pregnant women until they gave birth, often killing them afterward. The babies were then adopted by pro-military families to erase their 'disappeared' parents' ideals and instil more 'acceptable' values – a strategy that inspired Margaret Atwood's *The Handmaid's Tale.*

Named after the women who first stood in Plaza de Mayo (p58) in 1976 to protest and make visible the disappearance of their children and grandchildren is the powerful human rights organization **Abuelas de la Plaza de Mayo** *(abuelas.org.ar)*. They have successfully located and reunited over 130 children with their biological families, primarily through pioneering DNA work. Each child found (now in their 40s and early 50s) is celebrated in Argentina, but there are still thought to be over 300 more missing.

EATING IN COSTANERA NORTE: OUR PICKS

Ribs al río: Eat ribs on the river at this fun BBQ joint with an elevated outdoor terrace. *noon-midnight Sun-Thu, to 1am Fri & Sat* $

Espacio García: Peaceful glass-enclosed café bordering the Parque de la Memoria; usually filled with students from the nearby university. *9am-8:30pm Tue-Sun* $

Happening: Classic steakhouse dating back to the 1960s; try the *morcilla* (blood sausage) and *molleja* (sweetbreads). *noon-1:30am* $$

Gardiner: Another classic steakhouse on the coast with a large outdoor patio; top spot for a drink in the warmer months. *noon-1am Sun-Wed, to 2am Thu-Sat* $$

BEST OPEN SPACES

Parque Deportivo: Costanera Norte riverside skatepark complex with plenty of bowls and smooth paths for rollerblading and skating.

Parque de la Memoria: Peaceful and solemn memorial to the military dictatorship's 'disappeared'; one of the best outdoor spots on the river's edge.

Parque de Barrancas: Lush park to hang in once you're done with the Barrio Chino crowds.

Parque de Innovación: Still evolving park in Núñez with plenty of dedicated skate and rollerblading paths. View the impressive 34m-high public artwork *Arbórea Magna*. *(parqueinnovacionba.com)*

Museo Larreta: The museum's Andalusian-style garden is a shady oasis.

perfect for cycling or walking the coast. Start at the southern end of Aeroparque Internacional Jorge Newbery where you'll see the historic **Club de Pescadores** (Fisherman's Club) built in the 1930s atop the 500m pier. You'd be forgiven for thinking you are standing beside the sea as it stretches out to nearby Uruguay but, of course, the Río de la Plata is one of the world's widest rivers (220kms at its widest).

There are plenty of *carritos* (food trucks) offering *choripán* (chorizo sandwiches) or *bondiola* (pork) sandwiches which you can load with homemade sauces and salads. Other interesting spots along the Costanera Norte promenade include the soaring 17m tall **Christopher Columbus** monument in white Carrera marble.

DRINKING IN NÚÑEZ: OUR PICKS

El Pollo Gomez: Legendary late-night bar with a great vibe, plenty of music and a fun menu. *6pm-1am Mon-Thu, 7pm-2am Fri & Sat*

WIDE Cocina y Vinos: Top pick for low-intervention wines including whites and rose; also sip vermouth and snack on tapas. *5pm-1am Tue-Thu, 7pm-2am Fri & Sat*

Forma Café: Small and cozy cafe with top notch specialty coffee and sunny street-side seating; excellent service and tasty sweets. *8:30am-8pm*

CiTiO: Top coffee spot with brunch and breakfast options; take a seat at the counter or nab a table outside; don't miss the sourdough croissants. *8am-8pm*

DSAPRIN/SHUTTERSTOCK

Tierra Santa

Jerusalem in Buenos Aires

Visit the religious theme park Tierra Santa

Located along Costanera Norte, **Tierra Santa** *(Holy Land; tierrasanta.com.ar; 9am-7pm Fri, noon-8pm Sat & Sun)* is the only religious theme park in Argentina. Covering eight hectares, the site is a fascinating replica of ancient Jerusalem. It was blessed by Pope Francis when he was Archbishop of Buenos Aires.

Whether you're a believer or not, this one-of-a-kind kitsch spectacle is worth checking out. There are live shows, a 12m tall statue of Jesus who rises into the sky and opens his eyes and palms every half-hour and animatronic dioramas depicting Bible scenes from the Last Supper to the Nativity. Food is to theme with Middle Eastern fare on offer.

MOVIES & BOOKS ABOUT DICTATORSHIP ARGENTINA

El Secreto de Sus Ojos (2009): Campanella's Oscar-winning film (*The Secret in Their Eyes*; from the book by Eduardo Sacheri) is set in 1975 and details the events that lead to the start of the military dictatorship.

Hades, Argentina (2021): Daniel Loedel's novel about an Argentine who was involved in the torture of dissidents during the dictatorship, returning to Argentina and the ghosts of his past.

Argentina, 1985 (2022): Santiago Mitre's film is set during the landmark Trial of the Juntas, history's first instance of a civilian justice system convicting a military dictatorship.

Mauer: Warehouse bar with a 1960s Berlin theme and DJs; arrive early if you want a table. *6pm-1am Mon-Thu, 6pm-3:30am Fri & Sat*

Vereda Adentro: Natural wines, cheeses and charcuterie with seating on a wide corner footpath; book ahead on the weekends. *6pm-1am Mon & Thu-Sat*

Oporto Almacén: Bistro and wine bar; tasting room with 450 color-coordinated bottles. *noon-4pm, 8pm-midnight Mon-Sat, noon-4pm Sun*

Al Fondo: Scramble up the stairs at the back of Piedra Pasillo for this hidden gem of a cocktail bar with occasional DJs. *8pm-2am Mon-Sat*

Researched by
Rachel Tolosa Paz

PALERMO

NIGHTLIFE, PARKS, GLORIOUS FOOD AND SHOPPING

Palermo, Buenos Aires' largest neighborhood, has it all – restaurants, bars and shopping for all tastes, mighty museums, and parks that stretch for days.

Palermo is the city's most populated barrio but it extends wide across the BA map. It is filled with sub-neighborhoods that aren't quite official (it's more of a real-estate thing) but each has its own identity. Put simply, Palermo Viejo is the area west of Plaza Italia and Av Santa Fe. Within Palermo Viejo there are two neighborhoods, Palermo Soho (south of the train tracks on Av Juan Bautista Justo) and Palermo Hollywood (north of the train tracks). Both areas are brimming with nightlife and shopping. The more upscale area of Palermo is east of Av Santa Fe and here you'll find Palermo Chico (surrounding MALBA) and Palermo's museums and parks.

TOP TIP

Things tend to start later in the day in Palermo Viejo (given all that happens at night). Shops generally open from noon to 8pm.

DIEGO GRANDI/SHUTTERSTOCK

Palermo Soho

See page 198 for places to stay in Palermo

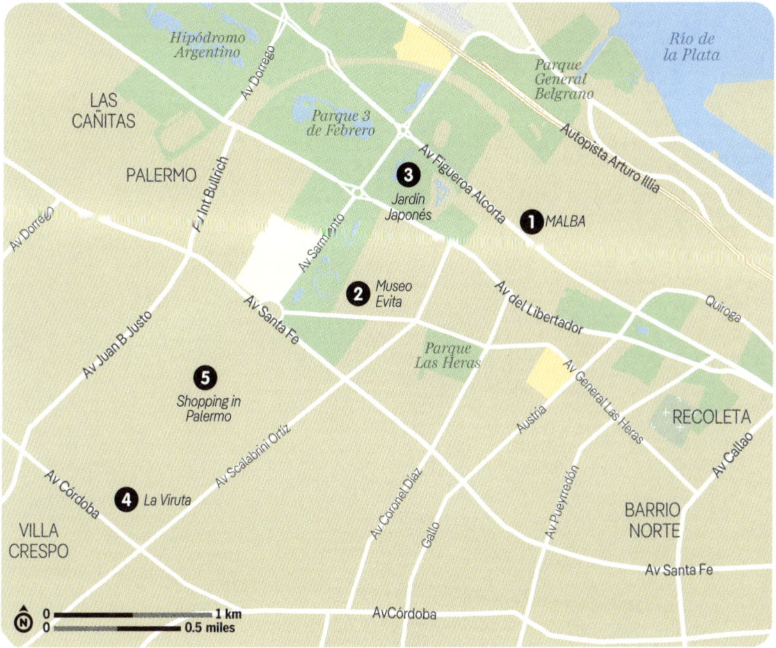

Highlights

❶ MALBA

Explore cavernous halls of Latin American art and a great museum store filled with locally-designed objects. **p168**

❷ Museo Evita ▶

Dive deep into the life of Argentina's most famous First Lady at this museum housed in a gorgeous 1923 mansion. **p165**

BRESTER IRINA/SHUTTERSTOCK

❸ Jardín Japonés

Immaculate Japanese gardens to wander and delicious sushi to savor on the terrace. **p164**

❹ La Viruta

Take a tango class at this basement venue then dance at their *milonga* until the sun comes up. **p173**

❺ Shopping in Palermo

Wander the streets to discover BA's hip boutiques, bookstores and hand-crafted art and design. **p169**

Getting Around

Bus

Take buses 29, 59, 64 and 152 from downtown to Plaza Italia; 39 and 111 from downtown to Palermo Viejo; 110 from Scalabrini Ortiz to Palermo Chico.

Subte

Línea D (green line) runs through the middle of Palermo along Av Santa Fe but you'll have to walk or bus into either side.

Walking

Palermo is a great barrio to walk but it is very spread out. Use buses to cross into different areas or hire a bike.

Lago de Regatas (1.5km)
Hipódromo Argentino
Lago de Rosedal
Av Pedro Montt
Parque 3 de Febrero
Av del Libertador
Soldado de la Independencia
Migueletes
Av Federico Lacroze
Olleros
Newberry
Matienzo
LAS CAÑITAS
3 de Febrero
Maure
Av Luis María Campos
Arce
Av Báez
Arguibel
Av Dorrego
Campo Argentino de Polo
Av Cabildo
Zapata
Ciudad de la Paz
Savio
Clay
Juan Seguí
Demaría
Av Cerviño
Sinclair
Av Int Bullrich
COLEGIALES
Arenal
Estación Ministro Carranza
Ministro Carranza
PALERMO
Juncal
Beruti
Av Santa Fe
Conesa
Nicaragua
Crámer
Dr Emilio Ravignani
Ángel Justiniano Carranza
Palermo
Estación Palermo
La Rural
Av Sarmiento
Av Dorrego
Arévalo
PALERMO HOLLYWOOD
Guatemala
Soler
Humboldt
Fitz Roy
Plaza Italia
Jardín Botánico Carlos Thays
JSM de Oro
Darregueyra
Uriarte
Thames
PALERMO VIEJO
Costa Rica
El Salvador
Honduras
Gorriti
Av Juan B Justo
Jorge Luis Borges
Charcas
Guatemala
Soler
Armenia
Malabia
Paraguay
José Antonio Cabrera
Niceto Vega
Bonpland
See Enlargement
Thames
Plaza Serrano
Gurruchaga
Serrano
Godoy Cruz
Av Córdoba
Plaza Palermo Viejo
Aráoz
J Álvarez
Costa Rica
El Salvador
Costa Rica
El Salvador
Honduras
Darwin
Av Juan B Justo
Castillo
Niceto Vega
José Antonio Cabrera
Gorriti
Jufré
Lerma
Gurrachaga
Acevedo
Malabia
Juan Ramírez de Velasco
Aguirre
Av Scalabrini Ortiz
Aráoz
J Álvarez
Lavalleja
Gascón
Acuña Figueroa
Av Medrano
Salguero
Av Corrientes
Av Estado de Israel
0 500 m
0 0.25 miles

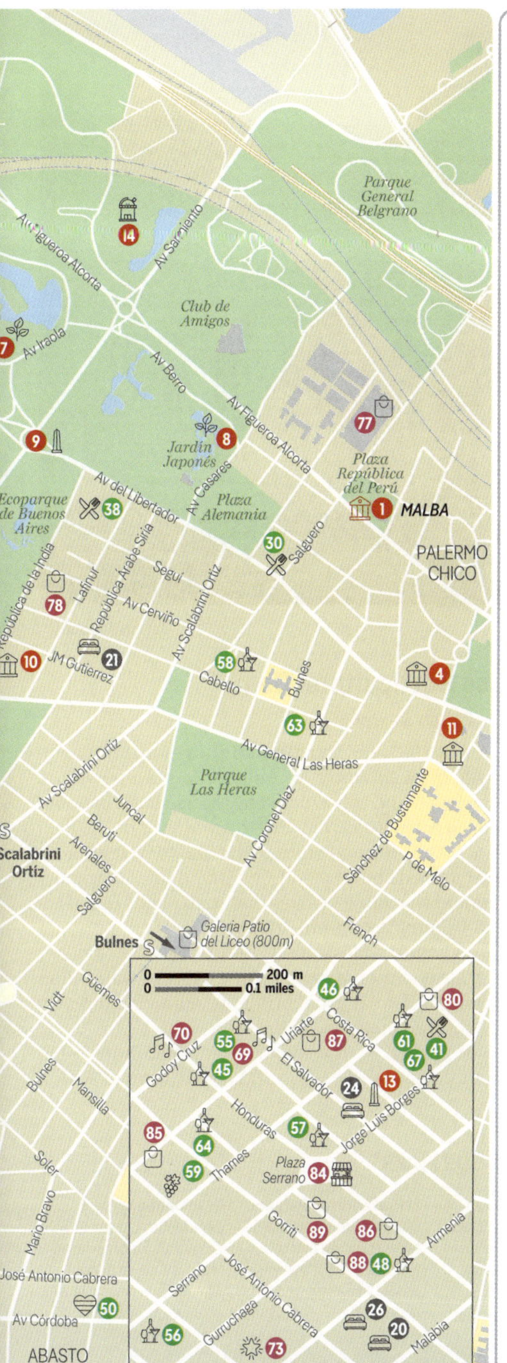

HIGHLIGHTS

1 MALBA
2 Parque 3 de Febrero

SIGHTS

3 Campo Argentino de Polo
4 Casa de la Cultura del Fondo Nacional de las Artes
5 Ecoparque
6 Jardín Botánico Carlos Thays
7 Jardín de los Poetas
8 Jardín Japonés
9 Monumento de los Españoles
10 Museo Evita
11 Museo Nacional de Arte Decorativo
12 Parque El Rosedal
13 Pasaje Russel
14 Planetario Galileo Galilei
15 Plazoleta Luna de Enfrente
16 Puente Griego
17 Tango Murals

ACTIVITIES

18 Boat hire for Lago de Rosedal
19 Graffiti Mundo

SLEEPING

20 Be Jardin Escondido by Coppola
21 Casasur Bellini
22 Duque Hotel Boutique & Spa
23 Ilum Experience Home
24 Malevo Muraña Hostel
25 Meridiano Hostel Boutique
26 Mine Hotel Boutique
27 Play Hostel Garden
28 Play Hostel SOHO

EATING

29 Arcos Del Rosedal
30 Casa Cavia
31 Cucina Paradiso Senza Glutine
32 Cuervo
33 Don Julio
34 El Preferido de Palermo
35 El Secretito
36 Fogón Asado
37 Gran Dabbang
38 Mishiguene
39 Moshu Treehouse
40 Sacro
41 Surry Hills
42 Varela Varelita

DRINKING & NIGHTLIFE

43 Amores Tintos
see 88 Blest Palermo
44 BOCHA Polo
45 Boticario
46 BrukBar
47 Club 69
48 CoChinChina
49 Crobar
50 Feliza
51 Frank's
52 Gris Gris
53 Harrison
54 Hole
55 J W Bradley
56 La Calle
57 La UAT
58 LPV Las Patriotas Vilardo
59 Pain et Vin
60 Peuteo
61 Post Street Bar
see 59 Rey de Copas
62 Rush
63 Social Wine Bar
64 Soria Bar
65 Tres Monos
66 Uptown
67 Victoria Brown

ENTERTAINMENT

68 Bar de Fondo
69 Bebop
70 Congo Cultural Club
71 El Despelote Tango
72 Hipódromo Argentino de Palermo
73 La Viruta
74 Makena Cantina Club
75 Thelonious Club
76 Virasoro

SHOPPING

77 Alcorta Shopping
78 Bolazo
79 Borges 1975
80 Dain Usina Cultural
81 Elementos Argentinos
82 Eterna Cadencia
83 Feria Palermo Viejo
84 Feria Plaza Serrano
85 Galería Mar Dulce
86 Las Pepas
87 Libros del Pasaje
88 NIMES
89 Sommelier en Bicicleta

PALERMO: SO MANY NAMES, SO LITTLE TIME

You name it, there's a sub-neighborhood of Palermo in every corner of the barrio – from **Palermo Zoologico** (surrounding the former zoo) to **Palermo Botánico** (surrounding the botanic gardens) and **Palermo Norte** (bordering Parque Las Heras). Perhaps the most fascinating micro-'hood is **Villa Freud**, sandwiched between Scalabrini Ortiz and Av Coronel Diaz beneath Alto Palermo. It's so called for the unusually high concentration of psychologist offices in the area (with a significant proportion of practitioners of the Freud and Lacan variants of psychoanalysis). A nation in love with therapy, Argentina has the most psychologists per capita in the world.

BRESTER IRINA/SHUTTERSTOCK

Jardín Japonés

Japanese Horticultural Gem

Stroll in the Jardín Japonés

First opened in 1967, the **Jardín Japonés** *(jardinjapones.org.ar; 10am-7pm; entrance fee but children under 12 are free)* was designed and constructed by the Japanese community in Buenos Aires as a tribute to the first visit of the then Crown Prince Akihito and Princess Michiko to Argentina. It is a well-maintained and peaceful spot where you can wander the gardens and charming bridges that span ponds full of koi and pose in front of the Shinto-style gate.

July sees the cherry blossoms in full force, September is when the azaleas put on a bright show, vibrant water lilies cover the ponds in January, and brilliant yellow ginkgo leaves are scattered throughout in April.

It's a small garden – an easy stroll in 30 minutes – but it is a tranquil gem in the city so take your time to soak it

EATING IN PALERMO VIEJO: OUR PICKS

Varela Varelita: Bohemian cultural hang that's been going strong for 70 years; mingle with unpretentious locals who come for the coffee, *empanadas* and chat. *7am-2am Mon-Sat* $

El Secretito: Sidle up with Racing football fans in this rustic closed-door neighborhood *parrilla*; bookings essential. *noon-3pm, 7:30pm-11pm Tue-Sat* $$

El Preferido de Palermo: Charming Palermo staple takes tradition and gives it a modern twist; bookings essential for this must-visit bistro *11:30am-4pm, 7pm-1am* $$

Gran Dabbang: Very popular tiny LatAm-Indian-Thai-Arab fusion joint; no reservations so queue with the hoards. *7:30pm-midnight Mon-Sat* $$

up. Also great for kids who will look in awe at the fish and flowers.

If you time your visit with lunch, there is a casual cafe in the grounds with the usual fare or treat yourself to fresh sushi and sashimi at the visitors center and take a spot on the veranda if the weather is nice. Don't miss the first-floor balcony for a stunning view across the manicured gardens. The visitors center also hosts origami, bonsai, manga, martial arts and taiko (Japanese drumming) workshops and occasional cultural exhibitions.

All About Eva Perón

Deep dive into Evita's life

Housed in the Eva Perón Foundation's former shelter for women and children, **Museo Evita** *(museoevita.org.ar; 11am-7pm Tue-Sun)* is a celebratory museum, well set-up for English-speaking tourists. An audio guide read by one of the performers from Andrew Lloyd Webber's musical, *Evita*, is easily downloaded via their wi-fi (take headphones) and failing that the wall descriptions are also in English. A small space, it takes about 45 minutes to tour the exhibition and building.

The tour chronicles María Eva Duarte's (later known as Eva Perón) short life from her humble provincial beginnings to her showbiz career and of course, her famed meeting and love affair with Juan Domingo Perón (they met at Buenos Aires' art deco stadium, Luna Park and later married in La Iglesia de San Francisco in La Plata) to her death in 1952. Love her or hate her (she is still very much a divisive figure in Argentina) she fought for women's suffrage, which led to the women's vote in 1951, workers' rights across the country and children's education and wellbeing. There's plenty of memorabilia on show including superb couture from her wardrobe and archival footage, including that of her funeral procession when Argentina ran out of flowers.

If you're hungry, there's a leafy patio cafe on the grounds and a gift store for those wanting a souvenir.

Green Escape

Visit the botanic gardens designed by Carlos Thay

At the top of Palermo Viejo, alongside Plaza Italia, you'll find the **Jardín Botánico Carlos Thays** *(@buenosairesjardin; free; 8am-6pm Mon-Fri; 9:30am-6pm Sat & Sun)* a green

BEST SHOPPING IN PALERMO

Galería Mar Dulce: Art gallery specializing in small works by local artists like María Luque and Consuelo Vidal.

NIMES: Sumptuous locally-made vegetable tanned leather bags and belts with minimalist design (p169).

Galería Patio del Liceo: This sprawling hidden gem off Av Santa Fe is home to dozens of specialty shops, artist and designer studios; best to visit in the late afternoons.

Elementos Argentinos: This store has been in the business of Argentine wool rugs for over 18 years; pick up a beauty to take home.

MALBA: The museum's (p168) shop has a well-curated selection of Latin American-designed objects, art books and posters.

Cucina Paradiso Senza Glutine: Gluten-free pasta from top Italian chef Donato de Santis; don't miss el Nino Bergese, a mega spinach-and-ricotta ravioli topped with truffle. *9am-midnight* $$

Sacro: Next-level gourmet vegan in a hip setting in Palermo Soho; incredible flavours abound like the eggplant starter. *noon-midnight Tue-Sun* $$$

Don Julio: Need we say more? The world's only grill with a Michelin star. Top tip: message direct via WhatsApp for more booking options. *11:30am-4pm & 7:30pm-1am* $$$

Fogón Asado: An incredible meat-eating experience with limited seating around the chef's counter. Booking essential, no lunch service Sun & Mon. *12:30pm-3.30pm, 7:30pm-10:30pm* $$$

SHOPPING TOURS

Like most things in BA, while you'll see many shops as you pound the pavement, many more are hidden away as *puertas cerradas* (closed door) stores and showrooms. It is not a concept well-suited to Western ideas of capitalism but here, shops are secreted away on top floors, in basements or in designer's homes. Some are more visible – like the hip art and design store Casa Social (p152), whose showroom is the front space of a Colegiales home – while others need a super sleuth to uncover. Try **Vanessa Bell** *(@cremedelacremeba)* or **Mani Boucher** *(@shophopba)* for curated shopping tours that deep dive into hidden BA.

refuge for Palermo residents and visitors alike with plenty of peaceful pockets to connect with nature or simply sit and chat with friends. Designed by renowned landscape architect Carlos Thays (he was responsible for many of BA's public green spaces) in 1898, there are thousands of botanical species on view including a garden devoted to yerba, the plant used to create Argentina's ubiquitous tea-like brew *mate*. There are plenty of sculptures positioned throughout the gardens. If visiting on the weekend, be sure to visit the **Invernáculo** *(4-5pm Sat & Sun)* a stunning late 19th-century art nouveau greenhouse and the **butterfly garden** *(noon-1pm Sun)*. Check their Instagram for upcoming events and workshops.

DRINKING IN PALERMO VIEJO: OUR PICKS

Amores Tintos: Wines by the glass at this fun Palermo spot with great service; choose from more than 23 wines on tap. *12:30pm-late Tue-Sun*

Post Street Bar: Fun grungy low-fi institution where the walls are chock full of graffiti. *6pm-1am Sun-Thu, to 2.30am Fri & Sat*

BrukBar: Late-night bartender's hang with a local but friendly vibe; there's a trivia quiz on Thursdays and the kitchen is open until 3am. *8pm-4.30am*

Pain et Vin: Intimate wine bar run by a couple who also host very knowledgeable wine tastings; menu pairings are exquisite. *4-11:30pm Wed-Sun*

MARIANO GASPAR/SHUTTERSTOCK

Ecoparque

Kids' Play

Park in a former zoo

Wander out the Av Gral Las Heras exit of Jardín Botánico Carlos Thays and enter the former Buenos Aires Zoo, rebranded as the **Ecoparque** *(@ecoparqueba; free; 11am-6pm Tue-Sun)*, an environmental education space. The sprawling 18-hectare grounds are a great place for kids to run off some energy (although there is little shade in summer) with the added bonus of a few exotic and native animal sightings like elephants, an Andean condor, turtles and nutrias (some animals were deemed too old to move when the 140-year-old zoo closed in 2016). Scattered throughout are the original Victorian-era

BEST BOOKSTORES IN PALERMO

Libros del Pasaje: A stalwart of Calle Thames; excellently curated bookstore with patio cafe opposite a colorful *pasaje* (alleyway) filled with murals.

Borges 1975: Dreamy bookstore with an excellent cafe and Backroom, a tiny bar that hosts live music almost every night.

Dain Usina Cultural: Excellent bookstore with a huge variety of cultural events and talks and a great terrace spot to sit.

Eterna Cadencia: Atmospheric timber-lined bookstore with a huge chandelier, a packed events schedule and a cozy bar.

MALBA: The museum (p168) gift store has a well-curated selection of art books including children's titles by local and LatAm illustrators.

Rey de Copas: Cavernous bar filled with ancient antiquities and reasonably-priced cocktails; try to nab a spot on the roof top. *8pm-2am, to 3am Fri & Sat*

Gris Gris: Palermo Hollywood vinyl listening bar; moody lighting with great drinks and music; booking essential. *7pm-1am Sun, Tue & Wed, 8pm-2:30am Thu-Sat*

Soria Bar: Fun bar with a boho vibe; grab some friends and settle in for cocktails and live music; no reservations. *7.30pm-late Tue-Sun*

Blest Palermo: For a classic craft beer hang, try Blest's beer all the way from Bariloche. Relaxed atmosphere in a former home. *5pm-late Mon-Fri, from noon Sat & Sun*

TRAVELING SOLO?

Where to meet people:

Mundo Lingo *(mundolingo.org)* is an international meet-up and a great spot to make friends and exchange language.

Book a **puerta cerrada** dinner; tables are usually shared and you'll be old friends by the end of the night.

Book into a specialty workshop like the food photography classes hosted by Argentine photographer, **Magali Polverino** *(magali polverino.com)*.

Head out on a bike tour with **Biker Street** *(biker-street.com)*; the guides are great fun and there's plenty of opportunity to socialize while cycling.

Learn how to cook an *asado* with **The Asado Experience** *(theasadoexperience.com)*; an all-female team who make *asado* intimate and welcoming.

pavilions that housed the animals, many in Moorish, Indian, Chinese and Greek/Roman styles. You'll also spot works by Argentine sculptress Lola Mora. Kids will love the playground and antique carousel by the Av del Libertador entrance.

One of BA's Finest Museums

Latin American Art at MALBA

MALBA *(malba.org.ar; 11am-8pm Wed, noon-8pm Thu-Mon)*, standing for Museo de Arte Latinoamericano de Buenos Aires, is home to the private art collection of Eduardo F Costantini, an Argentine property developer, arts patron and philanthropist who has gathered more than 400 Latin American works from the 20th century. For the visitor, it is a fascinating collection that also tells the story of local artists' responses to political and social unrest in Latin America over the last century. Must-see works include Argentine artist Antonio Berni's *Manifestación* (1934); Frida Kahlo's *Self-Portrait with Monkey and Parrot* (1942) – purchased by Constantini for US$3.2 million; Diego Rivera's *Portrait of Ramón Gómez de la Serna* (1915); and Brazilian artist Tarsila do Amaral's *Abaporú* (1928). World-class temporary exhibitions are shown across several galleries, and there's a cinema that shows an eclectic range of art-house films. Check the MALBA website for their film schedule, guided tour times, events and audio guides, and to pre-purchase your entrance ticket. Tickets are half-price on Wednesdays.

A haven on hot days, the modern limestone building with soaring ceilings is an easy place to while away an afternoon. For refuelling, Ninina MALBA has a great selection of casual eats – sit inside or on the deck overlooking the adjoining park.

Museum in a Beaux Arts Mansion

Impressive collection of decorative arts

The **Museo Nacional de Arte Decorativo** *(museoarte decorativo.cultura.gob.ar; free; 1-7pm Wed-Sun)* is testimony to the lifestyle of Argentina's upper classes at the start of the 20th century. It's housed in the stunning neoclassical Residencia Errázuriz Alvear, once the home of Chilean aristocrat Matías Errázuriz Ortúzar and his wife, Josefina de Alvear, and said to have been inspired by the Palace of Versailles. The mansion and part of the Errázuriz Alvear collection were donated to the state after Josefina's death in 1936 and the

DRINKING IN PALERMO: BEST COFFEE

Surry Hills: Top coffee at this pioneering Australian-style cafe; superb sourdough, mushroom melts and of course, amazing avo toast. *8:30am-8pm* $

Cuervo: Top coffee spot in Palermo South with sweet treats, ice-cream. Also has a branch in Chacarita. *8am-8pm Tue-Sun* $

Libros del Pasaje (p167): Bookstore cafe with great coffee, *medialunas*, soups and sandwiches surrounded by books. *10am-8pm Mon-Sat, 2-8pm Sun* $

Moshu Treehouse: Atmospheric cafe with an architecturally-designed treehouse vibe, good coffee and decadent cheese cakes. *8am-9pm* $

Museo Nacional de Arte Decorativo

museum opened one year later. Over the decades, further objects have been added, creating an impressive collection. Some of the outstanding pieces are the 16th century European miniatures and tapestries and the bronze clock gifted to King Louis XVI and Queen Marie Antoinette on their wedding day. Art heavyweights include works by El Greco, Manet and Rodin amongst many others.

Like many BA museums, it opens late in the day but, if you arrive early, the cafe in the gardens by the entrance is open from 10am. Daily guided tours in English start at 1:30pm.

STREET ART HIGHLIGHTS

Pasaje Russel: Wander this colorful alleyway from Thames to Gurruchaga for lots of wonderful wall works.

Plazoleta Luna de Enfrente: This little plaza is surrounded by soaring murals.

Post Street Bar: Pop into this stalwart bar (p166) to check out the walls, which are chock full of graffiti.

Tango Murals: Check out Alfredo Segatori's tango murals painted under the overpass on the way to the bars of Arcos del Rosedal or the Parque 3 de Febrero (p170).

Graffiti Mundo: To get some guidance, contact long-standing walking tour company @graffitimundo for wonderful street art tours around BA.

Shop Until You Drop

Boutiques and weekend markets

It's not the cheapest spot to shop but browsing Palermo's retail scene is certainly a whole heap of fun. Note most shops don't tend to open until lunchtime.

You'll find plenty of boutiques along Calle Gurruchaga and the surrounding blocks with favorites like Rapsodia, Complot, **NIMES** and **Las Pepas**. At the upscale mall **Alcorta**

EATING IN PALERMO CHICO: OUR PICKS

Casa Paradiso: On the third floor of Alcorta Mall, a smorgasbord of Italian treats from pizza to pasta and ice-creams; open-air terrace with great views to the river. *10am-midnight* $

Arcos del Rosedal: A whole host of eating spots built into the cavernous arches of the train tracks in Tres de Febrero park; plenty of outdoor seating. *noon-late* $$

Casa Cavia: Local favorite; classy cocktails and fine dining in an elegant historic building. *10am-midnight Tue-Sat, 10am-7pm Sun & Mon* $$

Mishiguene: Modern spin on Jewish immigrant dishes in an atmospheric and moody dining room; Shabbat blessings and live music on Fridays. *7pm-midnight* $$$

BEST LIVE MUSIC VENUES IN PALERMO

Thelonious Club: Iconic moody jazz spot; book tickets ahead online.

Bar de Fondo: Blues, *boleros*, jazz and folk with a corner restaurant out the front.

Makena Cantina Club: Palermo Hollywood club packed with weekly shows from DJ sets to rock and hip hop.

Bebop: Great jazz, great wine and open every night of the week.

Congo Cultural Club: Indie music in a fun outdoor garden in Palermo Soho.

Virasoro: Intimate venue for jazz in this art deco beauty that belonged to an architect.

Shopping all the popular Argentine women's clothing shops are represented. Head to **Bolazo** for a uniquely Argentine spin on women's gaucho wear. Taste and buy local wines at **Sommelier en Bicicleta** where the staff are knowledgeable, friendly and speak English. For slighter cheaper prices, many Argentine brands have outlet stores on Calle Gurruchaga, south of Castillo.

Be sure to check out both **Feria Plaza Serrano** *(@feria honduras_plazaserrano; 10am-8pm Sat & Sun)*, also known as Feria Honduras; and **Feria Palermo Viejo** *(@feriapalermo viejo; 10am-7pm Sat & Sun)*, held in Plaza Armenia. Both markets are filled with works by local artists and designers although the Plaza Armenia market has a primary focus on handmade objects. Surrounded by bars and restaurants with street-side seating, do a spot of shopping and then soak up the atmosphere while watching the world pass by.

Giddy up!

Palermo's home of horse racing and polo

If you've got a hankering to see some horse racing while in BA, look no further than the **Hipódromo Argentino de Palermo** *(palermo.com.ar; free)* where races are held every Monday. It's nestled between the **Parque El Rosedal** (rose garden) and the **Lago de Regatas** (both part of Parque 3 de Febrero, commonly known as the Bosques de Palermo, the largest green space in BA). Even if you're not a fan, a few hours in the glamorous grandstand makes for a fun afternoon. If you want to take a punt, bring your pesos. The course's biggest event is the Gran Premio Nacional held in November. It is one of the oldest and most influential races in Latin American racing and has been running since 1884.

The skill of the players, the power of the horses, the glamor and tradition of the game; polo has a special place in Argentina, and there's no better place than Buenos Aires to experience this incredible sport. Just across the road from the racetrack you'll find the **Campo Argentino de Polo**. Known in polo circles as the 'cathedral of polo', this polo field plays host to the Campeonato Argentino Abierto de Polo (November and December), the most prestigious international interclub tournament in the world, held here since 1928. Early season matches are often free but for later games purchase tickets via Ticketek.

DRINKING IN PALERMO VIEJO: BEST SPEAKEASIES

La Calle: A fun spot that simulates the street; it's hidden behind pizzeria La Guitarrita. *8pm-2am Sun-Wed, to 4am Thu-Sat*

The Hole: Inspired by the infamous Alcatraz prison, dine in cells and order drinks from inmates. *8pm-2:30am Mon-Thu, to 4am Fri & Sat*

Boticario: Located in an old pharmacy, this bar runs with a medical theme. *8pm-2am Sun, Wed & Thu, 9pm-3am Fri & Sat*

J W Bradley: All aboard the Orient Express, a train-themed time capsule speakeasy. *8pm-2am Wed & Thu, to 4am Fri & Sat*

TOUR THE PARQUE 3 DE FEBRERO

Explore this sprawling park, which includes a rose garden and lakes, on foot or by bicycle.

START	END	LENGTH
Monumento de los Españoles	BOCHA Polo	2.5km; 2-3 hours

Start beside the soaring 1 **Monumento de los Españoles** that stands in the center of the roundabout. Walk alongside the park and then enter the grounds of the otherworldly 2 **Planetario Galileo Galilei**, an iconic building that offers fascinating exhibits on astronomy.

From here, make your way across the charming 3 **Puente Griego** (Greek Bridge), a picturesque arched span that provides great views of the surrounding landscape, to the beautiful rose garden 4 **Parque El Rosedal**.

Rent a paddleboat to sail the 5 **Lago de Rosedal**, then head to the tranquil 6 **Jardín de los Poetas**, lined with the busts of famous poets including Shakespeare, Borges and Lorca and perfect for a pause.

For a bite to eat or an afternoon drink head to the 7 **Arcos del Rosedal** (p169) where there are a multitude of bars and restaurants set into the arches of the aboveground railway tracks. Alternatively, head across the road to the Campo Argentino de Polo and find a spot in 8 **BOCHA Polo** (p173), a gastro area nestled between the polo fields.

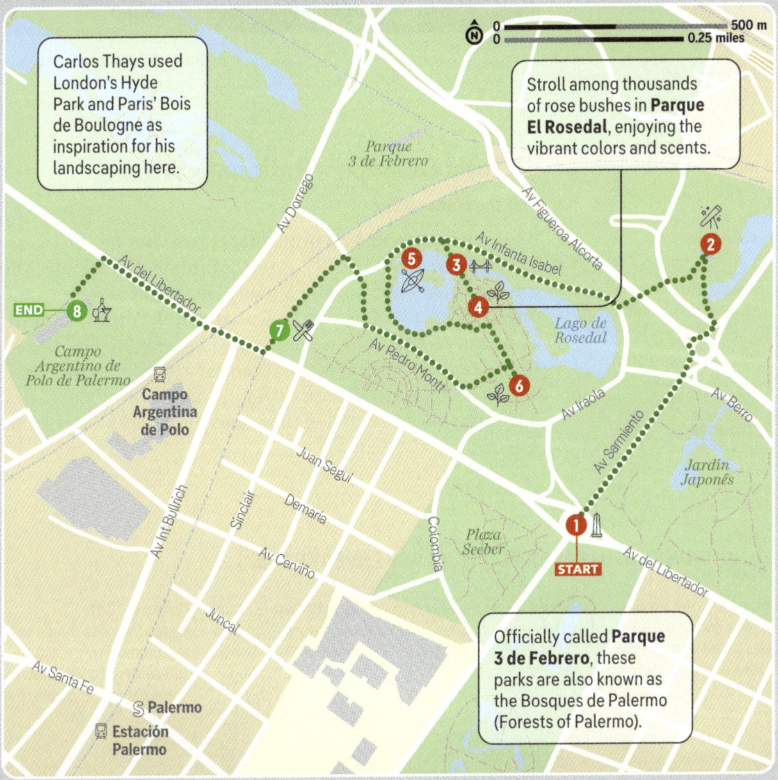

Carlos Thays used London's Hyde Park and Paris' Bois de Boulogne as inspiration for his landscaping here.

Stroll among thousands of rose bushes in **Parque El Rosedal**, enjoying the vibrant colors and scents.

Officially called **Parque 3 de Febrero**, these parks are also known as the Bosques de Palermo (Forests of Palermo).

0 500 m
0 0.25 miles
Parque 3 de Febrero
Av Dorrego
Av Figueroa Alcorta
Av Infanta Isabel
Av del Libertador
END
Campo Argentino de Polo de Palermo
Campo Argentina de Polo
Av Pedro Montt
Lago de Rosedal
Av Iraola
Av Sarmiento
Av Berro
Jardín Japonés
Juan Seguí
Demaría
Sinclair
Av Int Bullrich
Av Cerviño
Colombia
Plaza Seeber
START
Av del Libertador
Juncal
Av Santa Fe
Palermo
Estación Palermo

BEST LGBTIQ+ SPOTS IN PALERMO

Club 69: On Niceto Vega on the border of Palermo/Villa Crespo. Saturday nights.

Rheo: Regular gay dance party held at **Crobar** under the train tracks in Parque 3 de Febrero. Check @rheoba for upcoming events.

Rush: On Av Juan Bautista Justo in Palermo Hollywood. Saturdays.

Peuteo: Gay bar with drag shows in Palermo Soho. Wednesday to Sunday.

El Despelote Tango: Learn a few steps before taking part (or watching) the *milonga*. Check @eldespelotetango for up-to-date schedules.

Feliza: LGTBIQ+ social and cultural club has a schedule packed with DJs, live music and drag shows, karaoke, talks and films. Wednesday to Sundays.

ELI MEDEIROS/SHUTTERSTOCK

Parque El Rosedal (p170)

Victoria Ocampo's Rationalist Home

And the birth of *Sur*

While the titans of Argentine literature – Borges, Cortázar, Arlt, Sabato and Casares – often dominate discussions, the visionary contributions of Victoria Ocampo deserve equal recognition. The **Casa de la Cultura del Fondo Nacional de las Artes** *(argentina.gob.ar/cultura/fna/casa; free; 11am-7pm Mon-Fri)* was the legendary intellectual's home. At this heady cultural base Ocampo and her contemporaries, including Borges, founded the influential literary magazine,

DRINKING IN PALERMO VIEJO: BEST SPEAKEASIES

Frank's: Enter via a phone booth; decipher password from cryptic clues posted on social media. *8pm-2am Wed & Thu. 8pm-3am Fri & Sat*

Harrison: Out the back of Nicky New York Sushi lies this 1920s Prohibition-era bar with fine cocktails. *8pm-1am Mon-Wed, 8pm-2am Thu-Sat*

Victoria Brown: Elegant cafe by day, by night this is a steampunk-style bar accessed via a moving wall. *8pm-2am Tue-Thu, 8pm-4am Fri & Sat*

Uptown: 200% commitment to theme at this immersive speakeasy where New York's subway comes alive. *8pm-2am Sun-Thu, 8pm-4am Fri & Sat*

Sur – a cornerstone of the avant-garde bringing international writers to the country and promoting a generation of young Argentines.

Ocampo was not one to take no for an answer. She convinced architect Alejandro Bustillo to design the building Bustillo, who went on to design many of Argentina's public buildings and is considered the founder of Argentina's classical style (he is buried in Recoleta Cemetery, p140), agreed under duress – he never signed the work as his. Scandalous amongst its architectural neighbors (who were very much in their belle epoque era), this minimal white cube (not to mention the several cacti in the front garden) did not fit with the aspirations of the area. This doesn't appear to be the type of thing that fazed Ocampo.

In the 1940s, Ocampo moved to **Villa Ocampo** *(asociacion amigosdevillaocampo.org.ar)*, an eclectic-style mansion built in 1891 for her father Manuel Ocampo in San Isidro, on the outskirts of Buenos Aires. Today, this villa operates as a UNESCO-run museum, inviting visitors to delve more deeply into Ocampo's life and explore the rich legacy she left behind.

Tango in Palermo

Join the dance at La Viruta

For those wishing to get out on the dance floor and give tango a try, **La Viruta** *(@lavirutatangoclub)* is one of the city's most popular dance spots, going strong for 30 years and offering activities throughout the week. Located in a basement and known for its democratic approach to Buenos Aires' emblematic spectacle, it can get very busy with the less experienced – if you're an expert, aim for the early hours of the morning. La Viruta also has dance classes for a variety of different styles including rock and salsa and often has live music.

BAR-HOPPING IN PALERMO

Porteño **Lupe Domínguez**, who works in digital marketing, shares some of her favorite Palermo bars. *@sharingpiecesofme*

Tres Monos: The service is always wonderful, and I love the punk aesthetic. They use local produce for their innovative cocktails, have a community initiative where they train and employ people from Barrio Mugica, and have been named Latin America's best bar!

La UAT: This 1980s inspired drinking and dancing spot is hidden behind a restaurant. It's a lot of fun and they have great cocktails.

CoChinChina: This is Inés de los Santo's sublime east-meets-west bar. There's dancing, DJs, and heavenly cocktails. The space was designed by Eme Carranza, a well-known BA designer.

DRINKING IN PALERMO CHICO: OUR PICKS

Arcos del Rosedal (p169): A great drinking spot, ideal for an afternoon bevvy or late-night partying; beneath the train tracks in the Bosques de Palermo. *hours vary*

LPV Las Patriotas Vilardo: Head upstairs at this local favourite with live music (there's also a piano), great wine, tapas and an innovative cocktail list. *7pm-1am Tue-Thu, 8pm-2am Fri & Sat*

BOCHA Polo: Grab a drink at one of the many spots in the precinct nestled between the fields in the Campo Argentino de Polo. *hours vary*

Social Wine Bar: Intimate bar with a great natural wine list and delicious morsels like *bondiola* tacos. *7pm-2am Tue-Sat*

Researched by
Rachel Tolosa Paz

SOUTH OF PALERMO

EXPLORE THE EVERYDAY NEIGHBORHOODS OF BA

Lacking in top tourist sites, these areas continue to remain under the radar but they'll reward you with more authentic experiences of the city.

These barrios south of Palermo all have a flavour of their own but in general, they are more residential neighborhoods that provide visitors with a taste of everyday life for *porteños* (Buenos Aires residents). Chacarita is home to a sprawling cemetery filled with some of BA's most legendary musicians and a growing smorgasbord of hip eateries, cool bars and unique boutiques. Villa Crespo has been on the map for decades for its stylish scene, but it has managed to keep its *tranqui* (relaxed) vibe of shops and bars nestled among mechanic workshops. Almagro is home to bohemian tango spots and immigrant cuisine while Caballito is the rising star, a peaceful barrio with plenty of foodie spots popping up.

TOP TIP

Villa Crespo and Almagro are great options for accomodations that are cheaper than nearby Palermo but with easy access to the sights.

NATALIA SO/GETTY IMAGES

Pasaje Carlos Gardel, Abasto

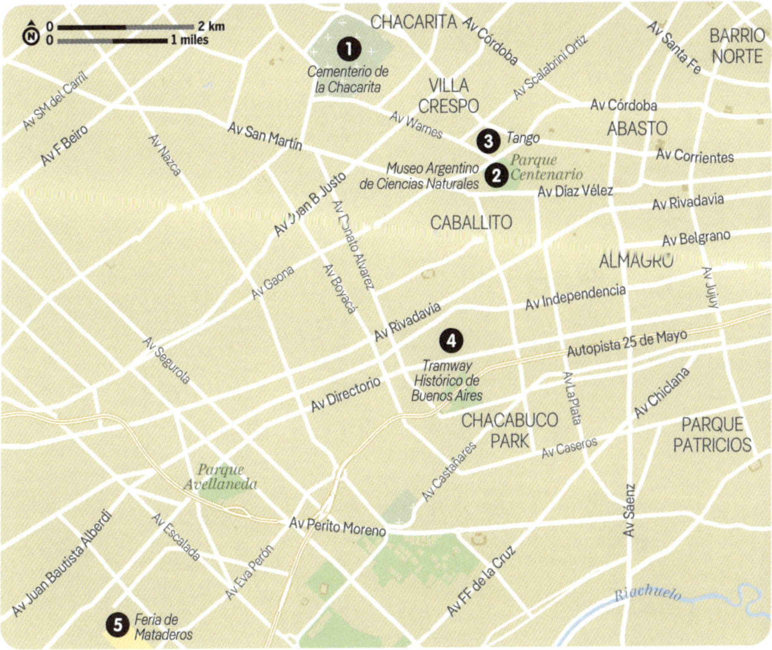

Highlights

❶ Cementerio de la Chacarita

Wander the cemetery and pay homage to tango legends like Carlos Gardel and Goyeneche. **p178**

❷ Museo Argentino de Ciencias Naturales

Kids will love the mechanical dinosaurs in this sprawling natural history museum. **p179**

BJANKA KADIC/ALAMY

❸ Tango

Nestle in with dancers, musicians and eccentric crowds in these historic tango bars of Almagro and Villa Crespo. **p180**

❹ Tramway Histórico de Buenos Aires

Ride this antique tram on weekends when it takes to the tracks to do a 20-minute loop back in time. **p180**

▲ ❺ Feria de Mataderos

Spend a Sunday soaking up Argentine folk culture and shopping for leather and hand-crafted knives. **p184**

Getting Around

Bus

From Plaza de Mayo take bus 140 to Villa Crespo and Almagro, bus 132 to Caballito; Bus 39 services Chacarita.

Subte

Líneas A, B and E service these neighborhoods.

Walking

It's safe to walk in these areas but be aware that sights are fairly spread out.

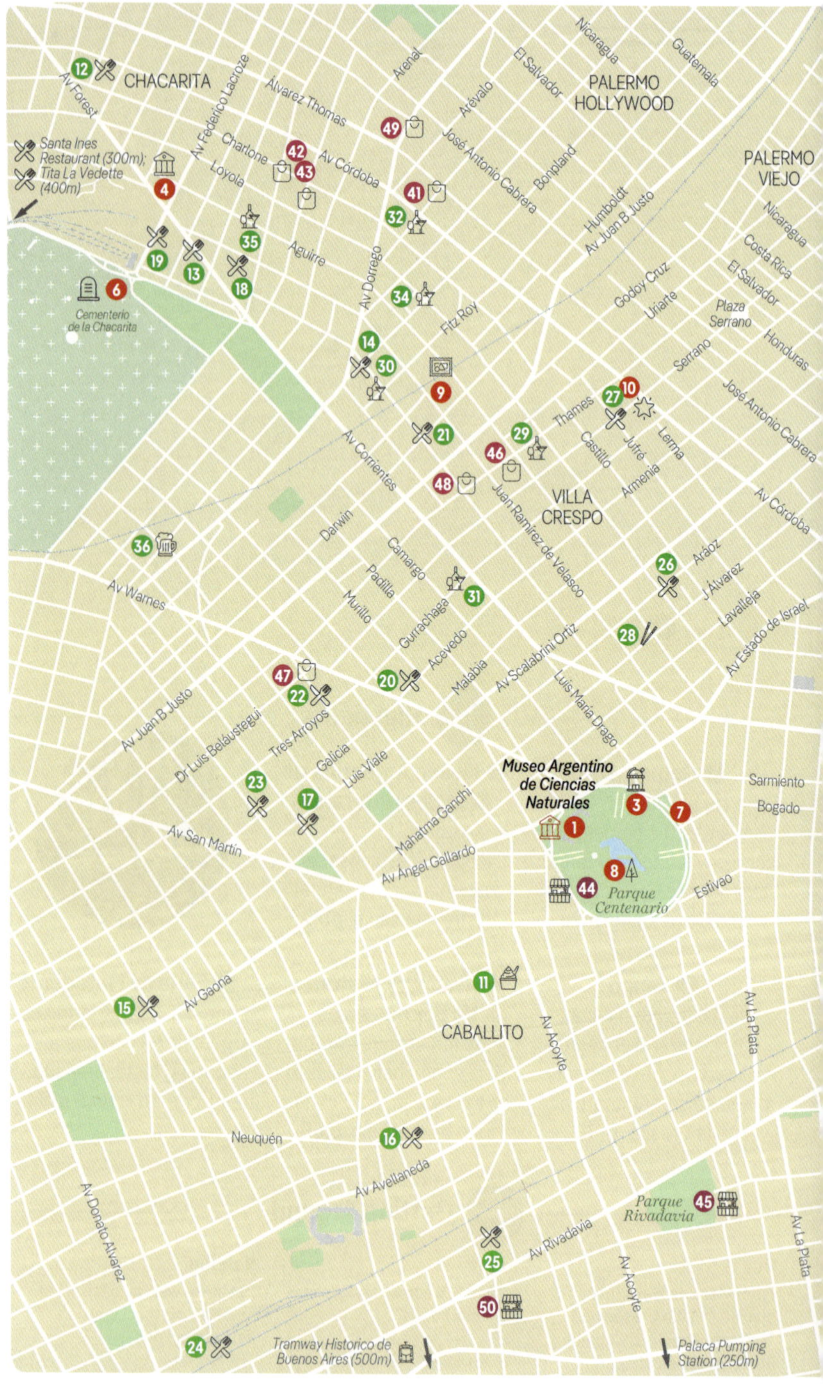
CHACARITA
PALERMO HOLLYWOOD
PALERMO VIEJO
VILLA CRESPO
CABALLITO
Santa Ines Restaurant (300m); Tita La Vedette (400m)
Cementerio de la Chacarita
Museo Argentino de Ciencias Naturales
Parque Centenario
Parque Rivadavia
Plaza Serrano
Tramway Historico de Buenos Aires (500m)
Palaca Pumping Station (250m)
Av Forest
Av Federico Lacroze
Álvarez Thomas
Charlone
Loyola
Av Córdoba
Aguirre
Arenal
Arévalo
El Salvador
Nicaragua
Guatemala
José Antonio Cabrera
Bonpland
Humboldt
Av Juan B Justo
Av Dorrego
Fitz Roy
Godoy Cruz
Uriarte
Serrano
Costa Rica
Honduras
Thames
Castillo
Jufré
Lerma
Armenia
Av Corrientes
Juan Ramírez de Velasco
Darwin
Camargo
Padilla
Murillo
Gurruchaga
Acevedo
Malabia
Av Scalabrini Ortiz
Aráoz
J Álvarez
Lavalleja
Av Estado de Israel
Av Warnes
Dr Luis Beláustegui
Tres Arroyos
Galicia
Luis Viale
Luis María Drago
Mahatma Gandhi
Av Ángel Gallardo
Av San Martín
Sarmiento
Bogado
Estivao
Av Gaona
Av Acoyte
Av La Plata
Neuquén
Av Avellaneda
Av Rivadavia
Av Donato Álvarez

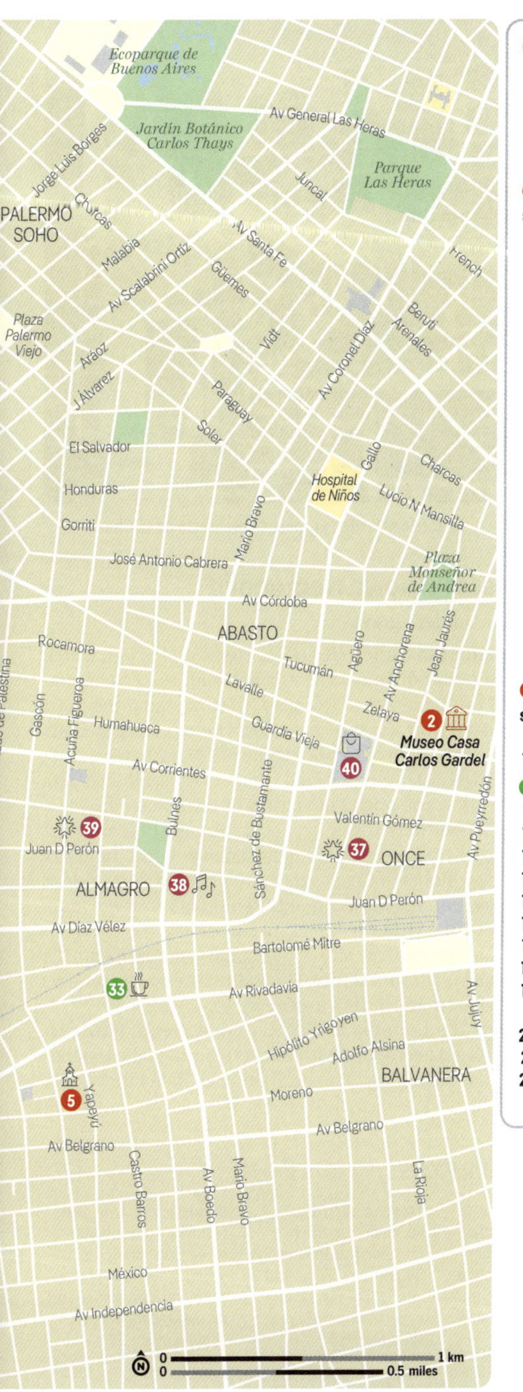

HIGHLIGHTS

1 Museo Argentino de Ciencias Naturales
2 Museo Casa Carlos Gardel

SIGHTS

see 1 Anfiteatro del Parque Centenario
3 Asociación Argentina Amigos de la Astronomía
4 Bar Palacio / Museo Fotográfico Simik
5 Basílica María Auxiliadora y San Carlos
6 Cementerio de la Chacarita
7 Hospital Naval
8 Parque Centenario
9 Ruth Benzacar Galleria de Arte

ACTIVITIES

see 40 Museo de los Niños
10 Villa Malcolm

EATING

11 1952 Helados
12 Ácido
13 Albamonte
14 Anchoíta
15 Barragán Café
16 CENTRO
17 Don Zoilo
18 Donnet
19 El Imperio de la Pizza
20 Fico
21 Gordo Chanta
22 Isla Flotante Comidas
23 Madre Rojas
24 Patio de los Lecheros
25 ROMA
26 Sampa
27 Sarkis
28 Tintorería Yafuso

DRINKING & NIGHTLIFE

29 878
30 Anchoíta Cava
see 21 Barcito Brutalista
31 Café San Bernardo
32 La Fuerza
33 Las Violetas
34 Naranjo Bar
35 SIFÓN Sodería
36 Strange 2

ENTERTAINMENT

37 Ciudad Cultural Konex
38 El Boliche de Roberto
39 La Catedral

SHOPPING

40 Abasto Shopping
41 Abrazando-cuentos
42 Facón
43 Falena
44 Feria Artesanal del Parque Centenario
45 Feria Parque Rivadavia
46 Fetiche Libros
47 Librería Punc
48 Mandrágora Libros y Cultura
49 Mercado de las Pulgas
50 Mercado del Progreso

HANDS OFF!

Former president Juan Domingo Perón (1895–1974) was also buried at Cementerio de la Chacarita until 2006 when his remains were moved to his former home in San Vicente. In 1987, his tomb there was raided and brutally, his hands were amputated with an electric saw.

On a side note, the Argentine revolutionary Che Guevara also had his hands severed from his body after his execution in Bolivia in 1967, for purposes of identification. After fingerprints were taken, the hands disappeared, never to be found again.

MARCELO TADVALD/SHUTTERSTOCK

Carlos Gardel's grave, Cementerio de la Chacarita

BA's Lesser-Known Necropolis

Visit Carlos Gardel's grave

Cementerio de la Chacarita *(free; 8am-5pm)* is well worth a couple of hours of your time – it holds all the charm and mystery of the cemetery in Recoleta (p140) without the tourists, spread out over a vast 95 hectares. The cemetery owes its existence to the yellow fever epidemic of 1871, when existing cemeteries were strained beyond capacity (upscale Recoleta refused to allow the burial of victims of the epidemic).

Many of Argentina's music greats are interred here: singer Carlos Gardel (p80); Ángel Villoldo (known as the father of tango); singer Roberto Goyeneche; and Gustavo Cerrati, lead singer of Soda Stereo and icon of the country's *rock nacional* who died in 2014. Other notables include artists Antonio Berni and Benito Quinquela Martín, legendary children's author María Elena Walsh, and Carlos Thays, the landscape architect responsible for many of BA's green spaces.

Don't miss the brutalist and otherworldly **Sexto Panteón**, an underground necropolis with 150,000 burial plots designed by one of Argentina's first female architects, Ítala Fulvia Villa.

EATING IN VILLA CRESPO: OUR PICKS

Isla Flotante Comidas: No-frills 1980s bar cafe with music and great food, try the tortilla sandwich. *6pm-1am Mon-Fri 11am-1am Sat & Sun* $

Gordo Chanta: Top-notch late-night pizza joint with a hidden bar in the basement; try the asparagus and mushroom pizza. *6pm-midnight Thu-Mon* $$

Trescha: With one Michelin star; this is fine dining as theater. Sumptuous dishes and interior details, savor every moment. *7-11pm Wed-Sat* $$$

Sarkis: Iconic Armenian restaurant that's been serving up classics for years; arrive early and try the *manti* (dumplings) and moussaka. *noon-3pm, 7pm-midnight* $$

Park at the City's Heart

Explore Parque Centenario

Almost the geographical center of Buenos Aires, **Parque Centenario** is a circular park that revolves around a lake with an artificial island. There's plenty of shade, a skate park and the observatory **Asociación Argentina Amigos de la Astronomía** *(check @asaramas for guided tour schedules and book ahead).*

Also here is **Anfiteatro del Parque Centenario** *(@elanfi.ba),* one of the most important amphitheaters in the city, hosting a wide variety of shows, including dance, live orchestras and all manner of music, which are mostly free and top quality; check their Instagram for what's on.

The park is at its best on weekends when **Feria Artesanal del Parque Centenario** (*11am-7pm Sat & Sun*) is in full force. It might look a little rough around the edges but some of the best secondhand clothing and objects can be found here if you've got the time for a good rummage. Street-side, you'll also find a whole strip of secondhand bookstands where you'll also need some hours up your sleeve to uncover little gems.

Across the road be sure to check out the Clorindo Testa-designed **Hospital Naval**, built to look like a ship with circular portholes.

A Date With Dinosaurs

Caballito's Natural History Museum

Housed in a historic building with marble staircases, charming dioramas and painted mural walls. **Museo Argentino de Ciencias Naturales** *(macnconicet.gob.ar; 2-7pm)* is a great outing for an hour or two. Kids will love the surprisingly lifelike mechanical dinosaurs and halls of dino bones and prehistoric animals discovered mostly in Buenos Aires (when the city excavated beneath Av Corrientes for the Linea B subway tunnel) and other provinces of Argentina. The small spider exhibition complete with examples of their intricate webs is another hit.

The museum also has fascinating exhibits (in Spanish) detailing Argentina's scientific achievements including a section on the Abuelas de la Plaza de Mayo (p157). This human rights organization pioneered the use of a DNA bank to assist in finding children who were stolen from their 'disappeared' parents during the military dictatorship and illegally adopted.

BEST BOOKSTORES SOUTH OF PALERMO

Fetiche Libros: Superb neighborhood bookstore with weekly talks and workshops, poetry readings and a used book table.

Falena: 'Closed door' bookstore in Chacarita in an architecturally inspiring space; focus on world literature in Spanish and rare art and design books.

Mandrágora Libros y Cultura: Focus on independent publishers, feminist titles and children's books in a charming building.

Abrazandocuentos: In English, it means 'hugging stories'! A divine children's bookstore run by an Italian expat with a full schedule of workshops and activities.

Sampa: A relaxed Villa Crespo spot with a focus on vegan dishes; no bookings, just turn up and sit at the bar around the kitchen. *8pm-midnight Tue-Sat* $$

Fico: Fun twist on the classics where every dish packs a punch; don't miss the doughnut dessert with *dulce de leche* ice cream. *8pm-11:30pm Tue-Sat* $$

Madre Rojas: Wagyu beef specialists, as the owner is a wagyu pioneer in Argentina; great wine pairings and sides. *7pm-12:30am, 12:30pm-4:30pm Sat & Sun* $$$

Tintorería Yafuso: Exquisite Japanese with only 10 seats in the chef's family's former dry-cleaning shop; dinner bookings via phone only, walk-ins at lunch. *noon-3pm & 8pm-midnight Tue-Sat* $$$

MORE ARTS & CULTURE SPOTS SOUTH OF PALERMO

Facón: The most unique selection of Argentine art and handcrafted objects in BA. Stunning handpainted flags, textiles, ceramics and books. A must-visit store.

Ruth Benzacar Galleria de Arte: Pioneering Argentine contemporary art space founded in 1965; now run by third generation. Closed Sundays and Mondays.

Bar Palacio / Museo Fotográfico Simik: Not just a museum with over 2000 cameras on display, it's also a *bar notable* with regular live music.

Punc: Gem of a comic bookstore with a great collection that includes many titles from BA's graphic illustrators.

Caballito's Historic Tram

Travel back in time

For over 100 years, the tram was king in Buenos Aires, but it disappeared, as in many cities, in the 1960s. In the 1980s, a group of tram enthusiasts got together and started to restore trams and offer historic rides around Caballito, a journey you can still do today. **Tramway Histórico de Buenos Aires** *(tranvia.org.ar/thba; free; 4-7pm Sat, 10am-1pm & 4-7pm Sun; hours vary slightly in winter and summer, check website)* offer rides on first-come, first-served system and you'll find the meeting point on the corner of Emilio Mitre and José Bonifacio in Caballito.

Entirely run by volunteers (who entertain the waiting crowds with tram tales) kids will delight in boarding the antique wagons and adults can indulge in a bit of harmless nostalgia. Trips take approximately 20 minutes. Arrive early or bring some snacks/hats for the kids if you have to wait. Afterwards, head to the **Patio de los Lecheros** by the railway line – a meeting spot for milk vendors until the 1960s – today it's filled with food trucks, live music and fun games to keep the kids entertained.

Dance & Sing With Locals

Bohemian tango in Almagro and Villa Crespo

Almagro and Villa Crespo's tango spots tend to be more laidback with a strong sense of community. **El Boliche de Roberto** *(@elbolichederoberto_almagro)* is a locals' favorite – tango musicians nestle in among the eclectic crowd of eccentrics (with the odd tourist or two). Arrive early if you want to nab a table, the audience usually spills out on to the street.

A grungy warehouse space with lashings of character, **La Catédral** *(@lacatedralclub)* is a bit of an institution. It hosts *milongas*, classes, tango shows, live music and parties. Head there in the wee hours of the morning when things get going. Check their Instagram for class schedules and upcoming events, there is no need to book ahead.

Villa Malcolm *(@villamalcolmtango)* is another iconic tango spot (with great neon street signage) located in a charming *club del barrio*, filled with kids playing indoor football. Tango musicians have been playing here since the 1940s and the tango community is tight knit. Check for schedules but Tuesdays are generally the night for classes and free practice.

DRINKING IN VILLA CRESPO: OUR PICKS

Café San Bernardo: *Bar notable* with an art school crowd vibe; filled with pool tables and ping pong including classes. *10am-3:30am Mon-Fri, from 8am Sat, 6pm-2am Sun*

El Limón: With a cracking cocktail list and down-to-earth vibes, at this bar the music is all part of the show. *6pm-1am Mon & Sun, 7pm-2am Tue, 7pm-3am Wed-Sat*

878: Pioneering speakeasy bar hidden behind an unmarked door; still going strong after two decades. *7pm-3am Wed-Sun*

Barcito Brutalista: Tiny hidden bar beneath late-night Villa Crespo pizza joint Gordo Chanta (p178). *8pm-1am Thu-Mon*

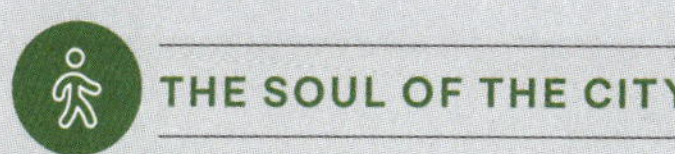

THE SOUL OF THE CITY

Wander – and eat your way – through Villa Crespo, Almagro and Abasto to step deeper into the soul of BA

START	END	LENGTH
Basílica María Auxiliadora y San Carlos	Jean Jaures 737	3.5km; 3-4 hours

Start in the morning at **1** **Basílica María Auxiliadora y San Carlos** (closed Monday mornings and between noon and 4pm daily). Buenos Aires' most beautiful church, it is nothing short of awe-inspiring. Around the corner, peep into **2** **Pasaje San Carlos**, a pedestrian alleyway with homes that date back to 1865.

Stop for a coffee at **3** **Las Violetas** (p185), an historic cafe that will instantly transport you back in time. Walk to **4** **El Boliche de Roberto** and make a mental note to return at night for an authentic experience of tango singers curled around the bar. Stroll through **5** **Plaza Almagro** and head to the **6** **Mercado De Flores De Ba**. The city's main flower market (founded here in 1940 by a coop of Japanese growers) was moved to Barracas in the early 2000s but many vendors remain.

If you're starting to get hungry, grab a quick slice and a fried *empanada* at iconic **7** **Pin Pun**. Stand at the bar at the front at this old school *porteño* pizzeria. Alternatively, wander a bit further into Abasto to **8** **El Banderin**, a *bar notable* decorated with hundreds of football banners. After lunch, stroll by the Gardel murals in **9** **Pasaje Zelaya** and finish up admiring the *fileatado* walls near the Gardel museum in **10** **Jean Jaures 737**.

There's a small secondhand market in **Plaza Almagro** on Saturdays (secondhand books on Sundays).

Pop into the **Museo Casa Carlos Gardel** (p79) in the home he bought for his mother.

Pope Francis was baptized at **Basílica María Auxiliadora y San Carlos**, and a young Carlos Gardel sang in the choir.

CABALLITO'S TRANSPORT LINKS

Caballito is a fascinating spot for public transport buffs. Its name (literally 'little horse') comes from the fact that 200 years ago there was a horse-shaped weathervane above a *pulpería* (country store) on the corner of Mitre and Av Rivadavia, which people used as a geographical marker in the days before Caballito was part of Buenos Aires city.

Built in 1913, BA's Línea A Subte (it ends in Caballito at Primera Junta) was the first subway line in Latin America and the third in all the Americas. Caballito also lays claim to the first bus route in Buenos Aires, the first trip was made in 1928. Today, the bus route Línea 1 starts in Caballito.

Historic Food Market Transformed

Eat kosher McD's at Abasto Shopping

Originally the site of the Abasto fruit and vegetable market (the Spanish verb *abastecer* means 'to supply' in English), this architectural wonder was completed in 1934 and operated as BA's largest food produce market until 1984. Today, the building has been transformed into a shopping mall, **Abasto Shopping** *(abasto-shopping.com.ar; 10am-10pm)*. As Abasto is one of the city's main Jewish neighborhoods, inside is the world's only kosher McDonald's outside of Israel –

EATING IN CHACARITA: OUR PICKS

El Imperio de la Pizza: A Chacarita classic. Grab a slice of typical Argentine pizza and stand at the bar with the shift workers. *6am-2am* $

Albamonte: An historic – and very busy – locals' *bodegon* where pasta is the specialty; book ahead or be prepared to wait. *noon-2:30pm Thu-Sun, 8pm-11pm Tue-Sun* $

Santa Ines Restaurant: Set in an old bakery, very unpretentious but delicious home-style dishes full of flavor; small seasonal menu for lunch only. *12:30pm-3pm Tue-Sun* $$

Donnet: Cool vegan and vegetarian joint where mushrooms are the star of the table (and it's all gluten-free); the tasting menu is a must. *8pm-midnight Tue-Sat* $$

WISKERKE/ALAMY

Abasto Shopping

look for the specific signage as there is another McDonald's in the mall.

For rainy days with kids, the top floor of the mall has an indoor games and rides park, **Neverland** (free to enter but pay to play). There's even a giant Ferris wheel set into the soaring ceilings. You'll also find the **Museo de los Niños** *(museoabasto.org.ar; entrance fee; closed Mondays and Jewish holidays)*, a play museum geared to kids up to 12 with a mini city that will keep the little ones entertained for a couple of hours.

BEST MARKETS SOUTH OF PALERMO

There are plenty of markets in this part of town.

Feria de Mataderos: A country-comes-to-the-city market filled with gaucho wear, silver and leatherwork and folklore music and dance performances. (Sundays; p184).

Mercado de las Pulgas: Indoor flea market packed with stalls; focus on furniture and interior objects (closed Mondays).

Feria Artesanal del Parque Centenario: Secondhand clothing markets (of the serious rummaging kind) on weekends (p179).

Feria Parque Rivadavia: A fascinating collectibles market in a park on Sundays.

Mercado del Progreso: A wonderful working produce market in Caballito (closed Sundays and between 1-3pm during the week).

Tita La Vedette: Divine colored plant-based pastas; totally Instagramable, they are almost too pretty to eat. *noon-7pm Wed-Fri, 11am-4pm Sat & Sun* $$

Yiyo El Zeneize: This restaurant is much further south of Palermo but the trip back in time to this hip family-run cantina in Parque Avellaneda is worth it. *8pm-late Thu & Fri, 1pm-late Sat, 1-6pm Sun* $$

Anchoíta: Much-hyped but incredibly special; the meat and fish here are worth wrangling a table for. Try your luck on the waiting list or turn up at opening; *8pm-1am Tue-Sat* $$

Ácido: Innovative small diner with share plates designed to combine incredible flavors; lots of vegetarian options and a great wine list. *8-11:30pm Mon-Fri* $$

HANDCRAFTED ART PIECES

Martín Bustamante works in Chacarita at his store, Facón (p180). *@faconargentina, @faconrugs*

Facón tries to be a bridge between Buenos Aires and the rest of the country. Through its handcrafted art and design pieces, entering our shop is a journey through Argentina; you'll wander its iconic routes, explore the Andes and the Patagonian steppe, and discover our fauna and flora. We try to represent every corner of the country and are proud of the history of our artisans and designers who make each piece. It is important for us to be in Chacarita, an area where already the visitor has stepped off the beaten path. And there are wonderful spots to be discovered like the fascinating *puerta cerrada* bookstore, Falena (p179), around the corner.

A Different Type of Musical Event

Book to see La Bomba de Tiempo

When everything else is closed in Buenos Aires on Mondays, book tickets to see the long-running percussion group **La Bomba de Tiempo** playing at **Ciudad Cultural Konex** *(cckonex.org)*. It is one of BA's most unique events and you'll find it impossible not to dance to the rhythms when the drummers get into their stride. It sells out quickly (being only one show a week) so book online to save lining up with the hoards before the show. It's open-air so be prepared to rug up or stay dry if the weather is inclement. There are security checks upon entering so it can take some time to arrive.

Gauchos & Folklore Music

Go country at Feria de Mataderos

If you're visiting BA but won't have a chance to venture beyond its limits, the **Feria de Mataderos** *(@feriadematadero s; 11am-6pm Sun; closed Jan & Feb)* is the perfect slice of country life. Due to its location – approximately 30 minutes by taxi from the city center, or take bus 55 or 126 (1 hour) – very few tourists make the trip. But for those who do, the market will satisfy your appetite for all things gaucho (the Argentine cowboy of the Pampa) and is filled with handcrafted objects, local produce and performances. The market stalls are centered around the main stage where Argentine folklore musicians perform alongside costumed dancers.

Arrive around noon, wander the stalls and then settle in for lunch – gobble a street-side *choripán* (chorizo sandwich) or head behind the stage (and down the street) to the crochet-hat wearing ladies of **Doña Maria** *(@donamaria.empanadas 11am-6pm Sun)* who serve up some of the city's best *locro* (hearty soup), *empanadas* and *tamales*. Stroll through the charming **Museo Criollo de los Corrales** *(10am-6pm Sun)* filled with artifacts of rural life and located in the building by the stage (it also has a cafe with tables on the corner).

While the market is perfectly safe, Mataderos is not a touristy neighborhood; use common sense and keep your belongings close.

DRINKING IN CHACARITA: OUR PICKS

La Fuerza: This crew makes their own vermouth, which you can try at this fun bar with outdoor seating. *6pm-1am Mon-Thu, to 2am Fri, noon-1am Sat & Sun*

SIFÓN Sodería: Vermouth bar in a modern, minimalist setting with delicious tapas and great service. *6pm-1am Mon, Wed-Fri, noon-1am Sat & Sun*

Naranjo Bar: Wine bar with a great vibe and impressive wine list (by the glass and bottle); nab a spot outside beneath the orange tree. *6pm-midnight Mon-Sat*

Anchoíta Cava: Mini wine bar with no reservations, drop by in the early evening to snaffle a spot; cellar of nearby restaurant Anchoíta (p183). *noon-midnight Tue-Sat*

HEMIS/ALAMY

Las Violetas

A Historic Cafe

Take tea at Las Violetas

Las Violetas *(@lasvioletasconfiteriaok; 6am-1am)* on the corner of Medrano and Av Rivadavia in Almagro, is one of the city's finest cafes. Originally built in 1884, it was reconstructed in the 1920s with stained-glass windows and closed altogether in the 1990s, when it was all but abandoned. Restored by the city in the early 2000s, today it is a charming spot for afternoon tea. The cafe also has an association with the Abuelas de la Plaza de Mayo (p157) who used the cafe as a meeting spot. In order not to draw attention to themselves, the women pretended to meet for birthdays, going as far as to laugh and sing happy birthday while exchanging 'presents'.

PALACE PUMPING STATION IN CABALLITO

You might have visited the Palacio de Aguas Corrientes (p81), the eclectic 19th-century palace built to hide the city's water pumping station. But did you know that there's another one in Caballito? Occupying an entire block between Valle, José María Moreno, Pedro Goyena and Beauchef, the **Caballito station** was opened in 1915 and sits 37m above sea level, a handy spot in flat BA for pumping water to the masses. Its palatial exterior was designed to hide 12 tanks (and reflect the style of the first in Av Corrientes) and it continues to operate today.

EATING IN CABALLITO: OUR PICKS

ROMA: This 100-year-old bakery has *alfajores* to die for and some of the best *sandwiches de miga* in town. *6am-9pm Mon-Sat, 7am-8pm Sun* $

Barragán Café: Atmospheric brunch spot with a Mexican twist in northern Caballito; be sure to try to the tacos and sweet treats. *8:30am-8pm Mon-Sat, 9:30am-7:30pm Sun* $

1952 Helados: Low-fi ice-cream parlour from the 1950s. Some claim this to be the best ice-cream in BA – they're not wrong. *9:30am-10:30pm Sun-Thu, to 12.30am Fri & Sat* $

CENTRO: Very sweet, unpretentious corner bistro with seasonal menu and plenty of creative vegetarian options. *4pm-midnight Mon-Fri, from 9am Sat & Sun* $$

Researched by Diego Jemio

Day Trips from Buenos Aires

The rich history of the city of La Plata, riverside walks in Tigre, and ranches where you can experience a day as a gaucho (cowboy) all surround Argentina's capital.

Places

Argentina's most connected city offers excellent day trips. La Plata, the capital of Buenos Aires province, is famous for its diagonal street layout and large parks. It is also home to Casa Curuchet, designed by Swiss architect Le Corbusier and a World Heritage Site. Tigre offers a large flea market, good restaurants, and the opportunity to sail on the river or practice nautical sports. To the northeast, Campana has wineries and *estancias* (ranches) where you can enjoy a day with the gauchos. It is also home to Parque Nacional Ciervo de los Pantanos, which protects more than 50 sq km of the Pampas.

DFLC PRINTS/SHUTTERSTOCK

La Plata (p190)

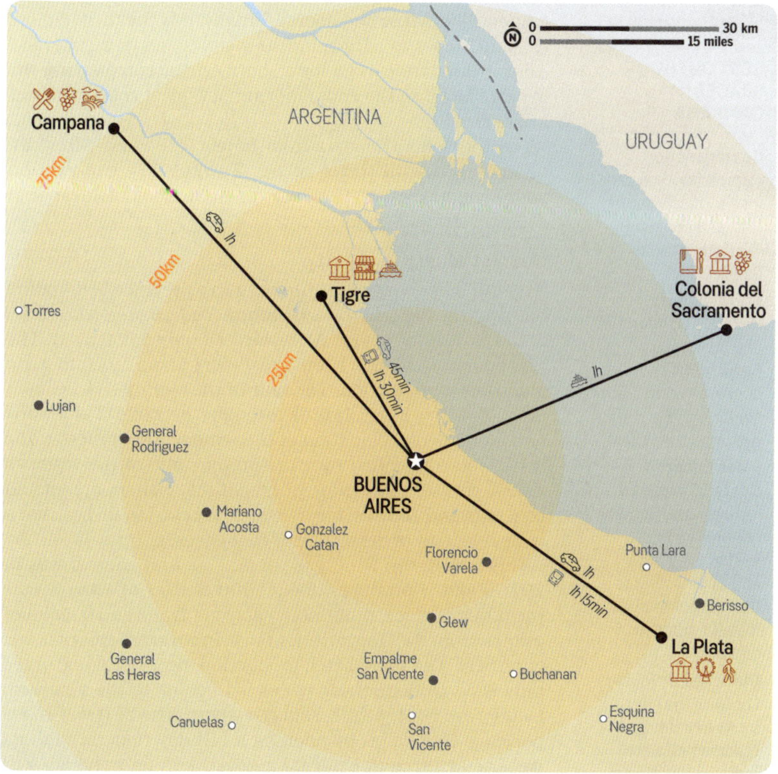

Campana

TIME FROM BUENOS AIRES: 1 HR

Spend a day on the ranch

Campana, 81km northwest of BA, combines rivers and islands, the immensity of the pampas and history. Along with the nearby town of Cardales, Campana is surrounded by *estancias* from the late 19th century, some of which are today open to the public. One of the best-known is **Santa Susana** *(estanciasantasusana.com.ar)*, a 350-hectare property dedicated to farming, horse breeding and tourism. Come here to learn about the customs of the gauchos and eat a typical *asado a las brasas* (barbecue).

Tours around the ranch, starting around 11am and lasting until 4pm, kick off with a snack of fried *empanadas* and a glass of wine or soft drink. Before lunch, there is time to walk around the *estancia*'s beautifully landscaped grounds which include an old chapel, a museum in the building where the ranch's first settlers lived, and a *pulpería* (old grocery store and bar) built with a thatched roof and adobe.

Lunch, which includes beef, chicken, chorizo and blood sausage, is served in a vast hall. This is followed by a folklore

TOP TIP

To enjoy the river and shopping in Tigre, try to avoid Sundays. It gets very crowded, and the river is packed with boats.

Find more day trips from Buenos Aires on lonelyplanet.com

BEST OUTDOOR SPACES IN CAMPANA

Costanera de Campana: Ideal park for a picnic, leisurely walk and observing the Paraná de las Palmas River.

Barrio Inglés: Historic neighborhood of picturesque English-style homes, built in the early 20th century for the staff of a meatpacking plant.

Plaza Eduardo Costa: Campana's main square. Notable features include a bust of Eva Perón and a monument to the first automobile manufactured in the country.

Plaza Italia: Square known in the city for its beautifully ornamented water tank, inaugurated in 1923.

Plaza España: Hosts food fairs and special celebrations, especially during carnival.

and tango show, with live musicians, a couple dancing and a demonstration with *boleadoras* (weapons used to ensnare cattle) full of vigor and energy. Finally, it is the turn of more than 20 horses to parade for the visitors and do a ring race. Those who dare can go for a short ride, accompanying the expert riders. In the end, *mate* and a typical country fritter are offered.

The tour plus transfers from hotels in Buenos Aires can be arranged with travel agency **Tangol**. You can visit on your own, but reservations are required. Book in advance at @estanciasantasusana.

Nearest winery to the city

Argentina has wineries in almost every province, but finding one near the capital is rare. **Gamboa** *(bodegagamboa.com.ar)* is the closest to Buenos Aires, located only 65km away. The team offers a guided visit to the winery and a lunch to learn about their production. The tour of the facilities lasts about an hour, with a leisurely walk through 6 hectares of vineyards and a detailed explanation of the winemaking process. The walk is accompanied by a tasting of some of the winery's wines, cheeses and fruits. At lunchtime, visitors are offered cold cuts and cheeses, meat, fish, or vegetarian dishes, and a wide selection of desserts and goat cheeses.

This family-run winery is young – its first harvest was in 2021 – and it produces about 1000 bottles of wine a year including malbec, pinot noir, cabernet franc and a blend of grapes from its vineyard. Its most innovative creation is a wine beer. The small batch production means that one of the only ways to taste these wines is to come to the vineyard, as they are not typically sold elsewhere. The best way to experience Gamboa is by booking a full-day tour through its website or through external guides like Viator, which will include transportation.

Home to South America's largest species of deer

Parque Nacional Ciervo de los Pantanos *(@pnciervodelos pantanos)*, with its grasslands and marshes, is an ideal spot to get to know the delta's biodiversity and the Río Paraná's islands. In this 50 sq km park you can walk three trails of 2km each, with viewpoints of the wetlands. If you are lucky, you may spot the *ciervo de los pantanos* (swamp deer) from which the park gets its name. This endangered species is the largest deer in South America at 1.27m. The deer have hooves especially suited to swimming in the park's river,

EATING IN CAMPANA: OUR PICKS

Italpast: Try their *cavatelli in formaggio*, pasta served in a hollowed out parmesan cheese. *11am-3pm, 8-11pm Tue-Sat & 11am-3pm Sun* $$$

La Catedral: Restaurant specializing in meat dishes and pasta. Breakfast options include *medialuna* and homemade cakes. *7am-1am* $$

La Pebeta: Organic farm-to-table restaurant, 22km south of Campana, offering seasonal dishes that change every week. Book online at lapebeta.ar. *hours vary* $$

Gamboa: The winery's restaurant offers a menu featuring traditional Argentine flavors, such as *empanadas* and *asado*. *11am-5pm Tue-Sun* $$

DIEGO GRANDI/SHUTTERSTOCK

Tigre

preventing them from sinking when walking through the swamplands.

You can also go bird watching – over 300 species have been spotted here. The most famous is the *pajonalera* (straight-billed reedhaunter), an endangered bird that attracts observers from all over the country. Don't forget to visit the native tree nursery, with specimens of talas, ceibos and ombúes grown to repopulate the park. The tour can be done with a guide or on your own. For security reasons, it is necessary to register at the entrance. Bring insect repellent!

Tigre

TIME FROM BUENOS AIRES: **45 MIN** / **1½ HR**

Explore world's third-largest river delta

Tigre, 32km north of Buenos Aires, and the surrounding delta is a popular weekend getaway for *porteños* (Buenos Aires residents). Always lively and energetic, the city has many colonial houses, rowing clubs and a busy **river station**. From there, boats depart to discover the incredible natural wonder surrounding it: the Río Paraná Delta. This succession of more than 350 rivers and streams is a complex water system that arises from the delta islands' formation and growth.

You can join a boat tour to learn about this landscape of latte-colored water and the culture of the people who live

BEST SHOPS IN TIGRE

Compañia Nativa: Offers a variety of home decor items, including handcrafted basketry and other decorative pieces.

La Casa del Mimbre: Long-running business in Puerto de Frutos selling handicrafts made of locally-grown natural materials, such as wicker and reed. They also work with imported materials, such as rattan and jute.

ArtesAna Hogar: Offers a variety of woven home goods, including armchair covers, lamps and bread baskets.

Galería Frutos Center: Home decor items, furniture and handcrafted jewelry.

Mercado Don Toto: The store is famous in Tigre for its antiques and also hosts workshops and cultural activities.

EATING IN TIGRE: OUR PICKS

Vivanco: In an old house with a large garden facing the river this restaurant specializes in grilled meats, pasta and fish. *hours vary* **$$**

Granero: Created from recycled materials, this restaurant is in Rincón de Milberg, a town near Tigre. Serves meat dishes and handmade pastas. *hours vary* **$$$**

María Luján: Housed in a charming 1890s residence, the standout dish is here is the house risotto featuring shrimp and mussels. *8:30am-midnight* **$$**

Almacén de Tigre: On a beautiful tree-lined street, this restaurant offers risottos, crêpes and homemade pastries. *9:30am-5pm Mon-Fri, 9:30am-8pm Sat-Sun* **$$**

CITY OF DIAGONALS

Founded in 1882, La Plata was the first planned city in South America. Locals call it La Ciudad de las Diagonales (City of Diagonals) because its streets follow an elaborate plan of diagonal avenues crossing a regular 5km-square grid pattern to connect the major plazas, creating a distinctive star design.

Architect Pedro Benoit planned this city grid as well as many of its public buildings, infusing his work with Freemason symbolism. His master plan for La Plata earned Benoit two gold medals at the 1889 Paris Universal Exposition, where it was honored as the 'City of the Future'. La Plata was also the first Argentine city to be lit by electric lightbulbs.

there. They are offered in small tourist booths around the river station and last about an hour with an audio guide and a brief visit to the **Museo Casa Sarmiento** *(@museocasasarmiento)*, a glass house, where former president Domingo Faustino Sarmiento lived.

If you have a sporty spirit, you can rent a kayak or canoe from some of the clubs in the area (the tourist information and excursion booths at the river station can help you with the hiring). Some local hotels also offer kayak tours to their guests. This option allows navigation through smaller, more peaceful rivers and canals, which motorboats cannot reach.

If you prefer a more immersive experience, arrange to stay overnight at one of the island accommodations or hotels. This way you can fully enjoy tranquility in the middle of the delta and the intricate river labyrinths.

Go shopping at the port

Despite its name, the **Puerto de Frutos** *(puertodefrutos-arg.com.ar)* does not sell fruit. Today, it is one of the most popular places in Tigre for locals and visitors to go shopping for decorative objects for their homes. However, until the mid-20th century, farmers unloaded fruit from the Río Paraná Delta here before selling it in Buenos Aires and the port's extensive concrete stairways remain in the place.

In the docks of Puerto de Frutos, over 500 shops sell mainly wicker and reed handicrafts (made from plants grown in the area), wood and iron furniture, plants and handmade food, such as honey and sweets. There are also small restaurants. On weekends, mainly on Sundays, it is usually full of people looking to buy some decorative objects for their homes and have lunch. Many shops only accept cash, so it's a good idea to have some bills on hand.

From BA to Tigre by boat

Sturla Viajes *(sturlaviajes.com.ar)* offer a two-hour boat trip straight to Tigre from Puerto Madero in Buenos Aires. It is a longer journey than the train, but the experience is worth it. After leaving BA's port you sail through the main neighborhoods that border the city's waterfront, such as Palermo, Nuñez and Saavedra. Then, when you navigate the open river, you finally start touring the Delta, with its houses, museums, and stories narrated by an audio guide throughout the trip. The trip ends at Tigre's river station (p189).

La Plata

TIME FROM BUENOS AIRES: **1 HR** (car) / **1¼ HR** (train)

Admire a Le Corbusier

Considered one of the best planned cities in Latin America, La Plata is 56km southeast of Buenos Aires. Home to a huge university, the city bustles with restaurants, craft breweries, a great music and art scene, and beautiful parks. Along its streets you'll find different species of trees, such as lime, plane, jacaranda and orange.

A great time to visit is on New Year's Eve when the festival **Quema de Muñecos** culminates with the burning of huge papier-mâché effigies after midnight.

LA PLATA ON FOOT

This walking tour of the City of Diagonals is a great introduction to the leafy, historic streets of La Plata.

START	END	LENGTH
Estación del Ferrocarril Roca	Catedral de La Plata	3.9km; 2 hours

Begin at the monumental, art nouveau ❶ **Estación del Ferrocarril Roca** dating to 1906. Head down Av 1 and turn right on Av 53 to arrive at ❷ **Casa Curutchet** (p192), the only Le Corbusier house in Latin America.

Continue along Av 53 to Plaza San Martín to reach the ❸ **Residencia de Gobierno**. Designed by Belgian architect Jules Dormal in a neo-Renaissance style, its white Corinthian columns and large balcony are accented by exposed red bricks. Also facing the plaza is the German Renaissance-style ❹ **Palacio de la Legislatura** and ❺ **Pasaje Dardo Rocha**, a former train station built in the Italian neo-Renaissance style. Now municipal offices and a cultural center, it sports an 85m long hall with a glass roof.

From the plaza, continue down Av 51 to reach the brutalist ❻ **Teatro Argentino**, a replacement after the original theater partially burned down. Proceed to Plaza Moreno where you'll see the ❼ **Palacio Municipal**, designed in German Renaissance style by Hanoverian architect Hubert Stiers, and the neo-Gothic ❽ **Catedral de La Plata** (p192). Relax in the grassy plaza and take in the gargoyles, stained-glass windows, and reliefs of saints' stories on the cathedral's facade.

Estación del Ferrocarril Roca's massive green dome with circular windows makes the station look like a large train itself.

Admire **Casa Curutchet**'s clean white lines and poplar tree, even if you don't venture inside.

Concrete **Teatro Argentino** boasts great acoustics and quality ballet, symphony and opera performances.

Hipódromo
Estación Ferrocarril General Roca
1 START
Av 1
Calle 50
Av 52
Paseo del Bosque
Av Iraola
Av 44
Diagonal 80
Av 7
Plaza Italia
Diagonal 77
Plaza Rivadavia
2
Av 51
Av 53
Av 60
5
3
Diagonal 79
Diagonal 74
Plaza San Martín
4
6
Av 51
7
Plaza Moreno
Diagonal 73
Plaza Dardo Rocha
Diagonal 73
Calle 15
Av 53
END 8
Av 60
Av 7
Av 13
0 500 m
0 0.25 miles

DIEGO GRANDI/SHUTTERSTOCK

Catedral de La Plata

One of the main reasons architecture buffs come here is to tour **Casa Curutchet** *(capbacs.com/capba-casa-curutchet)* one of only two works in the Americas by French-Swiss architect Le Corbusier (the other being Harvard's Carpenter Center for the Visual Arts). A pioneer of the modernist architectural movement, Le Corbusier made minimalist designs with industrial materials, like reinforced concrete. He hoped that this would make housing more affordable, something he was highly aware of as a city planner. The house was named a Unesco World Heritage Site in 2016, along with 17 other of Le Corbusier's works around the world.

Casa Curutchet is managed by the Colegio de Arquitectos (Buenos Aires Professional Association of Architects), with whom you can pre-arrange a brief guided tour that can sometimes be done in English – email casacurutchet@capba.org.ar for details. Afterwards, you can stay as long as you like to explore.

LOCAL FOOTBALL TEAMS

If you are a soccer fan, La Plata has two teams in the major league: Estudiantes de La Plata and Club de Gimnasia y Esgrima La Plata. For more about **attending a soccer match**, see p212.

South America's largest neo-Gothic church

Its formal name is Catedral de la Inmaculada Concepción, but everyone calls it **Catedral de La Plata** *(@fundacion.catedral.lp.museo)*. Located opposite Plaza Moreno, La Plata's nerve center, the cathedral is impressive for its dimensions: it covers 7000 sq meters and has capacity for 14,000 people making it the largest neo-Gothic church in South America.

The cathedral's cornerstone was laid in 1884 and it was inaugurated in 1932. The Gothic cathedrals of Amiens in France and Cologne in Germany influenced its design. In addition to its imposing dimensions, the cathedral's interior is impressive for its windows, an artistic work of 180 sq meters and 25,000 pieces of stained glass.

In the basement is an interesting **museum** with exhibits on the construction of the cathedral. Objects such as vestments and jewelry are also on display. The crypt holds the tomb of Dardo Rocha, the city's founder. You can also ride an elevator to one of the cathedral's towers, where you get a good view of the city from almost 100m high.

Visit an educational theme park

Some La Plata natives love to claim that the **República de los Niños** *(republica.laplata.gob.ar)* inspired Walt Disney to create Disneyland. The Argentine theme park was inaugurated in 1951, while the one in the United States was inaugurated in 1955. However, there is no concrete evidence to confirm the accuracy of this claim.

Today, families still visit this park in Gonnet on the outskirts of La Plata. The 53 hectare park is divided into rural, urban and sports zones, each one a miniature city designed for children. For example, the metropolitan zone has government houses, legislatures and municipal banks, while the rural area has a small farm where visitors can interact with farmyard animals and learn about different agricultural activities.

República de los Niños was the first educational theme park in Latin America, created by then-president Juan Domingo Perón as a recreational space and a place to learn about exercising rights and obligations as citizens. All the buildings and institutions (about 35) are to scale for children from 8 to 11 years old; some were built mixing different architectural styles of famous buildings worldwide. For families, it is a good option to spend the day or have a picnic, with a wide range of restaurants and ice cream parlours.

A cemetery full of symbolism

El Cementerio Municipal de La Plata was designed by Pedro Benoit, the Argentine architect who laid out La Plata. Built to be a mini version of the city, the cemetery emulates its placement of diagonal streets and small squares, using the same architectural styles of its buildings in its crypts: neo-classical, art deco, neo-Gothic, and Egyptian modernist, among others.

Benoit was a Freemason, and local guides will point you to masonic symbolism throughout, including mentioning the cemetery's location at the end of Diagonal 74, a street that starts at the La Plata River. The water represents birth and life, and the street's ending after heading east to the cemetery represents death.

LE CORBU'S FIVE POINTS OF ARCHITECTURE

Argentine surgeon Pedro Curutchet commissioned Le Corbusier to design his La Plata house in 1948. After the architect sent the plans, its construction was project managed by Amancio Williams, designer of Mar del Plata's famed Casa Puente.

Casa Curutchet is an example of Le Corbusier's five points of architecture: an open floor plan, long windows, open facades, pillars, and a roof garden. Sleek and functional with clean lines, it has a ramped walkway and four levels connected by a spiral staircase, with a poplar tree in the middle of the space. When you walk it, you might have a weightless feeling, something else for which his designs were known.

EATING IN LA PLATA: OUR PICKS

Lebrel: Specializing in *focaccia* bread Lebrel serves sandwiches, *bruschettas* and *milanesas* (breaded veal cutlets). *noon-1am* **$$**

Ostaria Valtellinese: Italian restaurant featuring seafood dishes, risotto and pasta as well as gluten-free dishes. *hours vary* **$$**

Chaucha & Palito: Its 12-course menu changes monthly and highlights local products. Reservations are essential. *hours vary* **$$$**

Carne: Burger restaurant featuring pasture-raised meats, organic vegetables and artisanal pickles. *11am-11.30pm Sun-Thu, to midnight Fri & Sat* **$$$**

COLONIA DEL SACRAMENTO'S HISTORY

Colonia was founded in 1680 by Manuel Lobo, the Portuguese governor of Río de Janeiro, and occupied a strategic position almost exactly opposite Buenos Aires across the Río de la Plata. The town grew in importance as a source of smuggled trade items, undercutting Spain's jealously defended mercantile monopoly and provoking repeated sieges and battles between Spain and Portugal.

Although the two powers agreed over the cession of Colonia to Spain around 1750, it wasn't until 1777 that Spain took final control of the city. From this time, the city's commercial importance declined as foreign goods proceeded directly to Buenos Aires.

RICUCCI MICHELE/SHUTTERSTOCK

Colonia del Sacramento

TIME FROM BUENOS AIRES: 1 HR

Explore Casco Histórico

This Uruguayan city founded by the Portuguese Manuel Lobo in 1860 is a pleasant ferry trip from Buenos Aires. Many Argentines come here for greater tranquility, especially after the pandemic. The heart of Colonia is the area known as **Casco Histórico**, which is 10 blocks long by five blocks wide on the banks of the Río de la Plata. With its historic facades and cobblestone streets the area seem frozen in time. Explore its irregular alleys, the famous **Calle de los Suspiros** (Street of Sighs), lined with tile-and-stucco colonial houses and **Faro**, the 19th-century working lighthouse which provides an excellent view of the old town and the Río de la Plata. There are guided tours, but it's also easy enough to stroll through these streets by yourself and dwell on every detail of its beauty and the brown river on the horizon.

Buquebus and Colonia Express, the leading shipping companies, organize day tours to Colonia del Sacarmento. These trips include a walking tour of the historic center, free bicycle transportation and health insurance.

Historic sports center reimagined

At the turn of the 20th century, Austro-Hungarian businessman and naturalized Argentine citizen Nicolás Mihanovich invested US$1.5 million building an immense tourist complex 5km north of Colonia at Real de San Carlos. It included a 10,000-seat bullring, a 3000-seat *frontón* (court) for the Basque

Colonia del Sacramento

sport of *jai alai*, a hotel-casino and a racecourse. The bullring operated until 1912 when bull fights were banned in Uruguay.

After a long restoration process, **Plaza de Toros Real de San Carlos** *(@plazadetoroscolonia)* was reopened 2021 as a center for conventions as well as cultural and sporting events. You can see the stage from the stands and visit restaurants below the grandstands. Very similar to the bullrings of Spain, it retains the traditional arches and some circumferential details. The complex, seen from the outside, is impressive.

Visit a winery

In Carmelo, 80km from Colonia del Sacramento, you'll find **Pueblo Tannat** *(pueblotannat.com.uy)* a boutique winery that made its first harvest in 2023. Located in a beautiful field, the winemakers here store some of their wines in 500-liter clay amphorae. A free guided tour is available, but if you prefer a tasting, there's a charge. Tannat is the typical grape of the winery and of Uruguay. Their restaurant, overlooking the vineyards, offers a menu based mainly on meats, with some homemade pasta options.

EATING IN COLONIA DEL SACRAMENTO: OUR PICKS

Casa Viera: Located in an old house and specializing in tasty meat and fish dishes. Has an extensive wine and drinks menu. *12:30-3pm & 7:30-11pm* **$$$**

Comarca Las Liebres: On the outskirts of Colonia this restaurant and winery offers meat, local fish and dishes made with organic flour. *11am-midnight* **$$$**

El Otro Portón: Dishes here feature local seasonal products, mainly pasta and meats. Offers a good selection of Uruguayan wines. *hours vary* **$$$**

Vinoteca de la Colonia: Small gourmet bar serving local wines, cheeses, sausages and preserves. *11:30am-10:30pm* **$$**

Where to Stay

Buenos Aires has no shortage of accommodations, from historic boutiques to ultra-modern suites. Booking in advance will guarantee availability and great prices in the most exciting neighborhoods.

Where to stay if you love...

Cobblestone streets and old mansions

San Telmo (p96) BA's once aristocratic neighborhood has gorgeous architecture, delightful and varied eating options, art galleries and flea markets.

Top-level eats and chic ambience

Palermo (p160) Where cutting edge restaurants meet innovative fashion designers. The daytime is for shopping; the nighttime for unforgettable meals and drinks.

Grand architecture and history

Recoleta (p136) The city's best museums coexist with lavish architecture and perfectly landscaped green spaces. Pricey but gorgeous.

High-energy, gritty nightlife

South of Palermo (p174) Nightclubs, rock and punk venues and underground theater, all within a few blocks of each other.

Quiet but close to the action

Belgrano, Núñez & Costanera Norte (p148) Residential and perfect for those who like a quieter place to rest. Costanera Norte has the hottest clubs in the city but isn't very accessible.

High-end dining and unforgettable views

Puerto Madero (p82) Some delicious classic restaurants and rooftop bars that look out onto the waterfront.

Great shopping and art galleries

Retiro (p122) The city's transport center and where iconic buildings mingle with upscale shopping and walkable streets.

Breathing along with the past

Centro Histórico (p54) Where everything happened in the Buenos Aires of yore. It can be empty late at night.

San Telmo & Centro Histórico

BUDGET

Viajero Hostel Buenos Aires $
MAP P56
Party non-stop at this hostel in the center of San Telmo, with a pool, daily activities, nightly parties and a restaurant. Both private and shared rooms available. Don't forget to get a drink at the bar!

Circus Hostel & Hotel $
MAP P98
Private and shared rooms abound, as do social opportunities, an outdoor pool, and a diverse lineup of weekly activities to get to know the city and its culture. Only a few blocks from Plaza Dorrego.

Hostel América del Sur $
MAP P98
Bright rooms, private or shared, as well as top-level amenities including a patio, a common area with lots of seating, a pool table and frequent events give this hostel a uniquely communal vibe.

BOUTIQUE

Loft Osteria by Sagardi $$
MAP P98
With exquisitely decorated rooms and a great location close to Plaza Dorrego, Loft Osteria by Sagardi offers a respite from the bustle. Features a great Spanish restaurant downstairs and an internal patio, but no lift.

Cassa Lepage $$
MAP P98
Set in a building dating back to the colonial era and with an archeological collection in its basement, this cozy boutique hotel has bright, simple but elegant rooms and a native plant garden on the roof.

Hotel Anselmo Buenos Aires $$$
MAP P98
A charming and 'secret' boutique hotel with a vintage, antique exterior and a sleek, modern interior located smack in the middle of San Telmo, facing Plaza Dorrego. Managed by Hilton, the rooms are luxurious but practical.

L'Adresse Hotel Boutique $$$
MAP P98
Small hotel set in a historic building whose interior has been refurbished by an expat French couple. There's only 15 rooms, each decorated with a unique flair. Very close to historic and lush Parque Lezama.

HOW MUCH FOR A NIGHT IN A...

boutique four-star
US$350

mid-range hotel
US$150

apartment hotel
US$80

hostel
US$30

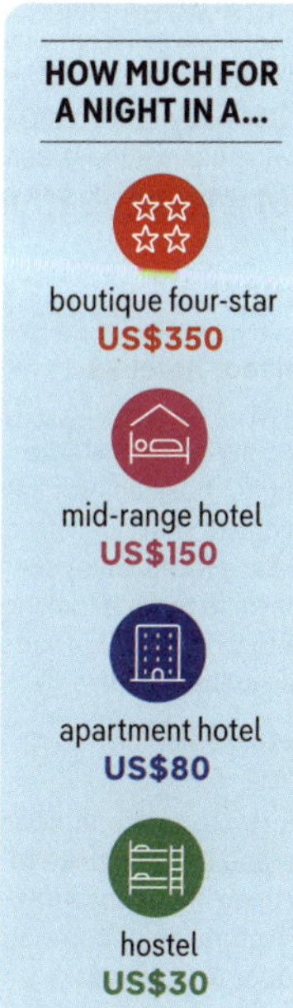

Recoleta & Retiro

TOP END TO SPLURGE

Palacio Duhau - Park Hyatt Buenos Aires $$$
MAP P138
Set in an iconic, French-inspired palace with a top-level restaurant, luxe gardens, private art collection featuring some of the best Argentine artists and a luxurious spa. Don't miss the afternoon tea service.

Algodon Mansion $$$
MAP P138
Offers impressive rooms, butlers for every guest and the amenities of larger establishments but with the intimacy of a boutique hotel. A short walk from BA's premier shopping boulevards, with a rooftop pool and fitness center.

Casa Lucía $$$
MAP P124
Spacious, sumptuously decorated rooms, a restaurant serving refined Argentine food, plus excellent cocktail bar, top wine cellar, spa and yoga studio. Regular events include jazz nights, bandoneon players and polo talks.

CONTEMPORARY

SuMa Recoleta Hotel $$
MAP P138
In the heart of Recoleta, a friendly and warm hotel that has all the essentials at an excellent price-point. Breakfast is included and glamorous Av Alvear is just around the corner.

Mio Buenos Aires $$$
MAP P138
Sporting a design inspired by Mendoza's rustic wineries, with doors crafted from wine barrels and hand-carved bathtubs. Also offers a top-level wine bar, wellness center and fully-equipped business center.

BUSINESS

Embajador Hotel $$
MAP P124
Classic-style comfortable lodging for business-focused travel only a short walk from Plaza San Martín. Enjoy the balcony and terrace looking out onto 9 de Julio, the widest avenue in the world!

Up Retiro $$
MAP P124
Comfortable, air-conditioned rooms and located close to everything in Buenos Aires' most historic neighborhood, next door to Galerías Pacífico and every mode of transportation.

Amérian Buenos Aires Park Hotel $$$
MAP P124
Close to the downtown business center and with every professional amenity. Rooms are comfortable and, if you're on one of the top floors, look out onto the Río de la Plata. Adaptive mobility rooms available.

APARTMENTS

Poetry Building $$
MAP P138
In a restored historic mansion, with a concierge, pool, garden and refined decor, these accommodations combine everything you expect in a top-level hotel with the privacy and independence of an apartment.

Attico Calas $$
MAP P138
A uniquely contemporary design, technology-forward focus on customer service, located in prime Recoleta next to innovative restaurant Néctar (p144). Don't miss the patio or the weekly events!

Palermo

COOL

Be Jardin Escondido by Coppola $$$
MAP P162
Owned and renovated by film director Francis Ford Coppola, this boutique has endless gardens, a heated pool, a parrilla and a terrace. In Palermo SoHo, close to the best fine dining in Buenos Aires.

CasaSur Bellini $$$
MAP P162
Next door to art galleries and museums, indie designers, adorable cafes and vibrant clubs in Buenos Aires' classiest neighborhood. Modern ambiance, spacious rooms, a pool and a top-level restaurant make it the complete package.

CAVAN-IMAGES/SHUTTERSTOCK

Palacio Duhau - Park Hyatt Buenos Aires (p197)

Duque Hotel Boutique & Spa $$$
MAP P162
Only 14 rooms in this cozy boutique in the middle of Palermo. With a pool and a garden, every room has hardwood floors and exquisite, unique design touches.

Ilum Experience Home $$$
MAP P162
A Buddhist-influenced design gives this boutique in Palermo Hollywood a soothing ambience. Don't forget the pool or to take a walk around the block to sample the best coffee in the city at Cuervo (p168).

Mine Hotel Boutique $$$
MAP P162
A gorgeous pool surrounded by plants and a rocky waterfall, with spacious rooms and lots of natural light. Walking distance from MALBA (p168) and other highlights as well as the subway.

HOSTELS

Play Hostel Soho & Play Hostel Garden $
MAP P162
Both locations are centrally located, offer private and shared rooms and are housed in historic, 19th-century houses with an open patio in the center. With spaces for watching TV, listening to music and hanging out.

Malevo Muraña Hostel $
MAP P162
Features a *parrilla* and bar, lots of options for partying and a hand-painted *fileteado porteño* design on the front. Shared and private rooms available, and only two blocks from nightlife hotspot Plaza Serraño.

ACCOMMODATION DISCOUNT
A lot of accommodations outside of the luxury tier will offer discounts if visitors pay with cash and will accept US dollars or euros, though not necessarily at favorable rates. Ask in advance.

Meridiano Hostel Boutique $
MAP P162
Housed in a historic building and offering a rooftop, tourism advice for Buenos Aires and the rest of the country as well as individual and shared beds, this is a hostel for travelers who want a little quiet.

Puerto Madero

LUXURY

Faena Hotel $$$
MAP P84
With carpets and hand-sewn drapes in every room, this ultra-deluxe hotel has a spa, French and Argentine restaurants and three character-filled bars. A lively events calendar includes tango dances.

Alvear Icon $$$
MAP P84
Look out into the Río de la Plata from spacious, light-filled rooms with beautiful, cosmopolitan design. The rooftop Crystal Bar (p89) has some of the best drinks in the city, and Glitter is the only glatt kosher fine dining establishment in Argentina.

Madero Hotel $$$
MAP P84
Only a walk away from the main attractions in Puerto Madero and overlooking the Río de la Plata, you can enjoy all the luxuries - spa, top-level restaurant, bar, events - with none of the fuss.

MINIMALIST STYLE

Believe Madero Hotel $$
MAP P84
No-frills decor and comfortably furnished rooms at the boundary between San Telmo and Puerto Madero make this four-star ideal for travelers who want the best of both worlds.

City Madero $$$
MAP P84
Spacious balcony rooms and minimalist design adorn pet-friendly rooms, with a view out to the river and the pool as well as fire pits and even a casino.

HAVANNA
CAMINITO

TOOLKIT

The chapters in this section cover the most important topics you'll need to know about in Buenos Aires. They're full of nuts-and-bolts information and valuable insights to help you understand and navigate Buenos Aires and get the most out of your trip.

El Caminito (p115)

IVO ANTONIE DE ROOIJ/SHUTTERSTOCK

Money

CURRENCY: ARGENTINE PESO (AR$)

Prices

High inflation and an unstable currency market means prices can change rapidly in Argentina. In this book, we give many costs as US dollar equivalents; the dollar is more stable than the peso and will give you a better idea of real costs. In most situations, you will be expected to pay in pesos, though, increasingly, some businesses also accept dollars.

Cash or Card

Most establishments will accept debit cards, but cash is still king in Buenos Aires and will often net you a considerable discount, especially in restaurants, convenience stores and other smaller establishments. Credit cards can be less useful but are also widely accepted. Ask if there's a cash price before you pay.

Credit or Debit

Visa and Mastercard credit and debit cards are widely accepted, while American Express and other cards are less welcome. Debit is almost always an option, but smaller convenience stores and other local businesses may not accept credit cards or will only accept them above a certain price threshold.

HOW MUCH FOR A...

museum entry
Usually free

private museum
US$3.50-US$12

Teatro Colón show
US$5-US$150

Subte ticket
US$0.50

HOW TO... Tip

Argentine tipping culture can be difficult to understand. At least 10% is standard in restaurants, and tipping is expected for valets and, if you're taking a bus, for the employee who gets your luggage into the bus' bag compartment. They are not necessary for taxis or in American-style coffee shops. Electronic tipping is a recent development and may not be available, so make sure to have enough cash.

LOCAL TIP

Many Argentines believe that pre-2009-design US$100 bills with a 'small face' of Benjamin Franklin are worth less. You may be offered a lower exchange rate, or they may not be accepted.

INFLATION-OMICS

The main characteristic of the Argentine economy over the decades has been inflation, which hovered around 200% year-on-year in 2024, a year in which the country's economy also went into recession. This has led to cyclical crises and caused many Argentines to distrust financial institutions. One of the causes of inflation is a lack of foreign currencies, which is why currency exchange is so tightly regulated. Travelers should double-check prices beforehand and know that they may have changed by the time of their arrival, and plan accordingly.

CLOCKWISE FROM TOP LEFT: MEHANIQ/SHUTTERSTOCK, RAME ALSAYED/SHUTTERSTOCK, EXESALAZAR/SHUTTERSTOCK

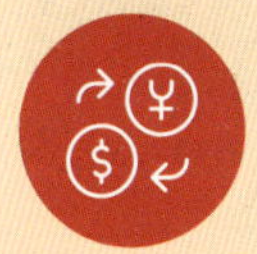

Currency Exchange in Argentina

Argentina has a wildly unpredictable and often incomprehensible system of currency regulation. Policies are in constant flux, with one government removing regulations and the next tightening them back up, while confusing dollar exchange rates multiply. The good news is that, by and large, the system favors travelers. Read on to understand the landscape and see below for resources with up-to-date information and the latest regulations.

Why?

Argentina's economy, broadly speaking, suffers from a significant export deficit, which leaves the country chronically short of dollars. Thus, to prevent dollars (and other foreign currencies) from leaving the country, governments have imposed restrictions on various kinds of currency exchanges, including small-scale consumer-level trading.

This produced, for consumers, a parallel or 'blue' market, which buys and sells dollars at a premium but without restrictions. There are also other rates meant for tourists coming to Argentina, Argentine tourists paying with their cards, financial institutions and exporters.

Restrictions are easing at the time of research, so make sure to check the current rates online before you travel.

What to Bring?

In Argentina, US dollars are always the best currency, though euros are almost as universal. Broadly, at the time of research, if you can avoid international transaction fees from your credit or debit card provider, you should feel free to use them: the rate that international card providers offer is roughly equivalent to the 'blue' rate.

You will often find that, in Argentina, cash is necessary for smaller transactions, so you should always have some pesos on hand. Many sellers prefer cash to cards, particularly taxis, street vendors and some restaurants, and may offer better prices.

How to Get Pesos

You may be able to get pesos from an ATM with your debit card, though make sure to check what rate your bank offers beforehand. It is also possible to use Western Union and similar wire agencies, though you should verify exchange rates and fees beforehand. Legal exchange houses – most famously clustered around Calle Florida in downtown Buenos Aires – will likewise offer a less attractive rate.

Many *porteños* (Buenos Aires residents) and visitors alike use *cuevas* (literally 'caves') or *arbolitos* ('little trees') – illegal exchange houses – to sell dollars at the more convenient 'blue' rate. However, their use is punishable with fines and even prison time.

RESOURCES

Because conditions in Argentina are so fluid, the wisest course of action is to find out the latest situation and rates before your trip. For English-language coverage of the country's latest economic news, the **Buenos Aires Herald** *(buenosairesherald.com)* and the **Buenos Aires Times** *(batimes.com.ar)* are the gold standard.

Most Argentine newspapers will list updated exchange rates, but **bluedollar.net** is a reliable English-language option.

Family Travel

Porteños adore children and the city is the perfect family-friendly destination. There are plentiful activities for children of every age group, a multitude of navigation alternatives and extremely friendly people who will happily help in a pinch. Relax at the city's parks and gardens, broaden your horizons with its many museums, or traipse through its bustling but welcoming streets.

Family-Friendly Facilities

Women's bathrooms mostly have diaper-changing stations, but they're rarer in men's bathrooms. Breastfeeding in public is completely acceptable, and nobody will look twice at you. Children are welcome in even the finest dining restaurants and some bars, especially all-day cafe-style establishments.

Pram-Friendly Buenos Aires

Though Buenos Aires sidewalks were once infamously bad, recent years have seen great improvements in their quality. Lifts are available at many subway stations and buildings, while taxis and buses are almost always happy to help out parents in need of a ride. Though family pack pricing for transport is not available, public transport in Buenos Aires is abundant and very accessible and children under five travel free.

Attractions

From an abundance of museums to beautiful parks and gardens to historic neighborhoods like La Boca and San Telmo, Buenos Aires is chock-full of activities open to all. Also you can get on a bus or train to one of many nearby towns, like San Antonio de Areco with its picturesque colonial streets dating from the early 18th century and preserved gaucho traditions.

BEST ATTRACTIONS FOR FAMILIES

Museo de los Niños (p183) Interactive miniatures of typical spaces in the city, from fast food restaurants to ports.

República de los Niños (p193) Educational theme park with rural, urban and sports zones.

Reserva Ecológica Costanera Sur (p88) The largest green space in Buenos Aires, with plenty of trails and bike routes.

Museo de la Imaginación y el Juego (p87) Puerto Madero museum dedicated to imagination and play.

Ecoparque (p167) Old zoo re-invented as an environmental education space.

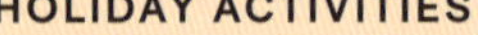

HOLIDAY ACTIVITIES

School summer holidays in Buenos Aires go from December to February while the winter ones are during July. Expect higher prices and occupancy in those seasons: book hotels at least two months in advance, and book any trips out of Buenos Aires with similar spacing.

The benefits of traveling during high season, especially the July break, is that you'll find a lot of special programming for children and families: from unique classical children's music, ballet and theater at Teatro Colón and along Av Corrientes to children's art and reading clubs at MALBA and the Museo de Arte Moderno.

Health & Safe Travel

ILLEGAL DRUGS

Cannabis is technically illegal, though possession for personal consumption cannot be prosecuted following a 2009 Supreme Court case; nonetheless, if you're caught with it, police will confiscate the substance. If you're found in possession of other illegal drugs such as cocaine, ecstasy or LSD, you will face stiffer penalties.

Vaccinations & Infectious Diseases

No special vaccinations are needed for travel to Buenos Aires. If arriving during the warmer months (November to March) beware of dengue fever, which can mess up a fun trip. Use lots of bug spray and cover up your skin, as the Aedes Aegypti mosquito that spreads the virus flies low.

Petty Theft

Buenos Aires is largely considered safe, but petty theft is widespread. Avoid using cell phones on the street when possible, especially on buses and other public transport, and particularly at night. *Pungas* (pickpockets) will take valuables from open purses and coat pockets in crowded subways, though snatching is also common.

RIDESHARING

Licensed, metered taxis are abundant and cheap, but only take cash. Use of ridesharing apps like Uber and Didi is widespread.

TRAFFIC LIGHTS

Red/orange light
Do not cross.

White/green light
Safe to cross.

Healthcare

Argentine public health is open to all but may not offer the speediest attention and, due to changing policy, may begin prioritizing Argentine citizens. Private healthcare is not expensive by international standards and widely available as well, so travel insurance of some kind is worth considering.

CAR GUARDS

A lot of venues do not have designated parking, and attendees leave their cars on the street to be guarded by *cuidacoches* or *trapitos*, sometimes hired by organizers. They'll request a specific amount of cash in exchange for watching your car for the duration – up front in most cases, pay only a small, discretionary tip they when hired by restaurants.

CLOCKWISE FROM LEFT: LJUPCO SMOKOVSKI/SHUTTERSTOCK, MALENKKA/SHUTTERSTOCK, FREE WIND 2014/SHUTTERSTOCK

Food, Drink & Nightlife

When to Eat

Breakfast (before 10:30am) Light – toast with cheese, jam or *dulce de leche* (milk caramel) or *facturas* with coffee or *mate*.

Lunch (12:30–4pm) Usually simple food. 'Executive' menu (food + drink + coffee or dessert) often available.

Merienda (4–7pm) Often *facturas* and toast or cakes with *mate*/coffee/tea.

Dinner (8–11pm) Two or three courses, often with wine, especially on weekends.

Where to Eat

Bodegón Rustic eatery serving simple homemade food like *milanesas* and pastas.

Parrillas Serve *asado* (barbecue) of grilled meats and, sometimes, vegetables.

Bar notable Historic cafe/bars, usually open from early in the morning until 2am and declared 'cultural patrimony of Buenos Aires'. Serve coffee and *medialunas*, some food and simple drinks.

Café American-style cafes serve latte-style coffee; traditional Argentine cafes often have lower-quality, non-specialty coffee, and are often also called 'bars' because they serve alcohol and are open late.

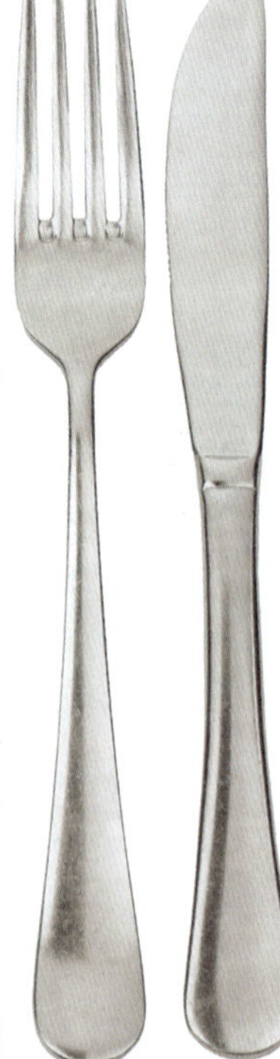

MENU DECODER

Medialunas Less flaky, smaller croissants. Can be *de grasa* (savory), made using animal fats, usually skinnier, or *de manteca* (sweet), made with butter and coated in syrup. Often stuffed with *dulce de leche* or ham and cheese.

Facturas Literally pastries, includes *medialunas* but also others often stuffed or topped with *dulce de leche*, jam, or crème pâtissière. Mostly eaten for *merienda*.

Guarnición Side. Mashed potatoes or pumpkin, *puré mixto* (half potato, half pumpkin), fries, Spanish-cut fries, or a three-ingredient salad.

Milanesa Breaded chicken or beef cutlet, usually fried. *Napolitana* is topped with ham, tomato sauce and cheese; *caballo* has two fried eggs on top; *suiza* has béchamel sauce and cheese on top.

Empanada Pastry turnover, traditionally fried. Usual stuffings: meat, cheese or veggies.

HOW TO... Order a Coffee

With the influx of American-style coffee chains and the boom in third-wave specialty coffee over the past decade, Argentine coffee culture has diversified. American-style coffee shops serve lattes and flat whites and 'global' confectionary, like cookies. They're often more expensive.

Traditional Argentine cafes also serve espresso, since *porteños* dislike brewed coffee. A *cortado* is a black coffee with a dash of milk foam; a *café con leche* is about equal parts coffee and milk; and a *lágrima* is milk with just a drop of coffee. They come in two sizes: *pocillo* or *vaso* are small cups for a shot of espresso and some milk, while *jarrito* is bigger. Your coffee will typically come with a small treat, like a cookie, and a small glass of carbonated water. Non-coffee options include *submarinos*: a glass of warm milk and a sliver of chocolate which the drinker melts into the milk.

CLOCKWISE FROM LEFT: SERGIY KUZMIN/SHUTTERSTOCK, BRESTER IRINA/SHUTTERSTOCK, BEARFOTOS/SHUTTERSTOCK

HOW MUCH FOR A...

cortado
US$2.50

medialuna
US$1

pint of beer
US$5.50

glass of wine
US$5

slice of pizza
US$2.50

parrillada for two
US$30

empanada
US$2

HOW TO... Order at a Parrilla

Argentina has an advanced vocabulary of terms for cuts of meat, preparations and points of readiness that must be mastered. There's the classic *ojo de bife* (rib-eye), *vacío* (flank steak), *tira de asado* or *asado* (kind of like short ribs), *colita de cuadril* (tri-tip), *entraña* (skirt steak), *choripán* (a sausage cut in half and grilled and placed between pieces of bread toasted on the grill), *morcilla* (grilled blood sausage), *mollejas* (sweetbreads), *chinchulín* (grilled pork tail), *bondiola* (pork shoulder), and various bits of chicken. You can request them at various degrees of doneness: *a punto* is medium, understood to be the correct degree of doneness in Argentina; *jugoso* is medium rare to rare; *bien cocido* is fully cooked. A *parrillada*, made to be shared, will include an assortment of cuts brought to the table on a hot portable grill.

The most common sides are *provoleta*, an oily cheese cooked on the grill and served molten and crispy; *papa al plomo*, a foil-wrapped potato cooked on the coals under the grill; and *ensalada rusa*, a salad with potatoes, carrots, peas, mayonnaise and lemon juice.

Fast Fact

The two main sauces in an *asado* are *salsa criolla* (chopped onions, tomatoes and bell peppers submerged in olive oil and vinegar) and chimichurri, which has chopped parsley and oregano, garlic, chili, olive oil and vinegar.

A NIGHT OUT IN BUENOS AIRES

Porteños love to have a good time, and they treasure their friends like no one else. Going out – whether that means a nightclub, a bar, or a long dinner with plenty of wine (or without!) – is integral to the identity of Buenos Aires, a city that really never sleeps.

The first thing to know is that *porteños* don't get very drunk. They'll certainly drink – wine, beer, vermouth with carbonated water in a siphon – but excessive inebriation is seen as uncouth.

Buenos Aires nights are long. *Porteños* have dinner late, clubs usually don't open until 2am and go until sunrise. A power nap before or after dinner, and a relaxed schedule the following day, are advisable. Expect bouncers at mainstream clubs to enforce relatively strict, gendered dress codes: pants and a button-up shirt for men, tights or black shorts for women. Expect an abundance of *cumbia* and Argentine dance music, with a smattering of foreign/global pop.

In recent years, less uptight *fiestas* have popped up. Playing less conventional, often slightly older music and global pop, with no dress code and meant to be 'queer-friendly' spaces, they usually begin slightly earlier, around midnight, and end around 4am, with changing locations, often outdoors. The largest are **Bresh** *(fiestabresh.com)*, **Cruza Polo** *(@cruzapolo_)* and **Cruza Recoleta** *(@cruzarecoleta)* – check Instagram for the latest dates and to book tickets, which often cannot be bought at the door.

Finde.club *(@finde.club)* and **baplanes** *(@baplanes)* on social media offer up-to-date summaries of social activities like concerts and parties happening every weekend.

LGBTIQ+ Travelers

Argentina was among the first countries in the world to legalize same-sex marriage, and Buenos Aires is a queer metropolis, full of life and with an LGBTIQ-friendly population. Pride is in November, commemorating the founding of Nuestro Mundo, the first gay rights group in Latin America. Nevertheless, catcalling and harassment are not uncommon on the streets.

Legal Rights

Argentina legalized same-sex marriage in 2010, following years of militancy by queer activists. In 2021, a law guaranteeing the right to employment of *travestis*/trans people passed, making it obligatory for 1% of all positions in the federal government to be held by *travesti*/trans folks.

Argentina has a strong anti-discriminatory framework that covers LGBTIQ+ discrimination. Recent changes in government have complicated enforcement of anti-discrimination laws, but that legal framework remains solid. You will almost certainly not have any issues checking into hotels, dining in restaurants or visiting attractions.

QUEER-FRIENDLY CITY

Buenos Aires does not have a 'pink zone' – LGBTIQ+ establishments are scattered across the city. Some parties, like Rheo at Crobar (p172) and **Fiesta Matilda** *(@fiestamatilda)*, started as gay events and have since become popular with wider audiences, though they retain an emphasis on openness and non-normativity.

Local LGBTIQ+ Resources

The cultural center **Casa Brandon** *(brandon.org.ar)* in Villa Crespo is a bar, library, publisher and great resource for any LGBTIQ+ traveler. The **Argentine LGBT Federation** *(falgbt.org)* has a well-kept website (in Spanish) full of resources for locals and travelers alike.

PORTEÑO BALLROOM

Buenos Aires has a nascent, small, but very active queer ballroom dance community, which organizes rotating events throughout the city and which are often free to attend. Follow @ballroombsas on Instagram to be the first to know when and where ballroom events are happening.

QUEER TANGO

Though tango has a reputation for being extremely heteronormative, when it began in the 1800s, two men danced together and women were not part of the ritual until later. Today, queer tango is kept alive in LGBTQI+ *milongas*, where you can watch a show, and even take a jaunt on the dance floor yourself. Try **La Marshall** *(@la.marshall.milonga)* or **El Despelote Tango** (p172).

Carlos Jáuregui

Jáuregui, after whom a subway stop is named, was a history teacher and Argentina's leading gay activist for much of the 20th century, obtaining among other things the inclusion of new rights for LGBTIQ+ people in Argentina's constitutional reform of 1994.

 NITO/SHUTTERSTOCK

Accessible Travel

Accessible travel has yet to fully arrive in Argentina. Historic sites and museums are prioritizing placement of lifts and ramps, as well as developing materials that are accessible to the visually and hearing impaired. Sidewalks can be uneven, though they've improved greatly in recent years.

Getting Around

Public transport has been revamped to prioritize accessibility, with ramps and elevators for subways and trains, Braille-coded navigation instructions in stations and stops, and wheelchair sections in all modes of transportation.

Airport

Buenos Aires' two major airports are both highly accessible and modern, with lifts, ramps, and visual and mobility aids. Help points are available throughout, with workers prepared to resolve most needs quickly.

Accommodations

With the exception of small boutique hotels set in antique buildings, many hotels will have mobility-prepared facilities. Many have special rooms for those with mobility difficulties, though they often must be requested in advance.

RESOURCES

turismo.buenosaires.gob.ar/en/article/accessible-tourism

BA's official tourism site has a guide for accessible tourism.

buenosaires.gob.ar/copidis/english

Accessible Tourism Guide for Buenos Aires and neighboring La Plata, Bahía Blanca, and Mar del Plata.

wheelchairtravel.org/buenos-aires

Guide for wheelchair accessibility in BA.

WATCH THE SIDEWALKS!

Those with mobility and visual impairments should be prepared for sidewalks that are not in perfect condition, especially in older neighborhoods like San Telmo, where they also tend to be narrow and in disrepair.

Guided Museum Tours

Both MALBA (p168) and the Museo Nacional de Bellas Artes (p147) have guided tours oriented towards those with visual, sensory and learning disabilities, and have revamped their galleries to be more navigable for those with mobility issues.

Haptic Maps

An increasing number of tourist spots, including museums and parks and historical sites, have been equipped with haptic maps that present information in Braille and macrotype so that those with visual impairments can enjoy them.

Porteños are a uniquely friendly people, and most locals you encounter on the street will happily go out of their way to give you a helping hand, from crossing the street to finding your way. Just ask!

KEEP YOUR FAITH

Multi-faith rooms are rare, but you can find Catholic/Christian spaces in most airports and hospitals. **halalfreak.com/halal-food-in-buenos-aires** has you covered for mosques and halal food, and **turismo.buenosaires.gob.ar/en/article/jewish-buenos-aires** has a list of Jewish sites in the city.

Responsible Travel

Climate Change & Travel

It's impossible to ignore the impact we have when traveling; Lonely Planet urges all travelers to engage with their travel carbon footprint, which will mainly come from air travel. While there often isn't an alternative, travelers can look to minimize the number of flights they take, opt for newer aircrafts and use cleaner ground transport, such as trains. One proposed solution – purchasing carbon offsets – unfortunately does not cancel out the impact of individual flights. While most destinations will depend on air travel for the foreseeable future, for now, pursuing ground-based travel where possible is the best course of action.

The **UN Carbon Offset Calculator** shows how flying impacts a household's emissions.

The **ICAO's carbon emissions calculator** allows visitors to analyze the CO_2 generated by point-to-point journeys.

Enjoy Indigenous Food

The restaurant Anchoíta (p183) grows most of its vegetables. They also hired an anthropologist to find sustainable ways to obtain and prepare overlooked ingredients autochthonous to Argentina, from fish to tubers.

Pedal Around

Bike rentals are very cheap in Buenos Aires, with rental stations available throughout the city and near high-tourism areas. Bike lanes run along most avenues with ample space. Remember to wear a helmet!

Help reduce the amount of waste generated in BA by separating recyclable items such as paper, metal, and glass and putting them in the green bins and green bell containers in the city.

If you want to browse the shelves of a nostalgic, cozy bookstore but can't read Spanish, head over to Walrus Books (p101), in San Telmo, which stocks thousands of new and used books in English.

An old saying, attributed to a French diplomat, says that Buenos Aires gives its back to the River Plate. Remedy this with a stroll along riverside Costanera, say hi to the fishermen and don't miss out on a *choripán* (chorizo sandwich).

Tigre (p189), a 30-minute drive away from the city, is part of the Río de la Plata delta with a thousand little islands. Head to the Puerto de Frutos for some local delicacies and catch a ferry upriver!

Japan in Buenos Aires

Jardín Japonés (p164) is a peaceful spot in Palermo for a stroll over pretty bridges spanning ponds filled with koi. The visitors center hosts occasional exhibitions and workshops on Japanese culture.

Meet the Ducks

Buenos Aires' largest green space, Parque 3 de Febrero (p170), has lakes and ponds populated by flocks of ducks and geese. It's a great place to enjoy a picnic or go for a run.

Blast From the Past

Encounter fragments of Buenos Aires' past and find unique souvenirs, including dusty trinkets, oddball antiques and rare vinyl records at the city's flea markets such as Feria de San Telmo (p100) every Sunday.

Sustainable Sexy

Buy yourself a handsome pair of jeans at Palermo-based **Limay Denim** *(limaydenim.com)*, which only works with cooperatively-owned suppliers to make their genderless pants and ensures every step of their zero-waste process happens in Argentina.

Earthly Delights

Sabe la Tierra *(sabelatierra.com)*, which has weekly events in Buenos Aires as well as the suburb of Vicente López, focuses on vegan and vegetarian foods and artisanal crafts as well as live events, including music and readings.

Jardín Botánico Carlos Thays (p165) in Palermo, hides history and natural wonder alike and has free entrance!

Many neighborhoods' central squares have small, quirky weekend fairs with local grocers and craftspeople selling their wares.

Green City

Buenos Aires has three ecological reserves, totaling 409 hectares, all of which are free to access and visit. If you take binoculars, you can even birdwatch for some of the 300+ species that inhabit the city.

RESOURCES

Turismo Buenos Aires
BA's official tourism site has tips on sustainable tourism.

BA Ecobici
Download this app to access BA's bike-share system.

C40 Cities: Buenos Aires
A short guide to ecological reserves in the city.

CLOCKWISE FROM BOTTOM LEFT: OLIVERDELAHAYE/SHUTTERSTOCK, DFLC PRINTS/SHUTTERSTOCK, FRANCESCO OCELLO/SHUTTERSTOCK

CELSO PUPO/SHUTTERSTOCK

Boca Juniors fans

HOW TO... Watch Live Soccer

The intensity of Argentina's obsession with *fútbol* is hard to overstate, especially since the men's national team won the Qatar FIFA World Cup 2022. It's impossible to understand without seeing it, and many travelers make attending a match their absolute priority.

When?

Argentina's first division club league tournament runs from May to December, while a League Cup is played from January to May and the Argentina Cup is played year-round.

Two continental competitions, the Copa Libertadores and the Copa Sudamericana, are played intermittently from February to November across the continent.

Dates for the national team are spread through the year.

What to Watch?

The best teams in Argentina play in the Primera A, followed by the B Nacional and descending into smaller regional leagues. The Cinco Grandes (Five Great) teams in Argentine football all hail from Buenos Aires: River Plate (p157) and Boca Juniors (p116) are the largest by fan base, while San Lorenzo, Independiente, and Racing Club also have sizeable fan bases and stadiums. Other notable teams from Buenos Aires and its suburbs include Vélez Sarfield, Argentinos Juniors, Lanús, and Huracán.

If cost is a priority, see smaller teams like Atlanta in Villa Crespo, and Argentinos Juniors (where Maradona got his start!) in Paternal. If quality your priority, you could try to attend a Libertadores Cup game.

To see Argentine *hinchadas* (fanbases) at their maximum intensity, consider attending a *clásico*, where local rivals play one another. Any game played between two of the Cinco Grandes is also regarded as a *clásico*.

Where to Find Tickets

Most teams (except Boca Juniors and River Plate) offer both early purchase and purchase at the stadium door for non-members. Prices vary. Avoid purchasing tickets on the black market; for most games, tickets will be cheaper from the home team themselves.

Boca and River mostly have a members-only policy due to demand. If you're determined to get the Boca or River experience, some tour agencies such as Homefans specialize in the experience and will offer tickets at a steep markup.

There are generally two types of stand. *Populares* are standing-only and cheaper, but usually rowdier and often for members only. *Plateas* are for seated watching; they tend to be calmer and more family-friendly.

GAME-DAY TIPS

- Arrive a few hours early if you're buying tickets on the day.
- **Bring cash:** although most will accept cards, stadiums often have poor reception and you may find a discount available for those who pay cash. There are also often concessions, including drinks and some simple foods like burgers, and those will be cash-only.
- **Watch out for pickpockets:** Football is a very safe spectacle, but crowds tend to attract *pungas* (pickpockets) so keep your valuables close just in case.

Nuts & Bolts

OPENING HOURS

Can vary throughout the year, so always check online for specific store hours, but broadly:

Banks 10am to 3pm (ATMS accessible 24/7)

Restaurants Lunch usually noon-3pm; dinner from 7pm to midnight, 1am to 2am on weekends

Bars Open at 6pm, close at 2-4am

Cafes Open at 7am or 8am; American coffee shops close at 8pm, Argentine cafes close around midnight or 2am

Shops 9am or 10am to 7pm or 8pm

Supermarkets 8am to 9:30pm

Convenience stores 8am to 10pm

Pharmacies 9am to 9pm, with many open 24hrs

Smoking

It is frowned upon to smoke indoors in restaurants, bars, cafes and even nightclubs, with the small exception of large-scale concert venues. Vaping is allowed, but doing so indoors will similarly earn you looks of disapproval.

GOOD TO KNOW

Time zone
Argentina Standard Time (GMT -3)

Country code
+54

Emergency number
911

Population
3.1 million

Internet

Free access to wi-fi at most establishments, though it's rare in outdoor spaces.

Weights & Measures

Argentina uses the metric system, with the exception of pints of beer.

Electricity 220v/50Hz

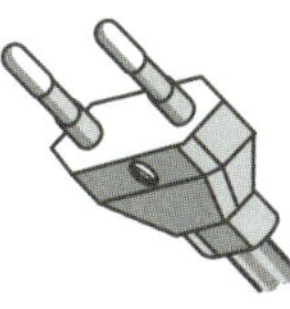

Type C

Type I

PUBLIC HOLIDAYS

New Year's Day January 1

Carnival Monday and Tuesday before Ash Wednesday

Malvinas War Veterans' Day April 2

Easter Thursday and Friday

Labor Day May 1

Revolution Day May 25

General Martín Miguel de Güemes Day June 17

General Belgrano Memorial Day/Flag Day June 20

Independence Day July 9

Day of the Immaculate Conception December 8

Christmas Eve and Christmas Day December 24 & 25

Three holidays are moved to the nearest Monday or Friday:

San Martín Memorial Day August 17

Day of Respect for Cultural Diversity October 12

National Sovereignty Day November 20

Language

Spanish is the national language of Argentina, and knowing some very basic phrases is not only courteous but also essential, particularly when navigating through rural areas. That said, a long history of North American tourists has made English the country's unofficial second language.

Basics

Hello. Hola. o·la
Goodbye. Adiós. a·*dyos*
Yes. Sí. see
No. No. no
Please. Por favor. por fa·*vor*
Thank you. Gracias. *gra*·syas
Excuse me. Con permiso. kon per·*mee*·so
Sorry. Perdón. per·*don*
What's your name? ¿Cómo se llama usted? *ko*·mo se *ya*·ma oo·*ste*
My name is ... Me llamo ... me *ya*·mo ...
Do you speak English? ¿Habla inglés? *a*·bla een·*gles*
I don't understand. No entiendo. no en·*tyen*·do

Directions

Where's ...? ¿Dónde está ...? *don*·de es·*ta* ...
What's the address? ¿Cuál es la dirección? kwal es la dee·rek·*syon*
Could you write it down? ¿Podría escribirlo? po·*dree*·a es·kree·*beer*·lo
Can you show me (on the map)? ¿Me puede enseñar (en el mapa)? me *pwe*·de en·se·*nyar* (en el *ma*·pa)

Signs

Abierto Open
Cerrado Closed
Entrada Entrance
Salida Exit
Servicios/Baños Toilets

Time

What time is it? ¿Qué hora es? ke *o*·ra es
It's (10) o'clock. Son (las diez). son (las dyes)
It's half past (one). Es (la una) y media. es (la *oo*·na) ee *me*·dya
Morning. Mañana. ma·*nya*·na
Afternoon. Tarde. *tar*·de
Evening. Noche. *no*·che
Yesterday. Ayer. a·*yer*
Today. Hoy. oy
Tomorrow. Mañana. ma·*nya*·na

Emergencies

Help! ¡Socorro! so·*ko*·ro
Go away! ¡Váyase! *va*·ya·se
I'm ill. Estoy enfermo/a. (m/f) es·*toy* en·*fer*·mo/a
I'm lost. Estoy perdido/a. (m/f) es·*toy* per·*dee*·do/a
Call ...! ¡Llame a ...! *ya*·me a ...
  a doctor un doctor oon dok·*tor*
  the police la policía la po·lee·*see*·a

Eating & Drinking

Can I see the menu, please? ¿Puedo ver el menú, por favor? *pwe*·do ver el me·*noo*, por fa·*vor*
What would you recommend? ¿Qué me recomienda? ke me re·ko·*myen*·da
Cheers! ¡Salud! sa·*lood*
That was delicious! ¡Estuvo delicioso! es·*too*·vo de·lee·*syo*·so
The bill, please. La cuenta, por favor. la *kwen*·ta por fa·*vor*

NUMBERS

1
uno *oo*·no

2
dos dos

3
tres tres

4
cuatro *kwa*·tro

5
cinco *seen*·ko

6
seis seys

7
siete *sye*·te

8
ocho *o*·cho

9
nueve *nwe*·ve

10
diez dyes

DISTINCTIVE SOUNDS

Note that *j* is a throaty sound (like the 'ch' in the Scottish loch), *v* and *b* are like a soft English 'v' (between a 'v' and a 'b'), and *r* is strongly rolled.

DONATIONS TO ENGLISH

Numerous – you may recognize armada, aficionado, embargo, fiesta, machismo, patio, plaza...

To Lisp or Not to Lisp

If you're familiar with the sound of European Spanish, you'll notice that Latin Americans don't 'lisp': where in European Spanish *c* (when followed by *e* or *i*) and *z* are usually pronounced th, they are pronounced as s in Latin America.

Río de la Plata

Spanish in the Río de la Plata region differs from Spain and the rest of the Americas, notably in the use of the informal form of 'you'. Instead of *tuteo* (the use of *tú*), Argentines commonly speak with *voseo* (the use of *vos*), a relic from 16th-century Spanish requiring slightly different grammar.

Where the @!*# is it?

Spanish-language and English-language keyboard layouts differ because the two alphabets aren't quite the same. This shouldn't generally be a problem, but for one pesky – all too useful in the age of email – key. The @ ('at') symbol – in Spanish this symbol is called *la arroba* (la a·ro·ba) – isn't necessarily labeled on keyboards or may not be accessed by simply pressing the keys you're used to. Try the F2 key, use an ALT code – or ask for help:

Where's the @ key? *¿Dónde está la arroba?* (don·de es·ta la a·ro·ba)

SPANISH AROUND THE WORLD

Spanish speakers in Argentina give the language its very own local flavor – the letters *ll* (pronounced 'ly' or simplified to 'y' in most parts of Latin America) and *y* are pronounced like the 's' in 'measure' or the 'sh' in 'shut' in Argentina. You'll get used to this very quickly by listening to and taking your cues from the locals.

THE BUENOS AIRES

STORYBOOK

Our writers delve deep into different aspects of Buenos Aires life.

Palacio del Congreso (p77)

HENRIK DOLLE/SHUTTERSTOCK

A HISTORY OF BUENOS AIRES IN 15 PLACES

The story of Buenos Aires is one of transformation and evolution, crisis and boom, synthesis and revolution. Though the city changes daily, if you look closely, you'll find traces of its history. These 15 locations provide insight into some of those radical upheavals over the city's 450-year history. By Federico Perelmuter

BUENOS AIRES WAS once a smuggler port, a small outpost used mostly by bootleggers whose main utility for the Spanish crown was for shipping out the precious metals being extracted from the mines of Potosí in present-day Bolivia. Yet following two failed English invasions in the early 19th century, winds of emancipation swept the nation and, after years of conflict, Argentina established itself as a burgeoning power in South America. A massive migratory wave in the late 19th and early 20th century exploded Buenos Aires into a metropolis: in 1855, the city had around 93,000 inhabitants; by 1914, the population had boomed to over 1.5 million. The city has continued to attract immigrants from all over the world since then – not only from other South American and Spanish-speaking countries, but also from China, Japan and, in recent years, Russia and Ukraine.

In the opening lines of his poem 'Las Calles' (The Streets) published in the 1923 collection *Buenos Aires Fervor,* Jorge Luis Borges writes, 'My soul is in the streets/of Buenos Aires.' For the young *porteño,* the city's languorous sunsets, its half-empty streets, miscreants and bandits, popular heroes and populist myths were his 'soul'. In the following list of places you, too, may find your soul lingering along the streets of Buenos Aires.

1. El Zanjón de Granados

TRACES OF THE (RE-)FOUNDING

Unlike most cities, Buenos Aires was founded twice. First, by Pedro de Mendoza, in 1536, but the Spanish colonists abandoned this settlement only a year later due to conflict with the area's indigenous populations. Buenos Aires was then re-founded in 1580 by Juan de Garay. El Zanjón de Granados is located in one of the city's original 14 squares, beneath an early 19th century house. Purchased and restored starting in the late 1980s by Jorge Eckstein, this network of tunnels and cisterns is one of the most significant archeological treasures of the city, with remnants going all the way back to the days of Garay in the 16th century.

For more on El Zanjón de Granados, see p102

2. Plaza de Mayo

THE LIFEBLOOD OF BUENOS AIRES

The oldest public square in Buenos Aires and the city's beating heart, Plaza de Mayo traces its founding to 1580. Though it would not become a single square until 1884, following the demolition of a building that split it in two, around it are clustered iconic buildings: the Casa Rosada, originally a river-facing fort and now Argentina's seat of government; the Catedral

Metropolitana, the city's premier Catholic church; the Cabildo, the seat of Buenos Aires' political life during the colonial era and now a museum; and the main branch of the National Bank, as well as the Buenos Aires seat of government.

For more on Plaza de Mayo, see p58

3. Plaza Dorrego

PLEIN AIR HISTORY

In the colonial era, Plaza Dorrego was one of Buenos Aires' first open-air markets because it was there that wagons would stop before crossing one of many now-buried streams in the city. In 1816, it was at that square that the people of the city officialized their commitment to the independence movement. Nowadays a site of historic interest following many transformations, the square, in the heart of traditional San Telmo, hosts a lively Sunday arts and crafts market and frequent tango-related events as well as busking and improvised performances by professional dancers.

For more on Plaza Dorrego, see p100

Plaza Dorrego (p100)

FEDERICO FERMEGLIA/SHUTTERSTOCK

4. Plaza San Martín

AN ANCIENT BATTLEFIELD

It's said that the first crime in Buenos Aires was committed at the Plaza San Martín by a soldier who then lived in a hermitage there, in penance. The English fruitlessly invaded Buenos Aires twice. The second time, in 1807, the main battle took place at the Plaza San Martín, in what is now the neighborhood of Retiro. General San Martín, leader of the Argentine Revolutionary Army, assembled his grenadiers regiment here. Over the next century its surroundings would become the city's poshest quarters, and the plaza was renovated to include an equestrian monument to San Martín and another to the Argentine soldiers who died in the Falklands War.

For more on Plaza San Martín, see p126

5. Cementerio de la Recoleta

RESTING PLACE OF THE GREATS

Once known as the North Cemetery, Cementerio de la Recoleta was Buenos Aires' first public graveyard, inaugurated in 1822 and named after a monastery in the vicinity. There, you'll find the tombs of many local luminaries, from Argentina's founding fathers like Domingo Faustino Sarmiento and Juan Manuel de Rosas, to Nobel Prize–winning chemist Federico Leloir and Eva Perón, whose remains were stolen and missing for 15 years before being returned in 1976. The cemetery's neoclassical architecture and many ornate mausoleums are an unforgettable attraction in themselves, icons of Buenos Aires' so-called belle epoque and the elaborate mortuary rituals of its elites.

For more on Cementerio de la Recoleta, see p140

6. Manzana de las Luces

ILLUMINATED BY GENIUS

Buenos Aires' frenzied intellectual life in the 19th century was concentrated in this central city block, baptized Manzana de las Luces (Square of Lights) by a newspaper in 1821. Tunnels for contraband and military activity dating back to the colonial era can also be found here, but its main attractions are the Colegio Nacional – Argentina's most historic and prestigious secondary school – the old building of the University of Buenos Aires, the city's first theater and first museum, a printing press that played a central role in the country's revolution, and Argentina's first National Library.

For more on the Manzana de las Luces, see p63

7. Cementerio de la Chacarita

THE GRAVES OF ICONS

When a yellow fever epidemic ravaged Buenos Aires in 1871, space was needed to bury the dead. The location that the Cementerio de la Chacarita now occupies was appropriated from the premises of a Jesuit school that then stood on the city outskirts. A 'funereal tram' was created to deliver bodies, and the cemetery became the city's main burial plot. Among its many renowned residents are tango singer Carlos Gardel, Soda Stereo singer Gustavo Cerati, and the great poet Alfonsina Storni, as well as a wide array of figures from Argentine culture and politics.

For more on Cementerio de la Chacarita, see p178

8. Museo de la Inmigración

MAKING MODERN ARGENTINES

Argentina received millions of immigrants from 1880 to around 1925, mainly from Spain and Italy but also from Eastern Europe, the British Isles, France and elsewhere, and most passed through the port of Buenos Aires. The Museo de la Inmigración is set in what was once the Hotel de Inmigrantes, where many new arrivals stayed for their first days in the city until they were able to get their bearings. Around 1 million people are thought to have lodged there from its inauguration in 1911 until it was closed in 1953, and the museum now stores the documents that registered immigrants' arrival in the country.

For more on the Museo de la Inmigración, see p130

9. El Caminito

BIRTHPLACE OF TANGO

After leaving the Hotel de Inmigrantes, many new arrivals headed to the port, where they were able to secure work quickly, without needing to speak Spanish. The neighborhood of La Boca, with its boarding houses and tenements where whole families often lived in squalor in single rooms, was a cosmopolitan melting pot. Here pre-existing cultures (African-Argentines and other creoles) met European immigrants and gave birth to tango and other pillars of modern Argentine life. In the 1950s in a project led by the famous local painter Benito Quinquela Martín, La Boca's most famous street El Caminito was renovated and revived with a colorful paint scheme. Today it's a 'street museum' and an unmissable landmark of Buenos Aires.

For more on El Caminito, see p115

10. Palacio Barolo

UNRIVALED ARCHITECTURAL AMBITION

An office building erected in the 1920s and designed by Italian architect Mario Palanti, the Palacio Barolo was, at the time, the tallest building in Buenos Aires. Its architecture and decoration brims with ornate allusions to Dante's *Divine Comedy,* and the building was designed as an allegory for the ascension of human souls from hell, through purgatory and towards heaven. Its elaborate dome, together with that of its twin building the Palacio Salvo in Montevideo, were designed as welcoming beams for migrants and new arrivals to the Río de la Plata – an allegory of the legendary Pillars of Hercules on either side of the Strait of Gibraltar.

For more on the Palacio Barolo, see p76

11. Obelisco

A MODERN LANDMARK

Standing upright and epic in the heart of the stunning Av 9 de Julio intersection with Av Corrientes, the Obelisco remains a beloved symbol of the city. Built in 1936 to celebrate the city's 400th anniversary by the distinguished local architect Alberto Prebisch, it stands where the Argentine flag first flew in 1812 following the revolution. *Porteños* head to the Obelisco to celebrate athletic and political victories – some climbed to its peak following the country's 2022 World Cup triumph. Brightly lit at night, it is simply impossible to miss as you traverse the city's most lively district.

For more on Obelisco, see p77

LOVELYPEACE/SHUTTERSTOCK

Café Tortoni (p62)

12. Café Tortoni

FREQUENTED BY GENIUSES

Founded in 1858 and named, probably, after a cafe in Paris, the Tortoni has been a landmark of Buenos Aires' aristocratic glamor for a century and a half. Sitting on the Haussman-inspired Av de Mayo, mere steps from the Casa Rosada and the Plaza de Mayo, under its roof congregated the country's great artists, including Benito Quinquela Martín, Jorge Luis Borges, Carlos Gardel and Roberto Arlt, among many others (including visitors like Albert Einstein and Arthur Rubinstein). Though lines are long nowadays, as it has grown in fame, its iconic interiors are witnesses to Buenos Aires' history.

For more on Café Tortoni, see p62

13. Biblioteca Nacional Mariano Moreno

BRUTALIST MASTERPIECE

Argentina's National Library, once headed by Jorge Luis Borges himself, was relocated to its current setting in tree-lined Recoleta in 1990, after decades of construction. The building is a brutalist masterpiece designed by visionary Italian-Argentine architect Clorindo Testa. Constructed on the site upon which stood Juan Domingo Perón's presidential residence, the Palacio Unzué, the Library resembles no other building in the world, and its floors of reading rooms and archives are second to none in South America. In its coffers are stored the libraries and archives of Argentina's founding fathers as well as many of its literary luminaries, including Borges' own personal collection.

For more on Biblioteca Nacional Mariano Moreno, see p141

14. Casa de la Cultura del Fondo Nacional de las Artes

CONTINENTAL ELEGANCE

Built as the headquarters of the *La Prensa* newspaper, a mainstay of the late 19th and early 20th century Argentine press and once regarded as a global benchmark publication, this French-style architectural masterpiece has hosted legends like Giacomo Puccini, who visited Buenos Aires in 1905 for the premiere of his opera *La Bohème*. The newspaper was closed by the Perón government in 1952 and reopened in 1956, though it had lost its preeminence. It is now a museum and gallery space adorned on almost every wall with paintings, and its Salón Dorado hosts the city's most elegant events.

For more on Casa de la Cultura del Fondo Nacional de las Artes, see p172

15. El Museo Sitio de Memoria ESMA

LEGACY OF THE DICTATORSHIP

Near the General Paz highway and the River Plate Estadio Mâs Monumental (where, in 1978, the soccer World Cup final was played) was the Argentine army's mechanic school. During Argentina's last civic-military dictatorship, which lasted from 1976 to 1983, thousands of left-wing militants, trade union activists, students and more were tortured and executed here, their bodies disappeared, never to be found. Though once the dictatorship ended, the school resumed its regular functions, it has since been turned into a museum, archive and 'memory center' of the atrocities committed during the dark abysses of recent Argentine history.

For more on El Museo Sitio de Memoria ESMA, see p155

MEET THE PORTEÑOS

How did the once-provincial, backwater town of Buenos Aires become a global metropolis brimming with people and their contradictions? Isabel and Eugenia Santana Goitia introduce their people.

WHY ARE PEOPLE from the city of Buenos Aires called *porteños*? The name derives from the word for port, and specifically from our port, set against the wide and turbulent Río de la Plata. When Juan de Garay founded Buenos Aires for the second time in 1580 (the first attempt by Pedro de Mendoza ended in disaster due to a siege by the Querandí people), he envisioned a destiny for this land and the Río de la Plata as a gateway to the other side of the world.

After our independence from Spain in 1816, wars were fought over control of Buenos Aires' customs office, source of the city's wealth. All Argentine trains lead to the Buenos Aires port, in line with the agro-export model championed by our elites. But, at the turn of the 19th century, the port became important for a different reason: millions of immigrants, mostly from Spain and Italy, arrived by ship, which meant most of the city's population had been born elsewhere. When the French-Swiss architect Le Corbusier visited Buenos Aires in 1929, he criticized the city's architecture for turning its back on the river. Funny, considering its importance throughout our history. But Buenos Aires is a land of contradictions and *porteños* are no exception.

Porteños can come off as proud and snobby and think themselves above the rest of the country. We can have a hard time acknowledging that other provinces have been as important as our city in Argentina's history. We can also be friendly and welcoming: after all, most of us were once newcomers ourselves.

For years Buenos Aires has been dubbed 'the Paris of South America' because of its architecture and cosmopolitan cultural scene. Some like this idea, as it matches their European aspirations, but others find it outdated and detrimental, as we have a long-established, non-European heritage, from rich African-Argentine and indigenous cultures to, in recent years, immigrants from places like Senegal and Venezuela.

Porteños make it a point to prove their open-mindedness, but some tend to favor traditional ways of life and are wary of change. We can also be melancholic regarding certain ideas of what the past looked like. However, every day historical buildings are demolished to build new, modern ones.

The new *porteño* gastronomic scene seems to have embraced both tradition and novelty. Innovative restaurants keep opening, but the old *bodegones* (taverns) remain popular. Foreign-style coffee shops coexist with *cafés notables* (historic cafes) that will exist as long as people want *tostados* and *cortados en jarrito*. *Porteños* are a patchwork of the old and the new in the ever-changing Buenos Aires landscape. The city is still young; who knows what the future holds?

Who & How Many

Buenos Aires has a population of 3.1 million people and is the most densely populated city in Argentina. The city is divided into 15 communes and 48 neighborhoods, each one with its own history and singularities.

A PORTEÑO FAMILY HISTORY

In many cases, including our own, the *porteño* family history doesn't start in Buenos Aires, but around the world. We were born and raised in Colegiales, Buenos Aires. Our parents were also *porteños*, but from very different backgrounds.

Our father was born in the working-class Constitución neighborhood to a Spanish immigrant mother and a father from the province of Tucumán. He worked from an early age, and even held a job at the port as a teenager. He spent his earnings on books, building the foundation for his career as an art critic and museum director.

Our mother was born in the fancy Retiro neighborhood. Her father was from Corrientes - her grandfather had been governor of that province. Her mother hailed from the province of Santa Fe, and one of her earliest recorded ancestors was mayor of Buenos Aires in 1621 before becoming Lieutenant Governor of Corrientes.

Tango dancers, Calle Florida
ALEXANDR VOROBEV/SHUTTERSTOCK

TANGO LIVES & BREATHES

The Río de la Plata's great music continues to evolve and transform, while its influence on Argentine culture remains supreme. By Federico Perelmuter

YOU KNOW THE sound – *bandoneones,* pianos, violins, upright bass all blasting in that unforgettable pattern – and you know the dance, its embraces and oscillations. Tango, from its origins in Buenos Aires slums to the great concert halls of the world and everywhere in between, is an icon. But don't let its iconic status deceive you: it is very much alive and well in Buenos Aires.

Tango's Origins

As with many other styles of music, such as jazz, tango was born from the great movements of history. It is impossible to pinpoint an exact birthdate, but we can say that a style of music recognizable as an early instance of tango emerged in the late 19th century. Its birthplace were the *arrabales* – slum-like suburbs near the ports of Buenos Aires and Montevideo; opposite shores of the Río de la Plata. Immigrants streamed into the city en masse during those years when Argentina's economy was devoted to exports. The city's port area and the poorer areas where its workers lived, many of them formerly enslaved African-Argentines, buzzed at all hours with people from all over the world.

In the mix was *candombe,* a style of drum-playing and dance originating in the 18th century among enslaved people, primarily from Central Africa, who were trafficked to Brazil, Buenos Aires and Montevideo. *Candombe* would, over decades, blend with other styles of music: the klezmer sounds of Eastern European Jewish immigrants; the *décima* poetic form, which originated in Spain and became integral to the oral poetic traditions of Latin America; flamenco music from Andalucía; and influences from Cuba, Italy, and beyond.

However, scholars agree that what came even before the music, which has since become globally known, was the dance, the beating heart of many social occasions. While first danced exclusively among men, tango soon evolved into a highly regimented model of heterosexual courtship. The turn of the 19th century is when professional musicians and skilled dancers began to synthesize and formalize what had, until then, been anonymous and proletarian music. This era is known as La Guardia Vieja (the old guard) and it lasted until the early 1920s.

The Evolution of the Music

As recorded music developed, tango became the Río de la Plata's hottest commodity. What had once been scorned-upon

working-class nightclub music became a symbol of the region both locally and around the world, much like jazz in the USA. This period, from the 1920s until the 1950s, is known as La Guardia Nueva (the new guard) and is remembered as tango's golden age, spawning some of the music's greatest icons including Julio de Caro, Carlos Gardel (p80) and Aníbal Troilo.

The most famous inheritor of this music was Ástor Piazzolla (p92), who combined the insights of his teachers, the composer Alberto Ginastera and the tango orchestra director and composer Troilo. Piazzolla intellectualized tango greatly, moving it away from dancing towards a more academic, 'listening' music.

MORE RECENT EVOLUTIONS INCLUDE QUEER TANGO, ELECTROTANGO, AND EVEN TANGO COMBINED WITH HIP HOP.

For a few decades tango experienced a downturn in popularity, replaced by folk music and, most of all, rock 'n' roll, which took Argentina by storm in the 1960s. Coinciding with the end of Argentina's dictatorship in 1983, the show *Tango Argentino,* directed by Claudio Segovia and Héctor Orezzolli, premiered in Paris and eventually traveled the world, reviving global interest in the music. As the country experienced a democratic, post-dictatorial cultural reinvigoration, a series of other tango productions revived interest in the music and dance. More recent evolutions include queer tango, electrotango, and even tango combined with hip hop.

Try it Yourself

Tango is not just a historical fact, it's a living, breathing cultural phenomenon in Buenos Aires. To get a glimpse into the tango world of the past, Villa Malcolm (p180), a tango club established in 1928, continues to offer lessons and social occasions in the Villa Crespo area.

La Catedral (p180), a much newer tango club, is based in the neighborhood of Abasto, where many tango greats lived, including the singer Carlos Gardel and the bandleaders Osvaldo Pugliese and Aníbal Troilo. Its majestic yet bohemian atmosphere evokes the origins of tango culture, and they offer both classes and spaces to dance freely as well as professional performances.

While you're in Abasto, don't hesitate to walk around: the Museo Casa Carlos Gardel (p79) and one of the singer's favorite bars, the (now closed) tanguería Chanta Cuatro, are nearby. Also in Abasto, El Boliche de Roberto (p180), a *bar notable* founded in 1893, still operates and hosts nightly *milongas* where you'll hear authentic singing and *bandoneón* and guitar-playing.

In another of tango's heartlands, at the intersection of Avs Boedo and San Juan, Esquina Homero Manzi *(esquinahomeromanzi.com.ar)* is named in homage to the lyricist of the famous tango Sur. Nightly tango shows of the highest quality are performed here. A short walk will take you to two more legendary *bares notables* – Quintino and Cafe Margot, both visited by tango's greatest.

In the tourist hotspot of Palermo, La Viruta (p173) dates back to the 1990s and offers classes, performances and other tango-related events on Wednesdays, Fridays and Sundays. Meanwhile, in the Barracas neighborhood, Los Laureles (p119) hosts tango events multiple nights a week.

New Directions

A new age of tango has opened the music and dance to other worlds. **Tango Queer Buenos Aires** *(@tangoqueerba)* offers a unique syntheses of queer culture and tango culture, and even hosts an international queer tango festival annually in December that attracts performers from across the city and the world. Unlike traditional tangos, queer tango involves frequent role reversals and deconstructs the rigid and often constraining gender scripts that much traditional tango relies on. Meanwhile, the **Festival Electrotango** *(festivalelectrotango.com),* which crosses electronic music with tango, takes place in February in the city.

Though much tango culture is steeped in nostalgia, tango is more alive than ever in Buenos Aires for those who care to look.

Tango orchestra, Plaza Dorrego (p100)

GM PHOTO IMAGES/ALAMY

CULTURE IN EVERY CORNER

An immense theatrical scene and more than 150 museums are just some of the attractions in this vibrant and culturally exciting city.
By Diego Jemio

BUENOS AIRES CAN boast many things – picturesque cobblestone streets in historic neighborhoods, tango, succulent meat and elegant architecture. Perhaps its most remarkable feature, however, is its impressive and effervescent cultural scene, which rivals major world capitals. Frank Sinatra once sang that New York is a city that never sleeps. He might have rethought that claim if he had spent more time in Buenos Aires. Despite the country's successive economic crises and cuts to the cultural budget, BA's vibrant artistic production has remained unstoppable.

Theater Scene

Tango (p224) is, of course, the most iconic gateway for travelers to experience the city's culture. However, Buenos Aires stands out in another aspect that may be less noticed by tourists but is enjoyed and consumed by locals: its theater scene.

Buenos Aires is, without a doubt, the capital of Spanish-language theater. According to BA's official tourism office, there are 287 theaters in the city, with the Teatro Colón (p61) the most famous. Considering that the city is 203 sq km, that's an average of more than one theater per

Teatro Colón (p61)

sq km. In London, for comparison, there's one theater every 5 sq kms.

Av Corrientes – the avenue that never sleeps in a city that rests very little – is the most visible theatrical phenomenon, lined with dozens of playhouses. The theatrical offerings are eclectic and for all tastes. In a small theater, you can find Argentine versions of Shakespeare's classics and, in others, stand-up shows, queer and trans shows, as well as comedy and drama plays. Within a few blocks are publicly-funded theaters, such as the Complejo Teatral de Buenos Aires, and commercial ones, such as Paseo La Plaza (p72), a center with several theaters and restaurants, as well as small and independent playhouses.

DESPITE THE COUNTRY'S SUCCESSIVE ECONOMIC CRISES AND CUTS TO THE CULTURAL BUDGET, BA'S VIBRANT ARTISTIC PRODUCTION HAS REMAINED UNSTOPPABLE.

Elsewhere BA is full of small theaters, each with a creative force and a unique and world-famous power. Argentine theater is an excellent focus for writers, actors and directors, and it is worth discovering on a visit to the city. See **Alternativa Teatral** *(alternativateatral.com)* for information about the plays and where to buy tickets.

Museo Nacional de Bellas Artes (p147)

FROM LEFT: DIEGO JEMIO/LONELY PLANET, YADID LEVY/ALAMY

Museums & More

About 150 museums operate in the city. The Museo Nacional de Bellas Artes (p147) and MALBA (p168) are the most popular. The former holds the primary collection of Argentine art, along with masterpieces by renowned artists from the history of world art, including Rodin, Manet, Monet and Picasso. Meanwhile, MALBA gathers some 700 pieces by crucial Latin American artists such as Tarsila do Amaral, Frida Kahlo and Antonio Berni.

In addition to the traditional museums, the visual and performing arts activities at ArtHaus, Fundación OSDE, Fundación Larivière and Fundación Medifé are remarkable. Meridiano, the Argentine Chamber of Contemporary Art Galleries, brings together scores of galleries in Buenos Aires. At the end of August, Buenos Aires hosts **Arteba** *(arteba.org)*, a major visual arts fair bringing artists, collectors, gallery owners, museum directors and curators together.

The neighborhood of La Boca, famous for its soccer club and El Caminito, has boosted its offering of museums and art galleries, such as Barro (p114) and Galería Sendrós (p117) in recent years. In addition to long-established venues like Fundación Proa (p117), there is now Colón Fábrica (p113), showcasing costumes and stage design from the Teatro Colón.

The are many cozy jazz clubs such as Bebop (p170), Prez Jazz (p147) and Borges 1975 (p167) where you can listen to live music while sipping a glass of wine. Movistar Arena, Luna Park and soccer stadiums host concerts by local and international rock, pop and folk musicians.

The scene does not end there. Cine Gaumont (p58), right in front of Plaza Congreso, is the home of Argentine cinema. It showcases local film productions and select films from the region. And literature lovers will find 380 bookstores, many offering lectures, courses and other cultural activities.

INDEX

C

Map Pages **000**

Map Pages **000**

NOTES

NOTES

NOTES

'I'd never felt as proud to be from Buenos Aires as when I tried Güerrín pizza (p67) for the first time. Here, at last upon my taste buds, was the perfect culinary creation.'

FEDERICO PERELMUTER

'I remember the first time I went to the market in San Telmo (p100). My sister and I wandered for hours upon hours, chatting with vendors and picking out precious things to take home.'

RACHEL TOLOSA PAZ

FROM LEFT: FELIPE CAMARA/SHUTTERSTOCK, DANIELCASTROMAIA/SHUTTERSTOCK

Mapping data sources:
© Lonely Planet
© OpenStreetMap http://openstreetmap.org/copyright

THIS BOOK

Destination Editor
Alicia Johnson

Production Editor
James Appleton

Image Editor
Compton Sheldon

Coordinating Editor
Simon Richmond

Assisting Editors
Imogen Bannister, Liana Cafolla, Jenna Myers, Charlotte Orr

Cartographer
Anita Banh

Assisting Cartographers
Rachel Imeson, Daniela Machová

Cover Researcher
Kat Marsh

Thanks Sofie Andersen, Fergal Condon, Gwen Cotter, Karen Henderson, Darren O'Connell, Katerina Pavkova

Paper in this book is certified against the Forest Stewardship Council™ standards. FSC™ promotes environmentally responsible, socially beneficial and economically viable management of the world's forests.

Published by Lonely Planet Global Limited
CRN 554153
9th edition - Oct 2025
ISBN 978 1 83758 390 4

10 9 8 7 6 5 4 3 2 1
Printed in China